BECOMING EQUIPPED *to* COMMUNICATE

A practical guide for learning a new language and culture

MICHAEL GRIFFIS, EdD

FIRST EDITION

Becoming Equipped to Communicate (BEC)

A practical guide for learning a new language and culture

First Edition (Revised 2022)

Contents

Preface 7

Introduction 9
Principles for learning 9
Becoming familiar with your new surroundings 11
How long will this take?. 14
Level Objectives - Pre-arrival and getting settled 16

Level 1: Relating through the Common and Familiar 19
Learning Exercises for Level 1 19
Level 1 Daily Learning Plans 1 to 25 30
Level 1 Daily Learning Plans 26 to 50 58
Self-evaluation for Level 1 100

Level 2: Relating through Daily Routines 105
Learning Exercises for Level 2 105
Daily Learning Plans for Level 2 106
Ideas for common daily activities for Level 2 learning 111
Procedure for using videos during Level 2 112
Level 2 Daily Learning Plans 1 to 40 114
Level 2 Daily Learning Plans 41 to 80 116
Self-evaluation for Level 2 121

Level 3: Relating through Sharing Life Stories 125
Four life perspectives to think about in Level 3 125
Learning Exercises for Level 3 133
Daily Learning Plans for Level 3 134
Level 3 Daily Learning Plans 1 to 20 136
Level 3 Daily Learning Plans 21 to 40 143
Level 3 Daily Learning Plans 41 to 70 146
Level 3 Daily Learning Plans 71 to 85 151
Level 3 Daily Learning Plans 86 to 100 154
Self-evaluation for Level 3 157

Level 4: Relating through Lifeview Conversation 159
Exploring the four life perspectives in Level 4 160
Learning Exercises for Level 4 169
Daily Learning Plans for Level 4 169
Level 4 Daily Learning Plans 1 to 20 170

Level 4 Daily Learning Plans 21 to 40 .177
Level 4 Daily Learning Plans 41 to 100 180
Level 4 Daily Learning Plans 81 to 100 (Instructions) 262
Self-evaluation for Level 4 263

Preface

Becoming Equipped to Communicate (BEC) is a language and culture learning curriculum that I originally developed while my wife and I were ourselves acquiring a minority endangered language in 2008-2009 in the Melanesian islands of Oceania. We subsequently worked with that language group in language development for many years. Since that first round of personal field-testing with the BEC curriculum, I have consulted for and tracked learners for more than a dozen years of successful implementation of the curriculum in many rural endangered and urban majority language contexts around the world. In the process, we have also verified that with proper implementation of BEC, learners can effectively and efficiently achieve worldview-level ability in the cultures and languages where they live.

Because of the proven effectiveness of the BEC curriculum over these many years and contexts, I am pleased to continue to make the program available to cross-cultural workers in this first edition book format, with a second edition on the way. As readers will note, BEC progressively leads learners into broader and deeper local relationships as the learners advance through the learning levels with the associated community-based activities. Even as learners grow in local relationships, BEC helps them move through key areas of culture toward a thematic worldview understanding of the local culture and language community. This approach provides learners with a robust foundation for effective communication and language development work. By the end of the BEC curriculum, learners who have followed the program will have cultivated many significant relationships in their new community as a part of identifying key themes of life in the worldview around them. In this sense, BEC acts as much more than a language learning program. Through this resource, cross-cultural workers grow to become a normal part of the life of the culture and language community: learning to understand, speak, read, write, and naturally interact in order to take an active and relevant role in people's lives for focused relationship-building and language development purposes.

The BEC curriculum:

- Explains the necessary foundations for deep communication

- Provides a comprehensive scope, sequence, and time schedule for the entire trajectory of culture and language learning

- Leads cross-cultural workers through successive levels of community-based activities that help them build deep relationships with others, such that learners grow to understand the community worldview as embodied in the local culture and language

- Includes detailed, step-by-step learning plans for each level

- Gives practical advice so that learners at any level can use the curriculum to continue to progress

- Includes self-evaluation checklists for each level in order to monitor learner progress

- Guides the learning process such that workers reach worldview-level communicative ability by the end of the curriculum (equivalent to Advanced High on the ACTFL scale of speaking proficiency)[1]

Finally, multiple unique features of BEC also distinguish this resource from other language learning curricula. Unlike other immersion programs, this curriculum:

- Presents a manageable, uncomplicated learning process for both urban majority languages and rural minority or unwritten languages

- Aligns learner progress with a proficiency assessment framework in order to help learners monitor and measure their growth in speaking proficiency as a baseline metric for growth in other proficiency areas

- Encourages the development of learner skills in reading and writing, in addition to listening and speaking

- Explicitly focuses on monitoring learner growth in social awareness, cultural insight, and key worldview themes for relationship-based language development goals

- Gives specific instruction to help learners develop high-level proficiency in advanced language functions for cross-cultural, worldview communication

- Positions learner investigation of worldview within an evaluative framework that prepares learners to build strong relationships in the local culture and language

- Integrates with an app to assist learners to organize their progress in the early levels of learning

As the author of BEC, I feel privileged to draw on postgraduate academic qualifications in linguistics and education, as well as many years of cross-cultural work, including learning three urban majority and two rural minority languages to an Advanced High level on the ACTFL scale. I have also been privileged to teach, coach learners, and travel for more than twenty years to evaluate and give direction for learners in second culture and language environments around the world. I would like to thank students, cross-cultural workers, and faculty colleagues for their diligent work, input, and support.

Michael P. Griffis, EdD

Fayetteville, Arkansas

July 2022

---

1. Based on field-tested proficiency outcomes over the last fifteen years of application, the target level of communicative ability for completing BEC parallels Advanced High on the ACTFL scale of speaking proficiency (see ACTFL Language Connects, "ACTFL Proficiency Guidelines 2012," American Council on the Teaching of Foreign Language, accessed May 13, 2022, https://www.actfl.org/resources/actfl-proficiency-guidelines-2012/english/speaking#advanced).

Introduction

Getting settled for learning

Welcome to the *Becoming Equipped To Communicate* program! For those of you using BEC in order to learn culture and language for long-term cross-cultural engagement and language development, I encourage you to reflect carefully on the challenging road before you. In order to effectively integrate into a second culture and language environment, you first will need to enter into the new setting with a plan for how you will progressively grow over time to become an insider in the life of that culture and language community. I created the BEC program expressly for that purpose. BEC guides you in how to intentionally and carefully learn the local culture and language in order to engage in cross-cultural communication at a worldview level. Only through these years of methodical learning can you expect local people to eventually deem you credible and competent to speak into worldview issues in their lives in a relevant way. So even as you plan for relevant cross-cultural work, I urge you to commit yourself to the years required for you to become culturally, socially, and linguistically proficient.

With those brief but important exhortations in mind, you may well now be at the point of arranging your departure from your home country. Before you leave, I encourage you to research and read or skim available books and resources to begin exploring the region, country, people, culture, and language you are about to learn. In terms of language specifically, be sure to look into the common writing systems (alphabets) for the language you will study, as well as any resources that describe the phonology (sound system), lexicon (dictionaries), and grammar of the language. Also, for culture, you can search for reliable resources that explain the cultures in the country and region where you plan to work. As you read or skim the books and articles, you should create an annotated bibliography by listing all of the resources in a document by category, and then noting in two to four sentences the value of each one, as well as how you can access them if and when you need to do so. While you won't try to learn the culture and language before you leave your home country, these resources can provide you with a very helpful overview of the new learning environment. This will enable you as an adult learner to build a broad mental picture of the culture and language content and context, all of which you will confirm as you implement BEC in the specific community where you will live.

After you depart from your home country and arrive in your new language learning environment, keep the following in mind as you warm up and get settled.

Principles for learning

As you enter the new context, I want to share four important principles that should guide you as you build a new way of life in this cross-cultural enviroment. These principles ultimately explain the approach that I take in BEC to train you to live, work, and relate effectively through the local culture and language. I trust that you will apply these principles thoroughly and consistently; and I believe that if you do, your learned abilities in culture and language will not distract local speech community members, but rather will greatly enhance your cross-cultural understanding and communication in light of the lived circumstances of those local communities.

Integrated into the local culture

First, I intentionally integrate the BEC program into the local cultural context. This principle makes the BEC program unique and explains why and how BEC will guide you to develop and implement learning activities specific to your local cultural environment as you progress through each of the four levels. While this may sound daunting, we have seen many learners enjoy and greatly benefit from this approach to culture and language learning in several ways. First, as a result of this principle, learners consistently have better opportunity to succeed in reaching our final BEC proficiency goal of Capable High, in contrast to other programs that aim for much lower target outcomes. Furthermore, we find that this culture-based approach best positions learners to contribute to culturally relevant conversations in the communities where they will live. Finally, deriving the learning curriculum from the local cultural context assists learners to not only effectively learn majority cultures and languages, but also, as necessary, to acquire minority or endangered languages where formal schools do not exist and where resources in the local language are lacking and need to be developed for the good of language preservation and development in those settings.

Based in local relationships

In the places where workers like you will locate, BEC encourages you to base your learning of culture and language on a strong foundation of local relationships. This means that BEC will direct you to strategically spend significant time building strong relationships with a wide and diverse group of local language speakers. Based on many years of working and consulting cross-culturally, I am convinced that this approach will serve you well to build necessary credibility as you experience your way into the lives of local people such that you can understand their worldviews and deeply held values. For these reasons, BEC not only explains how you should prioritize informal time with local people, but also how you will proactively seek out local people to serve as formal language helpers who can assist you to learn their culture and language. I believe this to be true and helpful for many of the same reasons listed above under the first principle of cultural integration. Additionally, I often find that the formal majority language schools that may already exist in a country lack the capability, desire, or resources to take learners to the worldview level of interpersonal understanding, relating, and communicating in the culture and language that I prioritize in BEC. Also, for obvious reasons, most of the pre-existing formal language schools do not consider the worldview implications connected to language development that you will need to explore as you build relationships in the community. For these reasons, I encourage you in the BEC program to ground your culture and language learning in deep relationships that you yourself form with members of the local community.

Comprehension anticipates production

In BEC, I believe that you will grown in speaking proficiency in culture and language as you first prioritize understanding the culture and language around you. In other words, I expect that you will learn to understand pieces of culture and language first, and that your learning to understand anticipates your learning to practice producing those pieces of culture and language. BEC will guide you in how to progressively increase the complexity of the culture and language that you focus on first understanding and then speaking. In the process, I will help you to know how to balance your comprehension and production in order to maximize efficiency and effectiveness in the progression of your learning.

Proficiency-focused outcomes

Finally, the BEC curriculum focuses on how proficiently you function in the local language in listening and speaking. Because functional proficiency matters more than what you formally know about the language, I set a specific and measurable speaking proficiency outcome for completing each one of the four BEC levels. As learners like you consistently apply the curriculum level by level, I find that you can indeed achieve these proficient targets as you move through BEC.

Become familiar with your new surroundings

With these four learning principles in mind, as you arrive in the country and begin to settle into your new community, I encourage you to invest the first four to six weeks into gradually becoming familiar with the immediate surroundings of your local environment. I trust that you have help finding a place to settle with your family, even if you need to first use temporary housing so that you can better get your bearings and evaluate your living options. As soon as you catch your breath, as you are out and about, pay attention to the sights and sounds of the culture and language around you. Here are a few specific encouragements as you get settled.

As you walk around the local community in your early days and weeks, rely on local people as much as possible to help you meet your immediate needs. Try to find one or two people who have some level of bilingualism in a language like English that you share in common with them. If possible, pursue friendship with these individuals in order to help make early communication easier.

As you think about long-term housing, I encourage you to look for options in neighborhoods where you have ample access to potential friends and language helpers from the local culture and language. Ask your new friends if they might show you around the area so you can get oriented to the geography and housing options. I encourage you to create a map of your local neighborhood so that you can organize your understanding of the area. As you make a longer-term housing decision, you may even consider staying in a compound or house with local hosts, if appropriate. In any case, I suggest that you avoid locating in expat neighborhoods with others from your own culture and language background. If you surround yourself with local people, you will have more natural opportunities to regularly interact with and live life alongside those from the culture and language you want to learn. And as you increase the regularity and volume of your interaction opportunities, your culture, language, and relationships can improve quite quickly as a result.

People

In your efforts to begin to explore the community around you in the first four to six weeks, begin making a list of people who might serve as potential friends and language helpers for you, including those you have already identified who have bilingual ability in a language like English that you share in common with them. Throughout BEC, you will need to intentionally and strategically spend significant time with local people. Even in the first four to six weeks of warming up and getting settled, I encourage you to begin building relationships with neighbors, host family members, work colleagues, shopkeepers, and other parents. Be eager to ask for and express openness to receive help from the community around you, even for meeting your basic needs. Approach people with a learner's attitude and a humble, caring heart. In most settings, when people believe that you are sincere, they are glad to offer input into questions you may have about furniture, shopping, cooking, schools, and so on.

These relationships are also important because in the coming levels of the BEC program, you will need to spend significant time with those who can help you both formally and informally to learn culture and language. First, some of these individuals will need to become formal language helpers who will work with you daily in language sessions in a controlled environment using focused learning activities that the BEC program will explain to you.

Second, many of those above will also become friends with whom you informally learn culture and language by intentionally investing in interpersonal interaction in community life together. As you do this, you will strategically use these less formal times to reinforce the culture and language that you have acquired through your controlled learning in language sessions. As you spend regular time with local people in community settings, BEC will encourage you to participate and document routine, relationally-based activities from ordinary life. You will do this because you want to grow not only in language proficiency, but also in relational and cultural proficiencies that will assist you in effective future language development work.

These relationally and culturally derived routines of life from your informal learning will form a framework for how you will apply BEC in all levels of the program. In Level 1 of BEC, for instance, you will observe and collect many examples of ordinary routines as you participate in daily life in the local community. This will provide you with a perspective of people's regular experience across a broad range of cultural categories. In Level 2, you will continue observing and collecting examples of life routines. You will also spend time in your formal language sessions with a growing number of local people to learn to explain these common routines from their lives. In Level 3, you will expand your relationship network to at least twenty local friends with whom you will discuss and debate life experiences and life complications common to local people based on their routines of life. Level 4 of BEC then bridges from these many relationships and life conversations into focused worldview discussions based on the significant rapport and trust you have established with local friends through their life stories derived from regular routines of life.

All of this means that investing time from the outset in getting to know the cultural routines of members of the local community serves as a crucial foundation for both formal and informal aspects of the BEC program. I designed the curriculum to help you to know how to engage and interact with the local community through these routines of life in a healthy and sustainable way as you move through BEC. These relationship expectations will feel challenging at the beginning, but will prove well worth the effort as you move toward worldview competency.

Places

As you get settled during your first weeks of meeting many potential friends and language helpers, you also should begin to identify common places where these local people congregate. Often I use the term "sociocultural institutions" to refer to these culturally predictable places for societal convergence. These locations are greatly beneficial because they serve as sites where local people tend to spend time together and therefore settings where you also can fit in naturally to spend time with local community members. Such locations might include:

- Your neighbors' homes and yards

- Your local street or suburb

- Local markets, parks, gardens, and playgrounds

- Nearby shops and stores

- Community centers, libraries, coffee shops, and places of religious observance

- Exercise, art, music, and dance facilities

As I previously mentioned, in your application of BEC, you will divide your time between these kinds of less formal learning settings where you participate in community life, and formal language sessions where you intentionally learn language and culture in a controlled environment. For now, note the sociocultural congregating places that you can begin to get to know and plan to engage more fully over time, both during and after your four to six weeks of settling in. Be sure to add these locations to the community map that you are creating.

Collect practical expressions

As you begin interacting with local community members in your first four to six weeks, you should relax and listen to the language rather than immediately trying to reproduce what you hear. Pay attention to how the language sounds when spoken by native speakers and not by you. You should realize that your accent and speech will differ from native speakers, since you do not have native speaker awareness of the sound system and rhythm of the language. You will need to acquire that ear and ability over time. In these first weeks, then, focus on observing and listening to how and when native speakers use the language socially and culturally, without feeling a pressure to immediately reproduce what you hear.

As you focus on listening to the language in the local community in the first four to six weeks, you should collect specific practical expressions that you will memorize and produce. Practical expressions are ordinary greetings and other everyday phrases that immediately help you begin to survive and function in the community. Common examples include: "Where is the bathroom?", "No, thank you," "Yes, please," "What is your name?", "My name is ...", "Good morning," "Good evening," or "How much does this cost?" Ask your friends to help you to decide which twenty to twenty-five expressions will assist you most in your first four to six weeks. Your friends can teach you how to say the expressions and can explain when you should use them. Ask one of your friends if he or she might also make a native speaker recording for you of the practical expressions in the local language, one at a time, spoken at a normal speech rate, with a pause between each one. Remember, you don't want to record your own voice, but rather record a native speaker saying the expressions for you.

When you have created the recording with the help of a native speaker, listen to it several times per day, pausing after each expression to practice repeating them one at a time, as correctly as possible. As you interact in the community, use the practical expressions at appropriate opportunities as frequently as you can. Get input from native speakers to correct your pronunciation.

Plan your schedule

In getting settled in the community by meeting people and visiting key places, you also need to plan to develop a broad schedule that will allow you, your spouse, your family, and possibly your teammates to invest as many daily and weekly blocks of time as possible into learning the local language and culture, while continuing with a healthy family and team life. In the coming years, you and your spouse and work partners will need to invest thousands of hours of consistent and focused time and energy into culture and language learning. This means that you should plan a schedule that will sustain you over the long journey.

If you have family responsibilities and other work you must do to maintain a viable identity and visa, you will need to strategize with your spouse and partners to collaborate together in a combined schedule that evens out your individual weekly and monthly investments in culture and language learning as much as possible. Look for opportunities to align the life activities for your family and team with the life activities and natural rhythms of the community around you. Observe how and when your local neighbors shop, cook, clean, wash, parent, study, work, and rest. Adjust your broad schedule to these rhythms so that you can learn to participate in the local way of functioning as you manage your home, family, team, and work.

Draw up your broad schedule in these early weeks, implement, and plan to modify as necessary. Try to relax and stay flexible. You will need to develop a routine of life that your whole family and team can manage together.

How long will this take, anyway?

In order to help you to plan your specific schedule, each level of BEC includes a recommended minimum number of learning plans for completing the level. For all levels, each of the learning plans requires eight hours to implement. I designed BEC to allow for multiple scenarios for how many weekly and monthly hours you as a learner put into culture and language acquisition. In an ideal situation, you should try to invest forty hours per week, meaning that you apply five learning plans per week. If you complete five learning plans per week throughout the entirety of BEC, you can expect that you will need between twenty-three and twenty-seven months to finish all the plans for all four levels.

Having said that, depending on your previous language learning experience, your aptitude, the relationship of the language you are learning to your native language, and other time commitments, you may find that you must add additional months and even learning plans to each level in order to achieve the level-by-level proficiency benchmarks that we recommend. In certain cases, the above time estimates may increase based on factors outside your control: lack of access to the language community, unforeseen illnesses, and other contingency events. As already mentioned, certain learners may need to work more slowly through the learning plans for one reason or another. Some learners may also find that they must manage other responsibilities in the second culture and language context, such as business or university studies for visa purposes. In these cases, learners may find that they can only complete three or four plans per week. Regardless of how many plans you implement per week, I recommend that you apply the BEC learning plans in eight hour increments, so that you engage with each plan for eight hours as a matter of habit, even if you subdivide plans over more than one day.

With eight hour increments in mind, if you can apply four learning plans per week instead of five, this means that you would implement thirty-two hours of weekly language learning on average. A schedule of four plans per week sometimes proves reasonable for husbands and wives learning language concurrently, as I highly recommend that spouses do everything they can to equalize the weekly hours each one invests as much as possible, since they both will need to learn the culture and language well in order to effectively work with men and women in the local environment. When husbands and wives intentionally collaborate together to balance out their schedules of learning with their other life responsibilities, often they find that they can each invest thirty-two hours per week, and in this way they can keep this relative pace and progress with one another.

In summary, as you plan your schedule for culture and language learning, keep in mind that you should (1) invest as many hours per week implementing BEC as possible; (2) allocate eight hours to each learning plan, such that you regularly complete all the sections for each plan before moving on to the next plan; (3) balance your weekly time investments for learning with your spouse and other work partners; and (4) do not regularly fall below a minimum threshold of weekly hours. I have found that when the pace of learning drops to less than sixteen hours per week (two learning plans), learner progress becomes extremely slow, likely not achieving a viable threshold of continuing to grow forward beyond a market level of fluency. For this reason, I recommend that you strive for twenty-four or thirty-two hours per week at the very least, and more ideally forty hours per week. As an encouraging word, I do believe that most adults can effectively learn a second culture and language in a reasonable timeframe if they persist in the diligent work that I am describing.

Looking forward: Preview of the four levels of the BEC program

As previously mentioned, after you complete your four to six weeks of getting settled, BEC will lead you through four successive levels of growing in culture and language based in your relationships to others in the local community. For each of the four levels, I break down the eight hour learning plans into four main kinds of learning activities: (1) Participant Observation, (3) Language Sessions, (3) Review, and (4) Planning. I will explain the time increments that you should allocate to each of these four segments of an eight hour learning plan as you progress through the learning plans in the four levels of BEC. In the meantime, below I briefly summarize the focus of the four levels of BEC for you.

Level 1: Relating through the common and familiar

Level 1 consists of 50 eight hour learning plans. During Level 1, you will relate to others through learning to comprehend and repeat the 1500 to 2000 most common words, familiar phrases, and simple sentence patterns that local community members use every day.

Level 2: Relating through life routines

Level 2 consists of 80 eight hour learning plans. During Level 2, you will relate to others through recognizing and creating simple descriptions of the scenes for common cultural routines of life, explaining the steps of the common routines from various points of view, and asking and answering simple questions about those routines. You will understand and create unique sentences at this level rather than relying primarily on words, phrases, and memorized content.

Level 3: Relating through sharing life stories

Level 3 consists of 100 eight hour learning plans. During Level 3, you will relate to others through understanding and producing paragraph-length speech in all the major time-frames: past, present, and future. At this level, you can understand and discuss overviews of life experience and specific situations in life with complications, all from multiple points of view. You can also understand and describe future plans and aspirations, and you can effectively compare and contrast life experiences.

Level 4: Relating through worldview conversation

Level 4 also consists of 100 eight hour learning plans. In Level 4 of BEC, you will learn to understand and talk about the values and beliefs that motivate the behavior of those with whom you build relationships. You can understand community member opinions about worldview questions, and you can support your own opinions about these kinds of topics. You can also understand and explain the benefits and difficulties of a variety of points of view for abstract topics. You can comprehend and explain reasons and results for many abstract issues affecting the community around you. You can also understand when community members hypothesize about potential or abstract topics, and you can talk about hypothetical world issues yourself. At this level, you can connect paragraphs together to form extended texts in conversation, talk about the bigger issues in the world, and can find ways to discuss concepts that are new to you but that you want to describe.

Level Objectives: Pre-Arrival and Getting Settled

At the end of each level of BEC, I provide a checklist of objectives that you can use to track your progress. In the following checklist for Pre-Arrival and Getting Settled, read and confirm that you have completed all the objectives. Remember, Pre-Arrival applies before you leave your country of origin, whereas Getting Settled covers your first four to six weeks in the local language community, prior to when you formally begin Level 1 in BEC. Only the first two objectives below relate to Pre-Arrival. The rest apply to Getting Settled.

1. Before my arrival, I researched and compiled a list of the best resources for the people, culture, and country where I plan to live, both on a national and local level. I reviewed and summarized the value of each of the resources in a brief paragraph or two (annotated bibliography). I can explain how and where I will access these resources should I need to do so.

2. Before my arrival, I specifically explored the language by compiling a list of available resources in areas of the writing systems (alphabets), sound systems (phonologies), dictionaries, and available grammars. I reviewed and summarized the value of each of the resources in a brief paragraph or two (annotated bibliography). I can explain how and where I will access these resources should I need to do so.

3. I have reviewed the four learning principles for BEC and can explain at least two implications for how each principle will impact my approach to learning culture and language.

4. I can list five to ten individuals from a range of backgrounds in my local community who may serve as future friends and language helpers for me.

5. I have drawn or marked a map that orients me to significant landmarks and points of reference in the local and surrounding language community.

6. I have specifically noted normal sociocultural congregating points where I can spend time in the future getting involved in community life.

7. I have worked with a language speaker to identify and record twenty to twenty-five practical expressions to help me begin to navigate in the local community. I have listened to those recordings daily for at least three weeks, seeking to repeat the expressions accurately. In the process of listening to the recordings, I have gotten help from a native speaker to learn to pronounce the expressions correctly.

8. I have memorized all the practical expressions and have practiced using them in the community many times.

9. I have a list of at least ten to fifteen common routines of life that I regularly observe in the lives of the local community members around me over a range of cultural categories.

10. Along with my spouse and/or teammates, we have observed regular life patterns in the community sufficiently to begin planning our language learning routine and time investments. We have determined our target weekly and monthly hours for Level 1 such that all of us have a comfortable plan for how we will use our time.

11. I can name the four kinds of activities that I will implement throughout my engagement with the learning plans in the BEC.

12. I can succinctly summarize the focus of each of the four levels of BEC.

LEVEL 1

Relating through the Common and Familiar

During level 1, you will relate to others through learning to comprehend and produce the 1500 to 2000 most common words, familiar phrases, and simple sentence patterns that local community members use every day.

Welcome to level 1! This chapter gives you step-by-step instructions for learning to understand and produce your first 1500 to 2000 words, familiar phrases, and simple sentence patterns from the local language community around you.

As mentioned in the Introduction, for each of the four levels of BEC, we break down the eight hour learning plans into four main kinds of learning activities: (1) Participant Observation, (2) Language Sessions, (3) Review, and (4) Planning.

As you get started with your level 1 learning, you will want to set up a simple, electronic learning plan notebook. This will be a place where you can plan for each day, record your community observations, organize your life routines list, and make other notes that will help you to track your progress as you learn. In this notebook, you should also include the sets of photos or pictures that you will use for each language session. Preferably, you will collect these photos in the community during your regular outings. But you also may need to supplement your photos with internet images, provided these images are culturally appropriate.

The first section of this chapter introduces the learning activities that you will use to progress through level 1. The second section provides learning plans that can guide you as you move through the level.

SECTION ONE

Learning Activities for Level 1

This section presents four learning activities for level 1 that you will apply in each of the eight hour learning plans. The next section, the learning plans, will describe the application of these four learning activities in greater detail.

Learning Activity 1: Participant Observation (three hours per learning plan)

Participant observation is very important to your entire learning process. The key to participant observation is to intentionally participate with community members in any routine activities that they regularly engage in. Most of these will be common life routines (e.g., shopping, cooking, banking, taking the bus), while a few will be special and formal routines (e.g., weddings, funerals, initiations, rituals).

As you begin your participant observation, it will be helpful for you to organize your life routines into cultural categories. I have created these categories as a way to cover the universal areas of culture no matter what the environment. All of the cultural categories that I list below, like food or transportation or work, can be broken down into a very large number of life routines that you should plan to observe, experience, and document from the local cultural point of view. As previously mentioned, you should also list in you learning plan notebook the common sociocultural settings where people live and work, such as shops, houses, markets, and other locations. These common settings will intersect with the cultural categories to produce many routines of life. You should already have a list of both sociocultural settings and common life routines that you've created during your time of getting settled. At this point, reorganize those routines in your learning plan notebook according to the twelve cultural categories below. Continue working on your list as you observe and participate in the community during level 1.

For your reference, I'm including in the cultural categories below some examples of life routines. These examples may or may not be relevant to the culture where you are living. If so, eliminate the irrelevant examples from the list. You will also notice that some life routines can fit into more than one cultural category. That's okay! Just make sure that you record them in a category and that you continue looking for additional life routines so that you can explore every cultural category on the list. You want to be sure that you are a well-rounded cultural observer moving forward, meaning you have many routines listed for each of the twelve cultural categories that are based in the cultural environment where you are living. Don't forget, any routine of life, as mundane as that routine may be, can serve as a routine that you can later document in twelve to fifteen steps. Almost any routine, even simple ones like brushing teeth or putting on clothes or combing hair, can be documented in steps like this. So don't discount the options in front of you; yet always make sure that you identify locally and culturally relevant routines, not ones that you import from your own culture! In the examples below, also realize that many of these routines can be further broken down into multiple smaller routines of life. So don't hesitate to subdivide complicated routines into multiple smaller life routines, even if you do also have an overview routine that covers the broad steps of the larger process.

The key question you should ask yourself is, "What are the twelve to fifteen steps that I might notice in this life routine from start to finish, based on how local community members do this task?" For example, if I were to document the routine of "How I brush my teeth" from my cultural context, I might note the steps like this: "When I want to brush my teeth, I first walk to the bathroom. Then I open the medicine cabinet. Next I pull out my toothpaste. I also get out my toothbrush. I turn the water on to get water on my toothbrush. I then take the cap off of the toothpaste. I put toothpaste on my toothbrush...". With this example, I would continue listing the steps to the end of the teeth brushing process. As I mention, you can see how you can easily derived twelve to fifteen steps from even the most ordinary of life routines.

Twelve Cultural Categories for Life Routines with Examples

1. Transportation routines: for example, taking a taxi or bus, how to drive or navigate to a destination, riding a bicycle or motorcycle, walking to work or a store, changing a tire, fixing a broken chain, making a repair, getting a vehicle or bicycle repaired

2. Work routines: common routines for jobs and work, building and construction processes, building items in carpentry, going to the market for buying food, selling a product, making a local product, helping someone move, working in a school or orphanage

3. Economic routines including finance, banking, marketplace, and ownership: getting

money from an ATM, opening a bank account, visiting a local business, exchanging currency, selling and buying, paying a bill, buying a car or motorcycle

4. Religious and ritual routines: weddings, funeral activities, religious observances and services, ritual activities, sacrifices

5. Education and knowledge routines: preparing to go to school, going to school, attending school, studying for an exam, buying school supplies, applying for a university program, going to a museum or zoo or cultural center

6. Art and entertainment routines, including sports and recreation: going dancing, going to a sporting event, going to the movies, taking a hobby class like art or calligraphy or martial arts, playing a sport, watching a sport, giving an invitation, accepting an invitation, going to a concert, going swimming, coaching a sport

7. Agriculture and food routines, including drinks, meals, drugs and alcohol: cooking on a stove, going out to eat, making a meal, planting food, raising animals, making drinks, buying and consuming drinks, smoking, placing a phone or internet food order, hosting a meal, attending a meal, hosting a party

8. Health and human biology routines, including stages of life: making a dental or doctor's appointment, attending a dental or doctor's appointment, ordering medicine in a pharmacy, buying medicine in a pharmacy, going to the gym, hosting a birthday party, attending a birthday party, attending an initiation or celebration event, getting married, graduating from some level of education, having a baby, attending a funeral, dating relationships

9. Social organization routines, including age, gender, race, caste, kinship, family, friends, government, law: voting, reporting a crime, interacting with the police, paying a fine, paying taxes, applying for a program, getting a visa, crossing a border, doing paperwork for some purpose, getting a driver's license

10. Physical environment routines: going to the beach, hiking, driving, doing yard work, gardening, sweeping the floor or street, washing dishes

11. Clothing and adornment routines: washing clothes, going to a laundromat, doing makeup, buying jewelry, getting piercings, getting tattoos, buying a uniform, getting a haircut, doing nails, styling hair, getting dressed

12. Tools and technology routines: receiving a phone call, making a phone call, buying a phone plan, adding phone minutes, checking your email, writing an email, using a computer or computer program, repairing a computer or phone, buying a computer, sending a picture over Whats App, connecting to the internet at a coffee shop

As you participate in these routines of life during level 1, here are a few notes of encouragement for how you can process and document your observations.

In your hours of participant observation, OBSERVE what is going on around you in a purposeful way. Who is speaking to whom, what tone are they using, what routines are taking place, and what people, actions, and objects are a part of those routines? As you participate, plan to take pictures of the life routines. Include a picture of each one of the steps of each routine, as well as two or three pictures of the broader routine settings. For example, if you are going to the pharmacy, get two to three setting pictures of the pharmacy exterior, a wide angle interior pharmacy picture, and perhaps a far away view of the area of the city where you find the pharmacy. Also, in taking pictures of the steps of the routine, capture at least twelve to fifteen steps for each routine, with one separate photo for each step. For each routine step, try to include an actor who is doing something specific with an object of some kind.

Once you have the photos, I encourage you to organize them in the order that the steps occurred, on the front side of just one to two pages. You should be able to drag and drop them into place with a simple word processing program. Insert the two or three setting photos first on the first page, before you begin the routine steps photos in order. Keep in mind that you probably will not want to document a routine with photos like this the first time you participate, as such may not be appropriate or helpful. You may want to wait until the second, third, or fourth time that you participate before you document the routine with photos, so that local community friends feel more comfortable with you. As you continue forward in level 1, plan to participate in the routines enough times to document all the life routines on your list as part of your participant observation. By the end of level 1, you will need to document more than forty routines in this way, approximately four per cultural area, as this photo documentation will serve as an important part of your learning content for level 2. Of course you should participate in lots more routines than forty, and you are well served to document as many as possible beyond forty in your participant observation. Also, keep in mind that your outsider's view of the steps of a routine may not represent how local people think of the process. So do your best to document the life routines through photos, all the while realizing that you may need to revise your photos when you begin learning the life routines in level 2. Finally, I encourage you to wait three or four weeks into level 1 before you begin documenting life routines with photos in this way, such that you can have a better chance of capturing how insiders understand the steps of these processes.

As you observe, participate in, and document routines of life, make an effort to LISTEN with understanding to the language you are learning.

In the process, RESPOND by showing friendship and appreciation to others. Genuinely participate as much as you can in what is taking place. Try to act in appropriate ways, while still being yourself. As you progress through level 1, you will grow in your ability to verbally respond and interact. Push yourself to practice speaking and repeating as much as you can. Don't forget to use your practical expressions!

Be very curious! NOTE down in your first language (English) what questions you might ask about who, with whom, for whom, what, with what, what kind, what color, when, where, how, how many, how long, how much, which ones, and why as you observe these life routines. Throughout most of level 1, I realize that you will not be asking these kinds of questions aloud in relevant ways in the local language, given your limited ability. However, as you move into level 2, having questions prepared in your first language will greatly help you to make the best use of these life routines for progressing forward. Also, continue noting down additional life routines for all the cultural areas that you do and can experience, identifying additional sociocultural settings, and recording people you can spend more time with. Finally, listen for and capture additional practical expressions related to the life routines that you can record from native speakers to add to your repertoire. Throughout level 1, try to capture at least five new practical expressions per week in this way.

Learning Activity 2: Listen and Act (two hours per plan for listening comprehension and speaking practice)

While participant observation is a critical form of informal learning, this second activity serves as a regular formal learning opportunity. In this activity, for each eight hour learning plan, you will intentionally set up two hour language sessions with local language helpers from the community. In order to do this, you may well need to make arrangements to pay these language helpers for their time according to the local wage scale. (I caution you to follow appropriate wage expectations for the local economy, not wage expectations from the country you are from.) You may also need to hire more than one language helper, since two hours per plan should amount to ten hours per week of language sessions for a full-time learner.

As you look for language helpers, begin with the list that you have created of friends from the community. You want to identify language helpers for level 1 who might be bilingual in their local language and your native tongue (English). They do not have to be highly proficient in English, though some level of bilingualism in English is very helpful. These language helpers do not need to be teachers by profession. In fact, sometimes teachers by profession have their own ideas about how you must learn the local language. But you need to find those who speak the standard local language clearly as their native tongue, who have good attention spans and memories, who are teachable and friendly, and who seem to catch on quickly to new ideas. When you first talk to a local person about serving as a potential language helper, I encourage you not to get into a long-term arrangement right away. Instead, ask the person if they might work with you for a set period of time, like four to eight weeks, to help you begin to learn their language and culture. As you work with the person in these early weeks, confirm that they demonstrate the characteristics that I listed above. As you find the right people, you can make longer-term arrangements to continue working with them as regular language helpers.

These language helpers will help you to apply this second activity, listen and act, as the primary way you will learn your first 1500 to 2000 words through your formal language sessions. In listen and act, you will use specific sentence frames to introduce new vocabulary in sentence contexts that are predictable enough for you to understand the new information being introduced by your helper. The vocabulary and simple sentences that you learn through listen and act will serve as the foundation for the bigger texts that you hear and learn from in level 2.

Here are the basic steps for listen and act:

1. Each learning plan will designate specific language areas for which you will learn basic vocabulary through the listen and act activity. I chose these vocabulary areas based on the general life experience of people around the world. In order to plan for your language sessions, then, you will need to collect relevant pictures for the specified language areas that represent 30-40 new vocabulary items for your two hour language session, as indicated in the learning plan for that day. (In some languages, learners find that they can process as many as 50-60 new vocabulary items in a two hour language session.) For the sake of this explanation, let's say that the learning plan for today indicates that you are learning the terms for the common fruits and vegetables found in the community. In order to prepare for your session, you should organize pictures of 30-40 common fruits and vegetables on the front side of no more than two printed pages, such that you can keep the two printed pages on the table in front of you and the language helper at all times during the session. (Note that you may want to keep a running master list in English in your learning plan notebook of all the vocabulary you have learned in all of your learning plans.)

2. Begin with one vocabulary item from the two printed pages and identify your first sentence frame. For example, let's say you will begin by learning to comprehend the word "banana" in the local language. For your sentence frame, you can ask your bilingual lan-

guage helper how he or she would say, "Point to the banana." Once the helper establishes the correct version of the frame in the local language, the helper then can say the frame with the vocabulary item: "Point to the banana." You will continue using this single frame for all the vocabulary items in your first two hour session. When the helper states the full sentence frame with the vocabulary item, you respond by pointing to the picture of the banana. The helper can repeat the sentence frame with the vocabulary item multiple times: "Point to the banana," "Point to the banana," "Point to the banana," "Point to the banana," "Point to the banana." Each time he or she says the sentence in the local language at a normal speech rate, you listen to what the helper says, and then you follow the instructions by pointing to the object that he or she designates with the sentence. At first, you will feel very lost and overwhelmed by the content of the full sentence. You won't even know which word is "banana"! You will be tempted to immediately write the sentence down to identify the individual words. You will be tempted to have the language helper only say single words instead of the complete sentence. You will feel that you must know how to say the sentence, too. But resist these three temptations to resort to writing, isolating single words, and repeating aloud! Trust me, those abilities will come over time as we introduce them to you. Instead, for now, simply listen to the vocabulary words as they occur in the context of the sentence frame, and then respond by pointing to the appropriate item. Respond eight or ten times by pointing as the language helper repeats the single sentence frame, "Point to the banana."

3. Now choose a second vocabulary item from the two pages. Direct the helper to use that item in the same spoken sentence frame. For example, the helper can now say, "Point to the apple." You will listen and point to the apple. As with "banana," the helper can repeat, "Point to the apple," multiple times. Each time the helper repeats the sentence, you point to the apple.

4. After eight to ten repetitions of the new item in the sentence frame, now have the helper alternate between "Point to the banana," and "Point to the apple." Each time the helper says one or the other at random, you point to the appropriate item. At this point, remind the helper that he or she should randomize the two sentences such that you can't predict which of the two he or she will use. Make sure that before you add another vocabulary item, you can consistently identify the ones that you have already included in the exercise as the helper says the sentences randomly.

5. After you can consistently respond to the difference between those first two sentences, the helper can add a third item: "Point to the orange." The helper should say this sentence eight to ten times, with you pointing to the orange each time. Now the helper should randomize the sentences with the three vocabulary items, always repeating the vocabulary item in the context of that complete sentence frame, "Point to the ...". Have the helper randomize these three sentences with the three fruits many times. At this point, you should be recognizing the sentences containing "banana," "apple," and "orange" at random when they appear in the "Point to the ..." sentence frame. You indicate your comprehension simply by pointing to the appropriate picture on the pages in front of you as the helper says the sentence.

6. You continue this way, adding one new vocabulary item at a time through your predictable sentence frame, "Point to the ...". As the helper adds each new item, he or she should first say the sentence frame eight or ten times with the new item. After you have heard that new item in the sentence frame eight to ten times, the helper can then add that sentence to the random repetition with all the other sentences, interspersed with the sentences containing the other fruits that you've previously heard, quizzing you at random

on all the fruits learned to this point in the process using the predictable sentence frame.

7. Gradually, then, you build up your comprehension of all of the 30-40 items in the set in this way, adding them one at a time with the sentence frame, "Point to the ...". As each item gets added through the frame, the helper should return to randomly quiz you on all the vocabulary that you have previously heard in that session, always in the context of the sentence frame. By the end of the two hour session, you should be able to confidently point to each vocabulary item when used at random in the predictable sentence frame. Keep in mind that this activity will seem quite monotonous for language helpers and for you. Most helpers and learners have no idea how many repetitions they will require in order to solidify their comprehension of vocabulary through this exercise. Suffice it to say, you will need dozens of repetitions of each vocabulary item used at random in the sentence frame during each language session! Persist in encouraging your helpers to continue forward with this process in the two hour session, trusting that over time, you will indeed internalize this vocabulary and the basic sentence structures.

8. In the last ten minutes of your two hour session, the language helper should create a single randomized recording of all the vocabulary items that you have learned in your session. In the recording, the language helper should repeat the sentence frame two times for every vocabulary item. (Tip: Many language helpers find that they can use tick marks on the printed picture pages to remember their progress through the recording. Each time they randomly repeat the frame with that vocabulary item, they can put a little mark by that picture on the pages. Thus, by the end of the recording, the helper should have put two tick marks by each of the items on the photo pages.) However, the two repetitions of the sentence with the same vocabulary item should not occur one after the other in the recording, but rather randomly in the recording. In other words, the sentence, "Point to the banana," should appear once in the recording randomly, and then another time elsewhere in the recording randomly, with no predictable pattern for when and where. Do this with all of the 30-40 vocabulary items for that day's learning plan, scattering the two repetitions randomly throughout the single recording. After each recorded sentence, the helper should leave enough of a space in the recording to allow you to mentally or audibly repeat the entire sentence at a normal speech rate in the local language in the blank audio space, before he or she moves on to say the next sentence. Remember, however, that you are only recording the voice of the language helper saying the sentences, not your own voice. The pauses in the recording are simply blank spaces long enough for you to later repeat the sentences mentally or audibly in your time of review as you hear them. In sum, a recording with 30-40 vocabulary items in sentence frames, repeated randomly two times each, with a sentence-length pause after each utterance, should be no longer than 3-5 minutes.

I need to mention three more important notes about listen and act before we move on. First, I encourage you to introduce one new sentence frame for every four learning plans as you move forward in level 1. This means that you will need to identify up to fifteen sentence frames for level 1. Here is a set of ideas for frames you can consider as you move forward.

(1) Point to the banana. (2) This is the banana. (3) That is the banana. (4) Pick up the banana. (5) Put down the banana. (6) Show me the banana. (7) Where is the banana? (8) Here is the banana. (9) Put the banana beside/on top of/beside/under the table. (10) Where is the woman holding the banana? (11) Which is the banana? (12) The banana is yellow. (13) Point to the banana beside the orange. (14) Don't put the banana on the table; put it on the floor. (15)

the man is putting the banana on the table. (16) The woman is putting the banana under the table. (17) The woman is putting the banana beside the table.

These sentences represent ideas for other frames you might explore. Remember, you will need to work with the language helper to be sure the frames are appropriate for the local culture and language. After you introduce the new frame the first day in a learning plan, the second day, bring all the other frames back into the possibilities for sentences the language helper can use at random, prioritizing the new frame more, but using the previous frames throughout to keep them fresh. By days three and four, the language helper should use all the frames that you have previously learned randomly in the language session. Your recording can also include all the frames used randomly with the new vocabulary for that day's learning plan.

Second, as you apply listen and act, you should keep in mind that you need to cover all the major parts of speech in the way that you construct sentence frames and learn core vocabulary through level 1. The specific learning plans in the next section will help you with that. However, remember that in a general sense, the common parts of speech include nouns, pronouns, verbs, adjectives, adverbs, prepositions, conjunctions, and interjections. For majority languages that are already documented, you may need to consult your grammar resources for the local language to overview how these features work in the context where you live.

Third, after about four weeks of working with and reviewing these familiar sentence frames as you learn new vocabulary, the learned frames should be familiar enough that you can mentally and silently repeat the sentences the helper speaks as he or she teaches you the new vocabulary. Your goal should be that as you review your recordings consistently and move forward with language sessions, you will begin to mentally and silently repeat the sentences like this in language sessions on a regular basis, even when you are learning new vocabulary.

As you can do this silent repetition consistently, by learning plan 26 at the latest, you will begin repeating aloud what you are hearing from the helper during your language sessions. The learning plans will guide you as to when to begin this repeating aloud in your language sessions.

Learning Activity 3: Review (two hours per learning plan)

As you collect good recordings for each vocabulary set of 30-40 items in sentence frames from your language sessions, you will need to review those vocabulary sets throughout the course of level 1 by practicing with your recordings on your own. I encourage you to practice reviewing your recordings of vocabulary sets for two hours for every eight hour learning plan. In other words, your hours of review with recordings should match your hours of language sessions for each learning plan. Here are some steps for you to consider for your time of review.

For the first four to six weeks of learning plans in level 1, simply listen and act, both in your language sessions and as you review your recordings. As previously described, the recordings should be random enough that you can listen to them many times without memorizing them per se. Be sure that as you review the recordings, you can consistently point to the appropriate item on the photo pages as the helper says the sentence containing that item. Plan to always review with the photo pages in front of you in all of the steps that follow.

1. As you feel more confident beyond four weeks, during your language sessions, you will mentally (internally and silently) repeat the sentences that you hear as you listen and

act. Also after about four weeks, practice this same habit while you review your recordings as well. At first, you may even whisper these repetitions aloud during your review. Remember, the recordings should be randomized, and they should have a space after each sentence that is long enough for you to do this mental or whispering repetition at a normal speech rate.

2. After about six weeks, begin repeating aloud as you listen and act, both in language sessions and in review of your recordings. This will require that you have internalized the sentence frames well enough to be able to repeat them aloud accurately, simply swapping out the new vocabulary items as you move forward.

3. After six weeks, you should also begin to transcribe your recordings completely, such that you fully clarify any unfamiliar words or phrases in all of your recordings. You can do this by writing out each recorded text word for word in a simple document. For every line of transcribed text in the local language, leave two blank line spaces. Then on the next line immediately below the original language text, write down the English meaning of just the unfamiliar words and phrases from that first line, placing each English translation of the unfamiliar word or phrase just below that word or phrase in the original language. On the third line below those two lines, you can then write out the full idiomatic meaning of the whole text in English, following the original language line by line in the process. In this way, you will confirm that you make all of your recordings fully comprehensible. You will also begin to learn to read and write correctly in the local language through this procedure. I encourage you to return to your earliest recordings first and work your way forward, writing down each recording as explained above, using the alphabet that represents the way local people write their language. You may need to consult local dictionaries and phonologies to ensure that you know how to write and spell the language correctly. In cases of unwritten languages, you may need to use the International Phonetic Alphabet (IPA) as a starting point for this process. While this transcription work will be painstaking at first, don't lose heart! Work with native speakers outside your language session hours to help you gain momentum for how to do this writing work. Confirm your transcriptions with these native speakers to ensure accuracy and clarity. While you can review these transcriptions of recorded texts during your language session hours, I encourage you to consider working with a native speaker outside of session hours for this purpose, so as not to consume your session learning hours with transcription correction. You might hire another language helper, or you might pay your one of your current helpers to extend your two session hours for this and for mimicry practice in (5) below.

4. After you begin transcribing your recordings in your review when you reach the six week mark, in this step, repeat the transcribed recording aloud sentence by sentence, pausing the recording between sentences to ensure that you can repeat the recordings accurately. For recordings at level 1, you probably won't need to pause the recording, as you have intentionally left sentence-length gaps for this purpose. Look at your transcriptions for help when you forget how to appropriately speak aloud what you have learned to understand in the recordings. Practice this step until you can repeat the recordings correctly sentence by sentence, without having to consult your transcriptions.

5. I also encourage you to set aside time each day to confirm pronunciation of the recordings sentence by sentence with a native speaker. In other words, sit with a native speaker and play the recording, pausing after each sentence so that you can repeat the sentence aloud in the presence of the native speaker. Solicit feedback from the native speaker as to how and where to improve your pronunciation. Try to mimic the native speaker's way

of saying the sentences. Work systematically through your recordings day by day with a native speaker, practicing your pronunciation. You can do this work in your language sessions if you very carefully limit the amount of time that you dedicate to this activity, not more than ten minutes per two hour session. Or as mentioned in (3) above, you may pay a language helper to extend your two hour session to include mimicry practice like this, along with correction of your written transcriptions.

6. Practice repeating the recording simultaneously with the native speaker's voice, without pausing the recording. (For level 1 recordings, you won't need to think about pausing, because you built pauses into your recordings.) In this step, you should be repeating the recording accurately without consulting your transcription any longer. When I describe repeating the recording simultaneously with the native speaker, I don't mean that you have memorized the recording word for word. Rather, I mean that while you listen to the recording at normal speed, you repeat slightly behind but overtop of the voice of the native speaker as you continue to listen, while not pausing the recording to "catch up" with the native speaker. You will improve in this skill of keeping up with native speakers the more that you practice.

7. In step 7, practice back-translating (by speaking aloud, not by writing) each recording into idiomatic English sentence by sentence, pausing the recording between sentences for your recordings beyond level 1. This is a high-level skill that develops your ability to listen and translate without having to consciously process your thoughts in the translation process. If you practice like this in level 1, this skill will pay great dividends as you move forward in later levels.

8. Finally, you should also practice simultaneously back-translating each recording aloud without pausing the recording. Again, as with simultaneous repetition, I mean that while you listen to the recording at normal speed, you translate into English slightly behind but overtop of the voice of the native speaker as you continue to listen, while not pausing the recording to "catch up" with the native speaker in your translation into idiomatic English. This step serves as your final confirmation of your grasp of the content of your recordings. I would encourage you to get all the way through step 8, simultaneous back-translation, with each of your recordings for level 1.

As you work through these eight steps for the review activity, I remind you of one important point to keep in mind: You shouldn't try to complete all eight review steps with each individual recording for level 1, before you begin the steps for other level 1 recordings. Rather, you should use your two review hours for a learning plan to work with three to five recordings, but take another step for each of those recordings so that you are not applying the same step with each recording. For example, in your two hours of review for a learning plan, you should certainly work significantly in review step 1 (mentally repeating) and/or step 2 (repeating aloud) with the session recording you collected today. But also in your two hours of review for today, you could work through the next step on your list with yesterday's recording, the subsequent step on the list with a recording from a day before that, and so on. You will find that certain review steps initially take more time, especially transcription. So you will have to work out your own plan for how much time to invest in each step of review with each recording. You should probably use a checklist of some kind to track your progress through the review steps for each of your recordings at all levels, such that you are sure to cover all the steps.

Also, after you complete step 8 with each recording, you should be able to move that recording to occasional review, such that you begin listening to the recording once every week, then every two weeks, then every month. I would encourage you to use step 6, simultaneous repetition without pausing, as your method of reviewing those recordings that you have moved to the occasional review phase.

Learning Activity 4: Planning (30 minutes to an hour per learning plan)

Finally, as you can see from the first three learning activities for level 1, you also will need to plan for your participant observation and language sessions for each learning plan. The process of planning for these two activities should take you between 30 minutes to an hour per plan.

In planning for your participant observation, you should set up times with local friends and language helpers to join with them in as many life routines as possible for each three hour increment of participant observation. I do encourage you to proactively plan these opportunities over the range of cultural areas, also accounting for the fact that you will take photos to document the life routines as previously described. You also should prepare to take notes of questions to self as you participate in the life routines. Keep in mind that often participant observation events do not occur in tidy three-hour segments. You will have to plan for multiple life routines for most days of this activity. Also, some life routines will stretch over much more than three hours, such as trips, major life events, meals and visiting, and other such occasions. In cases of extended routines, calculate the hours spent in participant observation for that event, divide the total by three hours, and allocate each of the three-hour segments to one of your learning plans. You can then focus on catching up on the other three learning activities besides participant observation for those learning plans, until you even out your investment of participant observation hours with the hours for the other learning activities across the plans.

In addition to planning for participant observation in that 30 minutes to an hour, you will also need to plan for language sessions for each learning plan. As you prepare for your language session for each plan, you should collect, organize, and print the picture sets of 30-40 items for that day of vocabulary learning on the front of two sheets. You will also prepare the sentence frames that you will use for learning the new vocabulary.

Conclusion for Level 1 Learning Activities

By applying these four learning activities in each of the eight hour learning plans for level 1, you can learn a large number of vocabulary items and basic sentence patterns in a period of just a few months. You will also have excellent opportunities to spend time with local friends in the context of their everyday lives. They will see you very much in a learner's role, and you will hopefully get to know them and their families and friends as well in the first few months. You will find that children love to help as you practice learning exercises like listen and act in informal settings, too.

As you hear and practice these words, phrases, and sentences in level 1 over and over in predictable frames, you will gradually begin to recognize and understand the learned vocabulary in unpredictable community interactions and settings as well. After many hundreds of repetitions in informal and formal contexts of learning, you will begin to pick out these items more quickly. Later, you will be able to think of the word or phrase appropriate for the context yourself, even before you hear it. Still later, you might remember the word or phrase out of context. Finally, months later in your practice, you will gain control of these words and phrases so that you can recall them at will for any context.

This is why repetition in the formal, familiar, and controlled context of language sessions first is so important. The process of hearing comprehensible pieces of the language repeated many times pushes you to first understand each word and phrase in a natural sentence before you own the pieces of language for yourself. When you do start repeating the sentence in level 1 after four to six weeks as stated above, your speaking will be based on your understanding of these components of language that you have heard repeated many times, and not on your forcing yourself to memorize them out of context. This thought should be an encouragement to you to relax and enjoy learning by first understanding. That is what the level 1 learning exercises are designed to help you to do. By spending a lot of time with these four learning activities in level 1, you are building your basic foundations for communication and are learning how to relate to others in natural situations. Learning to speak will come naturally as an outworking of all that you are understanding. By the time you finish level 1, my goal for you is that you at least reach the equivalent of Novice High on the ACTFL scale of speaking proficiency.[2] With proper implementation of the level 1 learning plans per the learning activities described, you can indeed achieve that goal.

SECTION TWO

Level 1 Learning plans 1 to 25

Now that you have been introduced to the four learning activities for level 1, let's move on to the level 1 learning plans. If you can work on culture and language full-time, you will spend forty or more hours each week implementing the learning plans for level 1. That would allow you to complete five learning plans each week, such that you finish all the learning plans for level 1 in ten to twelve weeks. Remember, even if you reduce your goal to three or four plans per week, be sure to implement each plan over eight hours so that you can consistently and correctly apply all four learning activities for each learning plan.

2. ACTFL Language Connects, "ACTFL Proficiency Guidelines 2012," American Council on the Teaching of Foreign Language, accessed May 13, 2022, https://www.actfl.org/resources/actfl-proficiency-guidelines-2012/english/speaking#novice.

Level 1 Daily Learning Plan 1

1) PARTICIPANT OBSERVATION: You can start by participating in simple daily activities like people greeting one another and saying goodbye, and by visiting common settings where people gather to talk to one another and to live their daily lives. You can accompany others as they wash laundry, cook, eat, clean up, go to work, go shopping, take children to school, ride public transport, chop firewood, work in gardens, gather food, hunt or fish, go to the market, build houses, visit with family and friends, visit people in hospital, go to a restaurant, go to the corner store, go to church or meetings, and do many such tasks that are a part of their daily routine in the community.

You may want to consider getting the basic tools and utensils that you see people using so that you can participate more effectively.

Here are a few goals for your participant observation:

> **OBSERVE** the common objects, positions of objects, people who are working with the objects, ways you would describe the objects, and actions that they use to work with the objects in the activities that you participate in.

> **LISTEN** for unique sounds, syllable stress, and general pronunciation.

> **RESPOND** by appropriately asking *WHAT, WHERE, HOW, WITH WHAT, WHEN*, and *WHO* questions in whatever second language you have in common with the community.

> **NOTE** common daily activities and categories of activities in people's lives, as well as *WHY* questions you have but shouldn't ask, and so on.

2) LISTEN AND ACT: Start by learning to understand words for people (like baby, child, young person, woman, man, old man, old woman) and common community animals (like pig, dog, chicken, bird, fish, snake). Include reference words like I, you, he, she, it, they, us. Never try to learn to understand words in isolation. Instead, always learn to understand new vocabulary in the context of a sentence, such as "Show me the man," "Point to the man," "Where is the man?" or "This is a man."

Here is an example of the way that you will apply this learning exercise. One of the sets of words you are learning to understand in this first *Daily Learning Plan* is words for people and common animals. In that case, start by using pictures of basic people from your *Photo Book* —baby, child, young person, woman, man, old man, old woman. Include the common animals that you see around the community in your pictures or photos (chickens, pigs, dogs, and so on) as well. Then pick two of the items, and point at them while the person uses them in a sentence - never try to learn words in isolation - only in the context of a sentence, like "This is a man" and "This is a woman." Or "Point to the man" or "Show me the man." It is often most helpful to use the same sentence pattern for the whole exercise so that you aren't confused. Remember, they are talking, you are just listening.

Listen to the community member several times as you point to the two people that they have first introduced, one at a time. Then they can say, "This is a man," and you try to point to the man. The person can say, "This is a woman," and you try to point to the woman. Once you succeed in pointing correctly to those two several times, you can add a third, then a fourth, and on up. The community member should attempt to go through the items as randomly and unpredictably as possible to maximize your learning. They probably won't realize that you need to hear these things many, many times in order to understand them well. So don't become bored or move on too quickly!

3) LISTEN AND ACT: Have the community member command you to perform basic actions. You do the action as he or she tells you to. Again, start with two commands and include new commands one by one as you are able. For example, common commands include such things as "Stand up, sit down, walk, run, crawl, lie down, go, come, jump, stop," and so on.

4) LISTEN AND ACT: Explain to the community member that you'd like to learn common greeting and leave takings. Hopefully you've noted some of these during your time of getting settled in the community. (You can practice by role-playing with the community member. That is, you work together to act out the greeting or leave-taking scenario and they tell you what each person should say.)

5) Each day you should take your last 20 minutes of listen and act to review previous listen and act exercises. Of course this doesn't apply to the plan for day 1, since you are just beginning.

6) At the end of each of your listen and act exercises 2 to 4, record a summary example of the community member practicing with you. These audio recordings should be short for Level 1 learning exercises (1 to 5 minutes per exercise task), since you only want to record an example of each exercise for later review.

7) Prepare for the coming day's learning plan for 30 minutes. This may require you to begin getting materials together, planning with community members for participant observation, making sketches for the coming day in your Daily Learning Plan Notebook, and so on.

Level 1 Daily Learning Plan 2

On day two you will continue to build on what you learned the previous day. This will be a pattern that you will follow throughout Level 1. Suggestions for *participant observation* are the same for your first two weeks of learning plans, since you will be getting a feel for how to plan to participate effectively with others in the community.

Most of your review for past daily learning plans is already built into the new *listen and act* exercises in the next learning plan for you. But as mentioned, you should plan also to spend the last 20 minutes of each day with the community member reviewing *listen and act* exercises from the day before.

Keep your goal in mind of learning to comprehend about 30 new vocabulary items each day. Remember, you won't be able to recall these whenever you want at this point! But by using *listen and act* in your learning, you will begin to increase your recognition of the words in a controlled environment, which is the first important step to learning and relating in the common and familiar.

THINGS TO DO FOR LEARNING

1) PARTICIPANT OBSERVATION: Continue participating in simple activities in the community like greeting others, saying goodbye, and by visiting common settings where people gather to talk to one another and to live their daily lives. You can accompany others as they wash laundry, chop firewood, work in gardens, go to the market, and do many such tasks that are a part of their daily routine in the community.

Here are a few goals for your participant observation:

> **OBSERVE** the common objects, positions of objects, people who are working with the objects, ways you would describe the objects, and actions that they use to work with the objects in the activities that you participate in.

> **LISTEN** for unique sounds, syllable stress, and general pronunciation.

> **RESPOND** by appropriately asking WHAT, WHERE, HOW, WITH WHAT, WHEN, and WHO questions in whatever second language you have in common with the community.

> **NOTE** common daily activities and categories of activities in people's lives, as well as WHY questions you have but shouldn't ask, and so on.

2) LISTEN AND ACT: Begin learning to understand words for common items that are in an ordinary household in the community. This will include items such as beds, tables, chairs, dishes, knives, fans, TVs, machetes, axes, mats, hammocks, baskets, and so on. Again, start with two items first and have the community member use a sentence like, "Where is the axe?" Or "Point to the hammock." Include new items until you have exhausted the common possibilities, up to 30 or so items that you can recognize interchangeably.

3) LISTEN AND ACT: Using the terms that you already understand for people, pronouns, and animals, draw pictures to combine the common command actions that you heard in the first lesson with the people and animal words. This should help you to hear what sentences sound like when the person tells what is happening rather than commands you to do something. You can start by acting out many of the common actions yourself and ask the person to describe what it is that you are doing. Then you can associate a picture of your own with that action. Continue adding actions one by one to include all those you are familiar with. (For example, the community member could say, "The man is walking," and you'd point to a picture of a man walking. Or they could say, "He is running," and you'd point to a picture of a running man.)

4) Spend your last 20 minutes of listen and act reviewing the previous day's exercises.

5) Record a summary example of each listen and act exercise.

6) Review your new recordings for 20 minutes and your older ones for 20 minutes.

7) Prepare for the coming day's learning plan for 30 minutes. This may require you to begin getting materials together, planning with community members for participant observation, making sketches, and so on.

Level 1 Daily Learning Plan 3

THINGS TO DO FOR LEARNING

1) PARTICIPANT OBSERVATION: Continue participating in simple activities like greetings, saying goodbye, and by visiting common settings where people gather to talk to one another and to live their daily lives. You can accompany others as they wash laundry, chop firewood, work in gardens, go to the market, and do many such tasks that are a part of their daily routine in the community.

Here are a few goals for your participant observation:

OBSERVE the common objects, positions of objects, people who are working with the objects, ways you would describe the objects, and actions that they use to work with the objects in the activities that you participate in.

LISTEN for unique sounds, syllable stress, and general pronunciation.

RESPOND by appropriately asking WHAT, WHERE, HOW, WITH WHAT, WHEN, and WHO questions in whatever second language you have in common with the community.

NOTE common daily activities and categories of activities in people's lives, as well as WHY questions you have but shouldn't ask, and so on.

2) LISTEN AND ACT: Begin learning to comprehend parts of common buildings. You aren't trying to learn to understand highly technical vocabulary, but just terms that are common to daily life and conversation. These would include things such as wall, window, door, floor, roof, ceiling, stairs, rafter, roof beam, eaves, posts, poles. Again, the community member can help you to determine commonly used and culturally appropriate words for parts of the house. A good sentence for learning is, "Where is the door?" Or "Show me the ceiling." Or "Point to the pole." Try to have the person use the same sentence throughout the exercise so that you aren't confused.

3) LISTEN AND ACT: Using a community house area that you are in as a model, begin learning the common rooms and areas in the house. First walk to two areas with the community member and have them tell you the name of the two areas. Have them begin with those two areas and tell you, "Walk to the sitting area," Or "Go to the sleeping area." Begin with two areas in this way and gradually include all those that you can. In cases where the bathroom is outdoors and the cooking house or other living spaces are separate from the house you are in, include those in your exercises as well. You can just have the person tell you to point to the ones that are far off because they will be too time consuming to walk to. You might want to also try drawing a house floor plan or area map to help with this exercise, depending on the ability of the community member to relate to that type of representation.

4) Spend your last 20 minutes of listen and act reviewing the previous day's exercises.

5) Record a summary example of each listen and act exercise.

6) Review your new recordings for 20 minutes and your older ones for 20 minutes.

7) Prepare for the coming day's learning plan for 30 minutes. This may require you to begin getting materials together, planning with community members for participant observation, and so on.

Level 1 Daily Learning Plan 4

THINGS TO DO FOR LEARNING

1) PARTICIPANT OBSERVATION: Continue participating in simple activities like greetings, saying goodbye, and by visiting common areas where people gather to talk to one another and to live their daily lives. You can accompany others as they wash laundry, chop firewood, work in gardens, go to the market, and do many such tasks that are a part of their daily routine in the community.

Here are a few goals for your participant observation:

OBSERVE the common objects, positions of objects, people who are working with the objects, ways you would describe the objects, and actions that they use to work with the objects in the activities that you participate in.

LISTEN for unique sounds, syllable stress, and general pronunciation.

RESPOND by appropriately asking WHAT, WHERE, HOW, WITH WHAT, WHEN, and WHO questions in whatever second language you have in common with the community.

NOTE common daily activities and categories of activities in people's lives, as well as WHY questions you have but shouldn't ask, and so on.

2) LISTEN AND ACT: Using the household objects that you are now familiar with, take a set and work with them to begin to learn to understand placement words. These placement words would include words like beside, under, on, between, with, in, out, here, there. For example, let's say you are now familiar with these ten household items—table, hammock, basket, chair, knife, machete, firewood, axe, spear, bread. The community member can say something like, "Put the axe in the basket." Or "Put the knife on the table." Or "Put the firewood beside the chair." You can learn to understand lots of new ways to talk about putting items in places in this way.

3) LISTEN AND ACT: Using words for parts of the house and rooms of the house, expand the exercise of having the community member tell you to do things related to those items. For example, they can tell you, "Close the door," "Open the door," "Sit in the chair," "Go down the stairs," "Come up the stairs," "Lie on the bed," "Open the window," and so on.

4) Spend your last 20 minutes of listen and act reviewing the previous day's exercises.

5) Record a summary example of each listen and act exercise.

6) Review your new recordings for 20 minutes and your older ones for 20 minutes.

7) Prepare for the coming day's learning plan for 30 minutes. This may require you to begin getting materials together, planning with community members for participant observation, and so on.

Level 1 Daily Learning Plan 5

THINGS TO DO FOR LEARNING

1) PARTICIPANT OBSERVATION: Continue participating in simple activities like greetings, saying goodbye, and by visiting common areas where people gather to talk to one another and to live their daily lives. You can accompany others as they wash laundry, chop firewood, work in gardens, go to the market, and do many such tasks that are a part of their daily routine in the community.

Here are a few goals for your participant observation:

OBSERVE the common objects, positions of objects, people who are working with the objects, ways you would describe the objects, and actions that they use to work with the objects in the activities that you participate in.

LISTEN for unique sounds, syllable stress, and general pronunciation.

RESPOND by appropriately asking WHAT, WHERE, HOW, WITH WHAT, WHEN, and WHO questions in whatever second language you have in common with the community.

NOTE common daily activities and categories of activities in people's lives, as well as WHY questions you have but shouldn't ask, and so on.

2) LISTEN AND ACT: Use the placement words that you've previously heard (in, beside, on, between, with, under, and so on) and the common household objects that you've learned to expand your previous exercise. Now you will include putting, moving, and taking out objects as part of the exercise. If there are other common household items that you didn't previously learn to understand, you can include those in the exercise as well. For example, the community member can tell you, "Put the knife in the basket," "Take the book off the chair," "Move the axe to the table." As always, only introduce two new actions at a time, then more as your comprehension grows.

3) LISTEN AND ACT: Walk around the general living area with the community member to observe terms for the outdoor house and yard area. You should note terms for things like shrubs, yard, grass, trees, flowers, path, rocks, dirt, ground, and so on. You can stand in the yard and go through the learning exercise if you like, or you could sketch the items on paper and use the exercise in that fashion.

4) Spend your last 20 minutes of listen and act reviewing the previous day's exercises.

5) Record a summary example of each listen and act exercise.

6) Review your new recordings for 20 minutes and your older ones for 20 minutes.

7) Prepare for the coming day's learning plan for 30 minutes. This may require you to begin getting materials together, planning with community members for participant observation, and so on.

Level 1 Daily Learning Plan 6

THINGS TO DO FOR LEARNING

1) PARTICIPANT OBSERVATION: Continue visiting common areas where people gather to talk to one another and to live their daily lives. You can accompany others as they wash laundry, chop firewood, work in gardens, go to the market, and do many such tasks that are a part of their daily routine in the community.

Here are a few goals for your participant observation:

OBSERVE the common objects, positions of objects, people who are working with the objects, ways you would describe the objects, and actions that they use to work with the objects in the activities that you participate in.

LISTEN for unique sounds, syllable stress, and general pronunciation.

RESPOND by appropriately asking WHAT, WHERE, HOW, WITH WHAT, WHEN, and WHO questions in whatever second language you have in common with the community.

NOTE common daily activities and categories of activities in people's lives, as well as WHY questions you have but shouldn't ask, and so on.

2) LISTEN AND ACT: Expand a previous exercise to learn to understand more about common containers, bags, baskets, and so on that are found in the living area around the house and yard.

3) LISTEN AND ACT: Using previously learned objects, learn to understand common ways to talk about carrying, picking up, and giving. You can begin with the community member giving you commands to carry, pick up, or give the objects that you already are familiar with. Work with this exercise for quite a while, sticking with the most common words for carrying, picking up, and giving.

5) LISTEN AND ACT: Since there are often lots of different ways to talk about carrying objects and giving objects depending on what you are carrying and to whom you are giving them, explore ways to talk about carrying and giving using a variety of objects and your words for different people. There are LOTS of options and possibilities with this exercise. Carrying can be done on the head, shoulder, in a strap, in a basket or bag, around the neck, and so on. Often languages use different words for these. You don't want to exhaust every possibility, but rather learn to understand the common terms for carrying and holding. Your friend can first model these for you. They can then command you to do the carrying actions using the objects that you know.

You can resort to using your sketches of people if you need to for describing different people and their giving actions. For example, the community member can say, "He is giving the axe to her," or "The woman is giving the book to the man." In each case, you can respond by motioning to the drawing who is doing what to whom with what object.

5) Spend your last 20 minutes of listen and act reviewing the previous day's exercises.

6) Record a summary example of each listen and act exercise.

7) Review your new recordings for 20 minutes and older ones for 20 minutes.

8) Prepare for the coming day's learning plan for 30 minutes.

Level 1 Daily Learning Plan 7

THINGS TO DO FOR LEARNING

1) PARTICIPANT OBSERVATION: Continue visiting common areas where people gather to talk to one another and to live their daily lives. You can accompany others as they wash laundry, chop firewood, work in gardens, go to the market, and do many such tasks that are a part of their daily routine in the community.

Here are a few goals for your participant observation:

OBSERVE the common objects, positions of objects, people who are working with the objects, ways you would describe the objects, and actions that they use to work with the objects in the activities that you participate in.

LISTEN for unique sounds, syllable stress, and general pronunciation.

RESPOND by appropriately asking WHAT, WHERE, HOW, WITH WHAT, WHEN, and WHO questions in whatever second language you have in common with the community.

NOTE common daily activities and categories of activities in people's lives, as well as WHY questions you have but shouldn't ask, and so on.

2) LISTEN AND ACT: Learn to understand terms related to common body parts, like hand, ear, nose, mouth, foot, eye, neck, back, stomach, hair, and so on. Try not to get into too many specifics—stick with the 15 to 20 terms that are most common. Realize also that often body parts have special markers on them depending on whose body you are referring to. Start then by having the community member refer to a picture you've drawn. Try to consistently learn to understand something that refers to the same person's body like "Point to HIS nose," "Point to HIS finger," "Point to HIS head," and so on. You shouldn't switch the person to whom you are referring so as to make the initial recognition easier for you. (You can also use appropriate Lexicarry pictures for this exercise.)

3) LISTEN AND ACT: In addition to body parts of people, try also to learn to understand some of the body parts of animals that are different from people. Four common animals that are good to start with in this way are a bird such as a chicken, a four-legged animal like a dog, a snake, and a fish. You can use sketches or other pictures to help you.

4) Spend your last 20 minutes of listen and act reviewing the previous day's exercises.

5) Record a summary example of each listen and act exercise.

6) Review your new recordings for 20 minutes and your older ones for 20 minutes.

7) Prepare for the coming day's learning plan for 30 minutes.

Level 1 Daily Learning Plan 8

THINGS TO DO FOR LEARNING

1) PARTICIPANT OBSERVATION: Continue visiting common areas where people gather to talk to one another and to live their daily lives. You can accompany others as they wash laundry, chop firewood, work in gardens, go to the market, and do many such tasks that are a part of their daily routine in the community.

Here are a few goals for your participant observation:

OBSERVE the common objects, positions of objects, people who are working with the objects, ways you would describe the objects, and actions that they use to work with the objects in the activities that you participate in.

LISTEN for unique sounds, syllable stress, and general pronunciation.

RESPOND by appropriately asking WHAT, WHERE, HOW, WITH WHAT, WHEN, and WHO questions in whatever second language you have in common with the community.

NOTE common daily activities and categories of activities in people's lives, as well as WHY questions you have but shouldn't ask, and so on.

2) LISTEN AND ACT: Using the body parts for people and animals, try to now expand your learning by using a variety of people combinations. You can use stick pictures for this exercise. You should also include yourself and the community member as two of the stick figures. Basic people words that you've already learned would include words like man, woman, baby, young person, older person, and so on. Also you should use the people reference words that you learned previously, such as his, her, its, our, their, and so on. For example, the person can say, "Point to his shoulder," and you would respond. Or "Point to the baby's leg." Or "Point to the dog's tail." Go through as many combinations at random as you can handle.

3) LISTEN AND ACT: Try to expand your previous learning of actions to understand actions related to body positions. This would include terms like walking, standing, sitting, kneeling, squatting, crawling, bending over, leaning, lying down, and so on. You could begin by having the community member act and describe what they are doing. Then they can give commands for you to carry out. The community member can use a sentence that is more complicated like "Point to the man who is leaning." Or if that is too difficult, begin with simple statements like, "He is crawling" and move toward the more complicated sentence type as you can follow the community member. (You can also use appropriate Lexicarry pictures for this exercise.)

4) Spend your last 20 minutes of listen and act reviewing the previous day's exercises.

5) Record a summary example of each listen and act exercise.

6) Review your new recordings for 20 minutes and your older ones for 20 minutes.

7) Prepare for the coming day's learning plan for 30 minutes.

Level 1 Daily Learning Plan 9

THINGS TO DO FOR LEARNING

1) PARTICIPANT OBSERVATION: Continue visiting common areas where people gather to talk to one another and to live their daily lives. You can accompany others as they wash laundry, chop firewood, work in gardens, go to the market, and do many such tasks that are a part of their daily routine in the community.

Here are a few goals for your participant observation:

OBSERVE the common objects, positions of objects, people who are working with the objects, ways you would describe the objects, and actions that they use to work with the objects in the activities that you participate in.

LISTEN for unique sounds, syllable stress, and general pronunciation.

RESPOND by appropriately asking WHAT, WHERE, HOW, WITH WHAT, WHEN, and WHO questions in whatever second language you have in common with the community.

NOTE common daily activities and categories of activities in people's lives, as well as WHY questions you have but shouldn't ask, and so on.

2) LISTEN AND ACT: Using a picture of your family or a sketch, try to begin learning to recognize basic terms for kinship relationships. This can be a very complicated area in languages, so try to begin with your or the community member's family members first. Think of the basic categories to comprehend, like my father, my mother, my grandfather, my grandmother, my wife, my child, my baby, my uncle, my aunt, my niece, my nephew, my father-in-law, my mother-in-law, and so on. Only expand the exercise as you are able to comprehend terms beyond the most common ones. (You can also use appropriate Lexicarry pictures for this exercise.)

3) LISTEN AND ACT: Explore ways of seeing and looking using house parts and house objects, as well as terms that you learned for the area around the house. You will likely find that there are multiple terms to describe seeing and looking depending on what you are looking at and your intensity in looking, and so on. Try to include common terms like see, look, stare, peek, watch, spy on, and so on. One approach is for you to act these out with the community member to create scenarios for the terms. Remember that you want to learn to understand the culturally appropriate terms and not just ones that coincide with your own language. (You can also use appropriate Lexicarry pictures for this exercise.)

4) Spend your last 20 minutes of listen and act reviewing the previous day's exercises.

5) Record a summary example of each listen and act exercise.

6) Review your new recordings for 20 minutes and your older ones for 20 minutes.

7) Prepare for the coming day's learning plan for 30 minutes.

Level 1 Daily Learning Plan 10

THINGS TO DO FOR LEARNING

1) PARTICIPANT OBSERVATION: Continue visiting common areas where people gather to talk to one another and to live their daily lives. You can accompany others as they wash laundry, chop firewood, work in gardens, go to the market, and do many such tasks that are a part of their daily routine in the community.

Here are a few goals for your participant observation:

OBSERVE the common objects, positions of objects, people who are working with the objects, ways you would describe the objects, and actions that they use to work with the objects in the activities that you participate in.

LISTEN for unique sounds, syllable stress, and general pronunciation.

RESPOND by appropriately asking WHAT, WHERE, HOW, WITH WHAT, WHEN, and WHO questions in whatever second language you have in common with the community.

NOTE common daily activities and categories of activities in people's lives, as well as WHY questions you have but shouldn't ask, and so on.

2) LISTEN AND ACT: Try to expand your previous kinship term exercise to include the description of someone's kinship relations besides your own using your sketches. For example, the community member can say "Point to the man's mother," in which case you will first point to a sketch of a man and then the equivalent relationship on the tree. Try to include terms sufficient to cover my, your, her, his, their, and our if possible. This can be difficult, but do the best that you can, because family relationships are important. (Also see Lexicarry.)

3) LISTEN AND ACT: Use your common household objects to comprehend terms for touching, such as touching, grabbing, hitting, kicking, rolling, throwing, pinching, squeezing, hugging, and so on. Begin by acting out these things with the community member only as appropriate! It is probably best for you to use sketches for some of them. (Also see Lexicarry.)

Include a review of your holding and carrying terms in your exercise as well.

4) Spend your last 20 minutes of listen and act reviewing the previous day's exercises.

5) Record a summary example of each listen and act exercise.

6) Review your new recordings for 20 minutes and your older ones for 20 minutes.

7) Prepare for the coming day's learning plan for 30 minutes.

Level 1 Daily Learning Plan 11

THINGS TO DO FOR LEARNING

1) PARTICIPANT OBSERVATION: Hopefully by now you will have a clearer understanding of how to use your time with others in the community more productively. Now would be a good time to return to previous listen and act exercises and more purposefully try to practice them while you are out participating in the community, if you haven't done so already. For example, if someone is building a house, you can assist and attempt to follow descriptions of house parts. You can take time to use listen and act. In any activity that you participate in, always listen for words that you've already been exposed to.

Here are a few goals for your participant observation:

OBSERVE the common objects, positions of objects, people who are working with the objects, ways you would describe the objects, and actions that they use to work with the objects in the activities that you participate in.

LISTEN for unique sounds, syllable stress, and general pronunciation.

RESPOND by appropriately asking WHAT, WHERE, HOW, WITH WHAT, WHEN, and WHO questions in whatever second language you have in common with the community.

NOTE common daily activities and categories of activities in people's lives, as well as WHY questions you have but shouldn't ask, and so on.

2) LISTEN AND ACT: Using body part words and kinship terms, use a family picture or sketch to combine kinship terms and body parts. For example, the community member can say, "Point to my aunt's foot," or "Point to your brother's face." Your goal is to be able to recognize the combinations successfully and respond appropriately.

3) LISTEN AND ACT: Take the opportunity to collect all the drawings, pictures, actions, and objects learned so far and try to work through a review of all the material. Of course you won't be able to get everything, but do as much as you can. This should be encouraging to you and the community member, since you likely can understand more than 300 basic words now in context. You will be surprised at how much you know!

4) Spend your last 20 minutes of listen and act reviewing the previous day's exercises.

5) Record a summary example of each listen and act exercise.

6) Review your new recordings for 20 minutes and your older ones for 20 minutes.

7) Prepare for the coming day's learning plan for 30 minutes.

Level 1 Daily Learning Plan 12

THINGS TO DO FOR LEARNING

1) PARTICIPANT OBSERVATION: Continue to participate in four hours of daily activities in the community. Incorporate your *listen and act* learning exercise into the activities as you can. If some activities end up lasting the entire day, don't worry. Just continue on using your other learning exercises the following day.

Here are a few goals for your participant observation:

OBSERVE the common objects, positions of objects, people who are working with the objects, ways you would describe the objects, and actions that they use to work with the objects in the activities that you participate in.

LISTEN for unique sounds, syllable stress, and general pronunciation.

RESPOND by appropriately asking WHAT, WHERE, HOW, WITH WHAT, WHEN, and WHO questions in whatever second language you have in common with the community.

NOTE common daily activities and categories of activities in people's lives, as well as WHY questions you have but shouldn't ask, and so on.

2) LISTEN AND ACT: Collect objects that represent a large variety of colors. You could use objects from the community around you, colored paper, crayons, cups, or pencils. Remember that colors are represented very differently from language to language. Try to incorporate options like spotted or striped as well. The community member can say, "Point to the red cup," or "Point to the blue cup," and so on. (Also see Lexicarry.)

3) LISTEN AND ACT: Collect an assortment of household and other objects that you've learned which represent adjective pair opposites. These would include large/small, heavy/light, long/short, cold/hot, rough/smooth, tall/short, thick/thin, round/flat, and so on. Work with the community member to find a generic phrase you can use such as, "Point to the thing that is hot," or "Point to the long one." In this way try to work through the sets of adjectives in random order.

4) Spend your last 20 minutes of listen and act reviewing the previous day's exercises.

5) Record a summary example of each listen and act exercise.

6) Review your new recordings for 20 minutes and your older ones for 20 minutes.

7) Prepare for the coming day's learning plan for 30 minutes.

Level 1 Daily Learning Plan 13

THINGS TO DO FOR LEARNING

1) PARTICIPANT OBSERVATION: Continue to participate in four hours of daily activities in the community.

Here are a few goals for your participant observation:

OBSERVE the common objects, positions of objects, people who are working with the objects, ways you would describe the objects, and actions that they use to work with the objects in the activities that you participate in.

LISTEN for unique sounds, syllable stress, and general pronunciation.

RESPOND by appropriately asking WHAT, WHERE, HOW, WITH WHAT, WHEN, and WHO questions in whatever second language you have in common with the community.

NOTE common daily activities and categories of activities in people's lives, as well as WHY questions you have but shouldn't ask, and so on.

2) LISTEN AND ACT: Using previously learned objects and simple sketches, learn to understand words for throwing to, showing to, taking to, bringing to, giving to, and so on. *Listen and act* as the community member tells you, "Throw the rock to me," or "Spear the ground with the spear," "Give the basket to him," or "Take the book to the boy." If others are around, include them in the exercise as well.

3) LISTEN AND ACT: Using a pouring container and a cup, learn to understand terms for drinking, dumping out, spilling, and pouring different types of liquids. The community member can use commands to work through this exercise with you, like "Pour me some coffee," or "Dump out the water."

4) LISTEN AND ACT: Collect 20 or so of the most common household food items to learn to understand their names.

5) Spend your last 20 minutes of listen and act reviewing the previous day's exercises.

6) Record a summary example of each listen and act exercise.

7) Review your new recordings for 20 minutes and your older ones for 20 minutes.

8) Prepare for the coming day's learning plan for 30 minutes.

Level 1 Daily Learning Plan 14

THINGS TO DO FOR LEARNING

1) PARTICIPANT OBSERVATION: Continue to participate in four hours of daily activities in the community.

Here are a few goals for your participant observation:

OBSERVE the common objects, positions of objects, people who are working with the objects, ways you would describe the objects, and actions that they use to work with the objects in the activities that you participate in.

LISTEN for unique sounds, syllable stress, and general pronunciation.

RESPOND by appropriately asking WHAT, WHERE, HOW, WITH WHAT, WHEN, and WHO questions in whatever second language you have in common with the community.

NOTE common daily activities and categories of activities in people's lives, as well as WHY questions you have but shouldn't ask, and so on.

2) LISTEN AND ACT: Using the words for common food items and pictures of animals and people, learn to comprehend sentences related to feeding and eating. The community member can begin by using commands such as, "Eat the salt," or "Feed me the sweet potato." Later they can relate the food items to pictures and you can pick the appropriate picture and food. For example, they can say, "The man (or woman) is eating the mango," in which case you'd pick up the mango and indicate that the man (or woman) was eating it by pointing to them and acting.

3) LISTEN AND ACT: Collect all the objects that you've learned that serve as tools or instruments for working. These should include things like broom, machete, shell, knife, fire, axe, planting tools, shovel, and so on. Begin to learn to understand the actions that are associated with the objects by having the community member use simple commands. Be prepared for multiple terms for cutting and chopping. Include ropes or vines to practice understanding tying and untying as well. Act out the commands as the community member gives them to you.

4) Spend your last 20 minutes of listen and act reviewing the previous day's exercises.

5) Record a summary example of each listen and act exercise.

6) Review your new recordings for 20 minutes and your older ones for 20 minutes.

7) Prepare for the coming day's learning plan for 30 minutes.

Level 1 Daily Learning Plan 15

THINGS TO DO FOR LEARNING

1) PARTICIPANT OBSERVATION: Continue to participate in four hours of daily activities in the community.

Here are a few goals for your participant observation:

OBSERVE the common objects, positions of objects, people who are working with the objects, ways you would describe the objects, and actions that they use to work with the objects in the activities that you participate in.

LISTEN for unique sounds, syllable stress, and general pronunciation.

RESPOND by appropriately asking WHAT, WHERE, HOW, WITH WHAT, WHEN, and WHO questionss in whatever second language you have in common with the community.

NOTE common daily activities and categories of activities in people's lives, as well as WHY questions you have but shouldn't ask, and so on.

2) LISTEN AND ACT: Using sketches and known food items, have the community member work through ways to describe possession and ownership with you. Begin with something such as "my knife," or "your axe," in which case you'd pick up the appropriate object and point to the respective owner. Expand this exercise with sketches of people, family, and animals.

3) LISTEN AND ACT: Using sketches and objects, learn to recognize differences in singular and plural objects. The community member can ask questions like, "Where is the stone?" or "Where are the sticks?"

4) LISTEN AND ACT: Collect 55 common objects to learn to understand the numbers one to ten. For example, get 55 stones and sort the stones into groups one to ten. Then the community member can say, "one stone," and you point to one stone. Then can say, "three stones," and you point to three. Do this until you can respond correctly to all ten numbers. The community member can also use a sentence like, "Show me three stones," or "Point to five stones."

5) Spend your last 20 minutes of listen and act reviewing the previous day's exercises.

6) Record a summary example of each listen and act exercise.

7) Review your new recordings for 20 minutes and your older ones for 20 minutes.

8) Prepare for the coming day's learning plan for 30 minutes.

Level 1 Daily Learning Plan 16

THINGS TO DO FOR LEARNING

1) PARTICIPANT OBSERVATION: Continue to participate in four hours of daily activities in the community.

Here are a few goals for your participant observation:

OBSERVE the common objects, positions of objects, people who are working with the objects, ways you would describe the objects, and actions that they use to work with the objects in the activities that you participate in.

LISTEN for unique sounds, syllable stress, and general pronunciation.

RESPOND by appropriately asking WHAT, WHERE, HOW, WITH WHAT, WHEN, and WHO questions in whatever second language you have in common with the community.

NOTE common daily activities and categories of activities in people's lives, as well as WHY questions you have but shouldn't ask, and so on.

2) LISTEN AND ACT: Learn to understand terms for days of the week and time (today, tomorrow, day before, day after, and so on). Also terms for common times of day, seasons, day, month, year, and so on. An easy way to learn today, yesterday, tomorrow, the day before yesterday, and the day after tomorrow is to draw five slots on a piece of paper and put the date on the center slot. The community member can randomly say one of the five terms and you point to the appropriate slot that corresponds. Start with two slots like this and work up to recognizing all five. You can do similar sketches for times of day, seasons, months, days of the week, and so on. (Also see Lexicarry.)

3) LISTEN AND ACT: Learn to understand terms related to the sky and weather using sketches and your environment, like sun, sky, moon, stars, clouds, rain, mist, fog, wind, and so on.

4) LISTEN AND ACT: Review your previous common instruments and actions with commands and try to add a few new ones, such as spear, eating utensil, rake, and so on.

5) Spend your last 20 minutes of listen and act reviewing the previous day's exercises.

6) Record a summary example of each listen and act exercise.

7) Review your new recordings for 20 minutes and your older ones for 20 minutes.

8) Prepare for the coming day's learning plan for 30 minutes.

Level 1 Daily Learning Plan 17

THINGS TO DO FOR LEARNING

1) PARTICIPANT OBSERVATION: Continue to participate in four hours of daily activities in the community.

Here are a few goals for your participant observation:

OBSERVE the common objects, positions of objects, people who are working with the objects, ways you would describe the objects, and actions that they use to work with the objects in the activities that you participate in.

LISTEN for unique sounds, syllable stress, and general pronunciation.

RESPOND by appropriately asking WHAT, WHERE, HOW, WITH WHAT, WHEN, and WHO questions in whatever second language you have in common with the community.

NOTE common daily activities and categories of activities in people's lives, as well as WHY questions you have but shouldn't ask, and so on.

2) LISTEN AND ACT: Use sketches or photos to explore terms related to people's emotions. As you work through the common terms, remember that these are culture specific. Take two of the pictures or sketches and have the community member ask questions like, "Who is angry?" or "Which person is crying?" You may need to negotiate what the terms actually mean to the person in your common second language if possible. Stick with the most common emotional behaviors, so try for ten of them. (Also see Lexicarry.)

3) LISTEN AND ACT: Learn to understand terms for common types of clothing. Obviously this will greatly vary from culture to culture. But try to generate a list of fifteen or more if possible. (Also see Lexicarry.)

4) LISTEN AND ACT: Combine your previous terms for colors, numbers, and adjective pair opposites. Try to combine them with actions related to the objects and food items that you've already learned. For example, the community member can say, "Point to the two long sticks," or "Show me the three black cups" or "Give me the two sweet potatoes." There are lots of options with this exercise, so think of the objects and actions that you can collect that will be the most helpful.

5) Spend your last 20 minutes of listen and act reviewing the previous day's exercises.

6) Record a summary example of each listen and act exercise.

7) Review your new recordings for 20 minutes and your older ones for 20 minutes.

8) Prepare for the coming day's learning plan for 30 minutes.

Level 1 Daily Learning Plan 18

THINGS TO DO FOR LEARNING

1) PARTICIPANT OBSERVATION: Continue to participate in four hours of daily activities in the community.

Here are a few goals for your participant observation:

OBSERVE the common objects, positions of objects, people who are working with the objects, ways you would describe the objects, and actions that they use to work with the objects in the activities that you participate in.

LISTEN for unique sounds, syllable stress, and general pronunciation.

RESPOND by appropriately asking WHAT, WHERE, HOW, WITH WHAT, WHEN, and WHO questions in whatever second language you have in common with the community.

NOTE common daily activities and categories of activities in people's lives, as well as WHY questions you have but shouldn't ask, and so on.

2) LISTEN AND ACT: Use your sketches of common words for animals to learn to understand several behaviors of animals. This is particularly useful for domesticated animals that people care for. You can include the common sounds that animals make as well. For example the community member can say "The cat hisses," or "The cat meows." Dogs bark and growl. Chickens scratch, cluck, and crow. Pigs root and grunt. Birds sing and fly. Fish swim and bite. Try to come up with a culturally appropriate set of five to ten animals with two action sketches for each one. These terms will vary greatly from language to language. (Also see Lexicarry.)

3) LISTEN AND ACT: Using sketches and examples, learn to understand names of common bugs and creeping things in the community. Make sure you limit this exercise to the 10 to 12 most generic terms, since often those who live close to the natural environment know many, many terms for such things. (Also see Lexicarry.)

4) LISTEN AND ACT: Using sketches, combine known objects with emotional states of individuals. A good way to do this is to use the action giving. The community member can state, "Give the rock to the sad man," or "Give the sweet potato to the happy man." Try to include a wide range of objects and the emotion words you've already learned. (Also see Lexicarry.)

5) Spend your last 20 minutes of listen and act reviewing the previous day's exercises.

6) Record a summary example of each listen and act exercise.

7) Review your new recordings for 20 minutes and your older ones for 20 minutes.

8) Prepare for the coming day's learning plan for 30 minutes.

Level 1 Daily Learning Plan 19

THINGS TO DO FOR LEARNING

1) PARTICIPANT OBSERVATION: Continue to participate in four hours of daily activities in the community.

Here are a few goals for your participant observation:

OBSERVE the common objects, positions of objects, people who are working with the objects, ways you would describe the objects, and actions that they use to work with the objects in the activities that you participate in.

LISTEN for unique sounds, syllable stress, and general pronunciation.

RESPOND by appropriately asking WHAT, WHERE, HOW, WITH WHAT, WHEN, and WHO questions in whatever second language you have in common with the community.

NOTE common daily activities and categories of activities in people's lives, as well as WHY questions you have but shouldn't ask, and so on.

2) LISTEN AND ACT: Using terms for insects, learn to understand terms related to what these creatures do to people. For example, centipedes sting, beatles pinch, wasps sting, ants bite, and so on. Try to use ten insects and comprehend one or two common aggressive behaviors for each one. If you haven't included animal aggressions, include those also. For example, dogs bite, snakes strike, and so on. Use simple sketches. (Also see Lexicarry.)

3) LISTEN AND ACT: Sketch landforms and parts of rivers and waterways to begin learning terms for these items. (Also see Lexicarry.)

4) LISTEN AND ACT: Apply the use of color and number to a wide range of items that you collect in numbers of 10. If possible, collect five different sets of items that are same but vary in color. For example, you can get 10 white stones and 10 black stones, 10 red leaves and 10 green leaves, 10 blue flowers and 10 yellow flowers, and so on. Go through an exercise where the community member commands you, "Give three yellow flowers to me," or "Give four red leaves to me." You can also include your sketches of people and relatives to apply this exercise to a broad range of people.

5) Spend your last 20 minutes of listen and act reviewing the previous day's exercises.

6) Record a summary example of each listen and act exercise.

7) Review your new recordings for 20 minutes and your older ones for 20 minutes.

8) Prepare for the coming day's learning plan for 30 minutes.

Level 1 Daily Learning Plan 20

THINGS TO DO FOR LEARNING

1) PARTICIPANT OBSERVATION: Continue to participate in four hours of daily activities in the community.

Here are a few goals for your participant observation:

OBSERVE the common objects, positions of objects, people who are working with the objects, ways you would describe the objects, and actions that they use to work with the objects in the activities that you participate in.

LISTEN for unique sounds, syllable stress, and general pronunciation.

RESPOND by appropriately asking WHAT, WHERE, HOW, WITH WHAT, WHEN, and WHO questions in whatever second language you have in common with the community.

NOTE common daily activities and categories of activities in people's lives, as well as WHY questions you have but shouldn't ask, and so on.

2) LISTEN AND ACT: Using 10 of an object that you already know, learn to understand your ordinal numbers 1 thru 10. The community member can use a sentence like, "Point to the third stone," or "Point to the seventh stone." Continue until you can recognize all ten readily.

3) LISTEN AND ACT: Using times during the day that you've previously learned, extend that exercise to include actual clock times if applicable. Use an example clock to begin learning how to tell time. The community member can tell you simply, "It is 2 o'clock," and you can respond by marking that time on the clock. This should combine your numbers and time in a useful way.

4) LISTEN AND ACT: Using many or most of the objects you have learned so far and your sketches of people, family, and animals, learn to understand the action wanting. For example, the community member can say, "The dog wants a chicken," and you'd indicate the dog and chicken in the proper order. Or "I want a rock," in which case you'd give the person a rock. Combine as many people, family, and animals as you can.

5) LISTEN AND ACT: Using the objects and sketches, practice your terms for seeing and location. The community member can ask, "Do you see a dog?" or "Where is your father?" Use this as a chance to review all the objects, sketches, and pictures that you can.

6) Spend your last 20 minutes of listen and act reviewing the previous day's exercises.

7) Record a summary example of each listen and act exercise.

8) Review your new recordings for 20 minutes and your older ones for 20 minutes.

9) Prepare for the coming day's learning plan for 30 minutes.

Level 1 Daily Learning Plan 21

In daily learning plans 21 to 25, you should try to plan for yourself. These plans should relate to specific activities in the community that you experience before you use the *listen and act* learning exercises in the plan. Your past experience should help you to decide what activity in the community is appropriate for your plan and what new words to focus on in your learning exercise.

For each plan, try to apply the *listen and act* learning exercise twice to introduce you to a total of 30 new words related to the activity. The first time, you can apply the exercise to new objects in the activity that you participated in. The second time, think of the common actions in that activity.

Then apply the *listen and act* learning exercise a third time to combine past materials in a useful way.

THINGS TO DO FOR LEARNING

1) PARTICIPANT OBSERVATION: Continue to participate in four hours of daily activities in the community.

Here are a few goals for your participant observation:

OBSERVE the common objects, positions of objects, people who are working with the objects, ways you would describe the objects, and actions that they use to work with the objects in the activities that you participate in.

LISTEN for unique sounds, syllable stress, and general pronunciation.

RESPOND by appropriately asking WHAT, WHERE, HOW, WITH WHAT, WHEN, and WHO questions in whatever second language you have in common with the community.

NOTE common daily activities and categories of activities in people's lives, as well as WHY questions you have but shouldn't ask, and so on.

2) LISTEN AND ACT: New objects from activity in the community.

3) LISTEN AND ACT: New actions from activity in the community.

4) LISTEN AND ACT: Combine previous day's material in a useful way.

5) Record a summary example of each listen and act exercise.

6) Spend your last 20 minutes of listen and act reviewing the previous day's exercises.

7) Review your new recordings for 20 minutes and your older ones for 20 minutes.

8) Prepare for the coming day's learning plan for 30 minutes.

Level 1 Daily Learning Plan 22

THINGS TO DO FOR LEARNING

1) PARTICIPANT OBSERVATION: Continue to participate in four hours of daily activities in the community.

Here are a few goals for your participant observation:

OBSERVE the common objects, positions of objects, people who are working with the objects, ways you would describe the objects, and actions that they use to work with the objects in the activities that you participate in.

LISTEN for unique sounds, syllable stress, and general pronunciation.

RESPOND by appropriately asking WHAT, WHERE, HOW, WITH WHAT, WHEN, and WHO questions in whatever second language you have in common with the community.

NOTE common daily activities and categories of activities in people's lives, as well as WHY questions you have but shouldn't ask, and so on.

2) LISTEN AND ACT: New objects from activity in the community.

3) LISTEN AND ACT: New actions from activity in the community.

4) LISTEN AND ACT: Combine previous day's material in a useful way.

5) Record a summary example of each listen and act exercise.

6) Spend your last 20 minutes of listen and act reviewing the previous day's exercises.

7) Review your new recordings for 20 minutes and your older ones for 20 minutes.

8) Prepare for the coming day's learning plan for 30 minutes.

Level 1 Daily Learning Plan 23

THINGS TO DO FOR LEARNING

1) PARTICIPANT OBSERVATION: Continue to participate in four hours of daily activities in the community.

Here are a few goals for your participant observation:

OBSERVE the common objects, positions of objects, people who are working with the objects, ways you would describe the objects, and actions that they use to work with the objects in the activities that you participate in.

LISTEN for unique sounds, syllable stress, and general pronunciation.

RESPOND by appropriately asking WHAT, WHERE, HOW, WITH WHAT, WHEN, and WHO questions in whatever second language you have in common with the community.

NOTE common daily activities and categories of activities in people's lives, as well as WHY questions you have but shouldn't ask, and so on.

2) LISTEN AND ACT: New objects from activity in the community.

3) LISTEN AND ACT: New actions from activity in the community.

4) LISTEN AND ACT: Combine previous day's material in a useful way.

5) Record a summary example of each listen and act exercise.

6) Spend your last 20 minutes of listen and act reviewing the previous day's exercises.

7) Review your new recordings for 20 minutes and your older ones for 20 minutes.

8) Prepare for the coming day's learning plan for 30 minutes.

Level 1 Daily Learning Plan 24

THINGS TO DO FOR LEARNING

1) PARTICIPANT OBSERVATION: Continue to participate in four hours of daily activities in the community.

Here are a few goals for your participant observation:

OBSERVE the common objects, positions of objects, people who are working with the objects, ways you would describe the objects, and actions that they use to work with the objects in the activities that you participate in.

LISTEN for unique sounds, syllable stress, and general pronunciation.

RESPOND by appropriately asking WHAT, WHERE, HOW, WITH WHAT, WHEN, and WHO questions in whatever second language you have in common with the community.

NOTE common daily activities and categories of activities in people's lives, as well as WHY questions you have but shouldn't ask, and so on.

2) LISTEN AND ACT: New objects from activity in the community.

3) LISTEN AND ACT: New actions from activity in the community.

4) LISTEN AND ACT: Combine previous day's material in a useful way.

5) Record a summary example of each listen and act exercise.

6) Spend your last 20 minutes of listen and act reviewing the previous day's exercises.

7) Review your new recordings for 20 minutes and your older ones for 20 minutes.

8) Prepare for the coming day's learning plan for 30 minutes.

Level 1 Daily Learning Plan 25

THINGS TO DO FOR LEARNING

1) PARTICIPANT OBSERVATION: Continue to participate in four hours of daily activities in the community.

Here are a few goals for your participant observation:

OBSERVE the common objects, positions of objects, people who are working with the objects, ways you would describe the objects, and actions that they use to work with the objects in the activities that you participate in.

LISTEN for unique sounds, syllable stress, and general pronunciation.

RESPOND by appropriately asking WHAT, WHERE, HOW, WITH WHAT, WHEN, and WHO questions in whatever second language you have in common with the community.

NOTE common daily activities and categories of activities in people's lives, as well as WHY questions you have but shouldn't ask, and so on.

2) LISTEN AND ACT: New objects from activity in the community.

3) LISTEN AND ACT: New actions from activity in the community.

4) LISTEN AND ACT: Combine previous day's material in a useful way.

5) Record a summary example of each listen and act exercise.

6) Spend your last 20 minutes of listen and act reviewing the previous day's exercises.

7) Review your new recordings for 20 minutes and your older ones for 20 minutes.

8) Prepare for the coming day's learning plan for 30 minutes.

Level 1 Daily Learning: Plans 26 to 50

In daily learning plans 26 to 50, you will begin to incorporate the *listen and act* with speaking learning exercise. This exercise will enable you to move from just listening and acting to actually repeating and rephrasing those small pieces of language now that you can understand them well. The daily learning plans will return to your early simple words and phrases and will gradually help you to build in speaking appropriately while you listen and act. Your *listen and act with speaking exercises* should consume 2 hours of your time each day.

You need to keep in mind that the *listen and act with speaking exercise* is NOT intended to help you 'memorize' what the community member is saying. This is simply a further step in reinforcing those pieces of language that you can already comprehend. Another purpose of *listen and act with speaking* is to allow you to loosen your tongue as you solidify your grasp on the comprehension of the language pieces.

Even though you will spend lots of time with the *listen and act with speaking exercise,* it is good for you to continue to introduce new vocabulary building exercises as well. For that reason, a new *listen and act* exercise is also included in each daily plan. The *listen and act* exercises will focus on common activities in the community and specific processes in those familiar contexts. Because these activities often vary from culture to culture, you might need to adjust the content of the exercise depending on the activities that are common to the community where you live.

Your goal for the new *listen and act* exercise can be reduced to your understanding 20 additional vocabulary items each day. Don't allow your *listen and act* exercise to take up more than 40 minutes of your time each day with the community member. You should spend an additional 20 minutes with the community member reviewing previous *listen and act* exercises, beginning with the most recent and incorporating others as you have time.

Daily time schedule for Level 1 (learning plans 26-50)

Learner time for daily learning plans 26 to 50 should break down each day as follows:

Participant observation exercise in activities in the community	4 hours
Listen and act with speaking exercises with a community member	2 hours
Listen and act exercise with a community member for 20 new vocabulary items	40 minutes
Review previous listen and act exercises with a community member	20 minutes
Review recorded listen and act exercises yourself	40 minutes
Preparing for the next daily learning plan	30 minutes
TOTAL:	8 hrs 10 min

Level 1 Daily Learning Plan 26

THINGS TO DO FOR LEARNING

1) PARTICIPANT OBSERVATION: Continue to participate in four hours of daily activities in the community.

Here are a few goals for your participant observation:

OBSERVE the common objects, positions of objects, people who are working with the objects, ways you would describe the objects, and actions that they use to work with the objects in the activities that you participate in.

LISTEN for unique sounds, syllable stress, and general pronunciation.

RESPOND by appropriately asking WHAT, WHERE, HOW, WITH WHAT, WHEN, and WHO questions in whatever second language you have in common with the community.

NOTE common daily activities and categories of activities in people's lives, as well as WHY questions you have but shouldn't ask, and so on.

2) LISTEN AND ACT WITH SPEAKING: Return to your sketches of words for people (like baby, child, young person, woman, man, old man, old woman) and common community animals (like pig, dog, chicken, bird, fish, snake). This includes reference words like I, you, he, she, it, they, us. Have the community member practice in the context of a sentence as before, such as "Show me the man," "Point to the man," "Where is the man?" or "This is a man."

As you practice with the community member, you yourself attempt to repeat as you are pointing in response to the appropriate person or animal. You may need to talk with the community member about the right way to say this if you are uncertain. For example, the person may say, "Where is the man?" to which you might point and respond simply, "the man," or you might say, "This is the man." Your goal is not to respond perfectly, but rather to begin to associate speaking with the appropriate person or animal.

3) LISTEN AND ACT WITH SPEAKING: Have the community member command you to perform basic actions for common commands (Stand up, sit down, walk, run, crawl, lie down, go, come, jump, stop, kneel, bend over, go up, go down, come up, come down, and so on). You do the action as he or she tells you to.

As you are following the commands from the community member, begin repeating out loud the commands that they are giving in the same way that they are giving them to you. In other words, if the community member says, "Stand up," you stand up and repeat the command out loud, "Stand up." Toward the end of the exercise, you can try telling them to do some of the things to practice giving commands yourself.

4) LISTEN AND ACT WITH SPEAKING: Practice again your common greetings and leave takings. These should be very familiar to you. You can practice by role playing with the community member. That is, you work together with him or her to act out these things.

5) LISTEN AND ACT: Begin to learn to understand terms related to tending the fire or cook area. If for a fire, you can think through all the objects and actions related to this activity. Set up a fire and draw a picture of a fire to help you. Objects would include things like match, lighter, fire, firewood, ash, coal, smoke, floating ash, and so on. Actions with the fire would include starting the fire, blowing on the fire, fanning the fire, putting the fire out, splitting the firewood, putting wood on the fire, putting the firewood together, scattering the firewood, and so on.

6) Record a summary example of your new listen and act exercise. DON'T record your listen and act with speaking exercise. You only want recordings of speaking from your community member, not from yourself.

Each day you should take 20 minutes to review the previous day's listen and act with the community member. Add more listen and act material as time permits. Don't try to review listen and act with speaking exercises, as that review is already a part of daily learning plans.

Also, listen to your new listen and act recordings for 20 minutes and your previous ones for 20 minutes.

7) Prepare for the coming day's learning plan for 30 minutes.

Level 1 Daily Learning Plan 27

THINGS TO DO FOR LEARNING

1) PARTICIPANT OBSERVATION: Continue to participate in four hours of daily activities in the community.

Here are a few goals for your participant observation:

OBSERVE the common objects, positions of objects, people who are working with the objects, ways you would describe the objects, and actions that they use to work with the objects in the activities that you participate in.

LISTEN for unique sounds, syllable stress, and general pronunciation.

RESPOND by appropriately asking WHAT, WHERE, HOW, WITH WHAT, WHEN, and WHO questions in whatever second language you have in common with the community.

NOTE common daily activities and categories of activities in people's lives, as well as WHY questions you have but shouldn't ask, and so on.

2) LISTEN AND ACT WITH SPEAKING: Using the words that you understand for common items that are in an ordinary household in the community (beds, tables, chairs, dishes, knives, machetes, axes, baskets, hammocks, and so on), go through an exercise with the community member. Have the person use a sentence like, "Where is the axe?" Or "Point to the hammock" for the review.

Have the person help you to frame an appropriate spoken response to the exercise using the object in a sentence. This could be a response like "There is the hammock," or "This is the bed," "That is the table," and so on. As the person works through the objects at random, try to point and speak appropriately in response.

3) LISTEN AND ACT WITH SPEAKING: Practice understanding the terms for people, pronouns, and animals along with common command actions that you reviewed in the previous lesson (Stand up, sit down, walk, run, crawl, lie down, go, come, jump, stop, kneel, bend over, go up, go down, come up, come down, and so on). Using sketches, the community member could say, "The man is walking," and you'd point to the sketch. Or they could say, "He is running," and you'd point to that sketch.

As you go through the exercise, try to repeat out loud each statement that the community member is making as you point to the proper picture. (**Also see Lexicarry.**)

4) LISTEN AND ACT: Review for 20 minutes your understanding of terms for fire and common actions for tending and working with the fire. Then find two or three foods commonly cooked on the fire to include into a new exercise for 40 more minutes. Most likely the foods will require certain objects or tools for working with them (knives, shells, tongs, graters, and so on), positions of the foods (on, in, under, and so on), preparatory steps (peeling, shucking, splitting or slicing, washing, and so on), as well as steps for managing the cooking process. For example you can flip or turn the food, watch over it, scrape it, cut it, taste it, and so on. Also, you can include combinations of previously learned adjectives (hard, soft, hot, cold) with new ones like burnt, raw, ripe, cooked, and so on. Your goal is to work with the activities of fire and cooking over the fire to have the community member help you understand terms for these five areas (objects or tools for working with the foods, positions of the foods, preparatory steps for cooking the foods, actions to work with the foods in cooking, and adjectives that describe the food that you are cooking.)

For objects or tools for working with the foods, the community member can have you show them the tools as they name them. For positions of the foods, preparatory steps for the foods, and steps for managing the cooking process, you can have the person command you to perform the actions that are associated with the food you are working with. For adjective descriptions, you could draw or have on hand food samples that represent the various options so that the person can help you understand the alternatives.

5) Record a summary example of your new listen and act exercise. DON'T record your listen and act with speaking exercises. You only want recordings of speaking from the community member, not from yourself.

6) Listen to your new recordings for 20 minutes and previous recordings for 20 minutes.

7) Prepare for the coming day's learning plan for 30 minutes.

Level 1 Daily Learning Plan 28

THINGS TO DO FOR LEARNING

1) PARTICIPANT OBSERVATION: Continue to participate in four hours of daily activities in the community.

Here are a few goals for your participant observation:

OBSERVE the common objects, positions of objects, people who are working with the objects, ways you would describe the objects, and actions that they use to work with the objects in the activities that you participate in.

LISTEN for unique sounds, syllable stress, and general pronunciation.

RESPOND by appropriately asking WHAT, WHERE, HOW, WITH WHAT, WHEN, and WHO questions in whatever second language you have in common with the community.

NOTE common daily activities and categories of activities in people's lives, as well as WHY questions you have but shouldn't ask, and so on.

2) LISTEN AND ACT WITH SPEAKING: Practice understanding the parts of common buildings (wall, window, door, floor, roof, ceiling, stairs, rafter, roof beam, eaves, posts, poles, and so on). A good sentence for the community member to use is, "Where is the door?" Or "Show me the ceiling." Or "Point to the pole."

As you are practicing, respond to the question or statement by the person while you point. For example, you can point and say simply, "the door," or more fully "That is the door."

3) LISTEN AND ACT WITH SPEAKING: Practice understanding the common rooms and areas in the house. If the bathroom is outdoors and the cooking house or other living spaces are separate from the house you are in, include those in your review. You can just have the person tell you to point to the ones that are far off because they will be time-consuming to walk to. You might want to also try drawing a house floor plan or area map to help with this exercise, depending on the ability of the person to relate to that.

As you practice, you should try to repeat the item or area in a sentence such as "That is the bathroom," "This is the sitting room," and so on.

4) LISTEN AND ACT: Review your terms for fire and for cooking over the fire for 20 minutes. For 40 more minutes, learn about one or two other common ways of cooking that you have previously observed. These could include cooking in a pan of some kind (boiling or frying), cooking in leaves, cooking in bamboo, cooking in bark, cooking with hot stones, and so on. Use drawings or actual objects to work with the methods of cooking similar to the way that you'd previously done for cooking on the fire. The community member can use commands for teaching you positions, objects, preparatory steps, and cooking actions, and descriptive phrases to teach you adjectives that tell about the cooking.

5) Record a summary example of your listen and act exercise to review later.

6) Listen to your new recordings for 20 minutes and previous recordings for 20 minutes.

7) Prepare for the coming day's learning plan for 30 minutes.

Level 1 Daily Learning Plan 29

THINGS TO DO FOR LEARNING

1) PARTICIPANT OBSERVATION: Continue to participate in four hours of daily activities in the community.

Here are a few goals for your participant observation:

OBSERVE the common objects, positions of objects, people who are working with the objects, ways you would describe the objects, and actions that they use to work with the objects in the activities that you participate in.

LISTEN for unique sounds, syllable stress, and general pronunciation.

RESPOND by appropriately asking WHAT, WHERE, HOW, WITH WHAT, WHEN, and WHO questions in whatever second language you have in common with the community.

NOTE common daily activities and categories of activities in people's lives, as well as WHY questions you have but shouldn't ask, and so on.

2) LISTEN AND ACT WITH SPEAKING: Practice understanding terms for household objects and placement words (beside, under, on, between, with, in, out, here, there, and so on). The community member can say something like, "Put the axe in the basket." Or "Put the knife on the table." Or "Put the firewood beside the chair."

As you practice, try repeating the command that the person is giving to you exactly as they are saying it. As you become more familiar with repeating the commands, try commanding the person to perform actions with the objects.

3) LISTEN AND ACT WITH SPEAKING: Using words for parts of the house and rooms of the house, practice the expanded exercise of having the community member tell you to do things related to those items. For example, the person can tell you, "Close the door," "Open the door," "Sit in the chair," "Go down the stairs," "Come up the stairs," "Lie on the bed," "Open the window," and so on.

As you are practicing, repeat the commands that the person is giving you. You can try giving them some commands with the objects and actions as well.

4) LISTEN AND ACT: Spend an hour reviewing all that you have learned about the fire and cooking. This would include the positions of the foods, objects used, the preparatory steps taken, the cooking actions, and descriptive phrases that tell you about the cooking process. If there are other kinds of cooking that you have yet to understand, include those in the exercise as well.

5) Record a summary example of new material from your listen and act exercise, if any.

6) Listen to your new recordings for 20 minutes and previous recordings for 20 minutes.

7) Prepare for the coming day's learning plan for 30 minutes.

Level 1 Daily Learning Plan 30

THINGS TO DO FOR LEARNING

1) PARTICIPANT OBSERVATION: Continue to participate in four hours of daily activities in the community.

Here are a few goals for your participant observation:

OBSERVE the common objects, positions of objects, people who are working with the objects, ways you would describe the objects, and actions that they use to work with the objects in the activities that you participate in.

LISTEN for unique sounds, syllable stress, and general pronunciation.

RESPOND by appropriately asking WHAT, WHERE, HOW, WITH WHAT, WHEN, and WHO questions in whatever second language you have in common with the community.

NOTE common daily activities and categories of activities in people's lives, as well as WHY questions you have but shouldn't ask, and so on.

2) LISTEN AND ACT WITH SPEAKING: Use the placement words that you've previously heard (in, beside, on, between, with, under, and so on) and the common household objects that you've learned to expand your previous exercise. Now you will include putting, moving, and taking out objects as part of the exercise. If there are other common household items that you didn't previously learn to understand, you can include those in the exercise as well. For example, the community member can tell you, "Put the knife in the basket," "Take the book off the chair," "Move the axe to the table." As you practice in this way, repeat what the person is saying as you respond to the commands. If you are able, you yourself can give some commands to the person toward the end of the exercise.

3) LISTEN AND ACT WITH SPEAKING: Walk around the general living area with the community member to observe terms for the outdoor house and yard area. You should note terms for things like shrubs, yard, grass, trees, flowers, path, rocks, dirt, ground, and so on. You can stand in the yard and go through the exercise if you like, or you could sketch the items on paper and use the learning exercise in that fashion. As you go through the exercise with the community member, practice responding using the item in a sentence like "This is grass," or "That is a flower."

4) LISTEN AND ACT: Think of a common exercise in the community that you have already observed where the community members are building something. For example, in the community where you live people may build houses, make canoes, and so on.

Let's use the building of a house as our example. Think through the steps of building a house as you have observed them. Gather sample tools and materials and prepare pictures, photos or images for the process. You should already be familiar with many of the common parts of the house, tools and materials for building. As a review exercise, the community member can have you show them the tools as they name them. For actions associated with building, you can have the person command you to perform the actions and you can pretend to do that thing, or can point to the appropriate sketch. Actions would include digging holes for posts, standing up posts, tamping posts, nailing, tying vines, making leaf roof segments, putting up rafters, putting on house siding, and so on. Don't try to exhaust every possibility, but rather focus on the actions that represent common steps in the process.

5) Record a summary example of new material from your listen and act exercise.

6) Review your fire and cooking activity for 20 minutes.

7) Listen to your new recordings for 20 minutes and previous recordings for 20 minutes.

8) Prepare for the coming day's learning plan for 30 minutes.

Level 1 Daily Learning Plan 31

THINGS TO DO FOR LEARNING

1) PARTICIPANT OBSERVATION: Continue to participate in four hours of daily activities in the community.

Here are a few goals for your participant observation:

OBSERVE the common objects, positions of objects, people who are working with the objects, ways you would describe the objects, and actions that they use to work with the objects in the activities that you participate in.

LISTEN for unique sounds, syllable stress, and general pronunciation.

RESPOND by appropriately asking WHAT, WHERE, HOW, WITH WHAT, WHEN, and WHO questions in whatever second language you have in common with the community.

NOTE common daily activities and categories of activities in people's lives, as well as WHY questions you have but shouldn't ask, and so on.

2) LISTEN AND ACT WITH SPEAKING: Practice your previous exercise for understanding more about common containers, bags, baskets, and so on, that are found in the living area around the house and yard.

Practice repeating the objects in an appropriate sentence as you indicate the container, bag, basket, and so on.

3) LISTEN AND ACT WITH SPEAKING: Using previously learned objects, practice understanding common ways to talk about carrying, picking up, and giving. You can begin with the community member giving you commands to carry, pick up, or give the objects that you already are familiar with. Work with this exercise for quite a while, sticking with the most common words for carrying, picking up, and giving.

As you respond to the commands, you yourself repeat the commands. Toward the end of the exercise, you might try giving commands to the community member.

4) LISTEN AND ACT WITH SPEAKING: Practice understanding the many ways to talk about carrying and giving using a variety of objects and your words for different people. Carrying can be done on the head, shoulder, in a strap, in a basket or bag, around the neck, and so on. Often languages use different words for these. Your friend can first model these for you. They can then command you to do the carrying actions using the objects that you know.

You can resort to using your sketches of people if you need to for describing different people and their giving actions. For example, the community member can say, "He is giving the axe to her," or "The woman is giving the book to the man." In each case, you can respond by motioning to the drawing who is doing what to whom with what object.

As you go through the exercise, repeat the command or statement that the community member is making.

5) LISTEN AND ACT: Think of a common activity that you have already observed where the community members are making something. For example, in the community where you live people may weave bed mats, weave baskets, make clothing, sew bags, and so on.

Let's use the weaving of a bed mat as an example. Think through the steps as you have observed them. Gather sample tools and materials and prepare sketches for the process.

For the items related to the process, the community member can have you learn to understand them with a phrase like "Point to the knife." For actions associated with weaving, you can have the person command you to perform the actions and you can pretend to do that thing, or can point to the appropriate sketch. Actions would include cutting the frond for the mats, splitting the frond stems, heating the fronds over the fire to soften them, bending the frond leaves, weaving the fronds together, setting the mat in the sun to dry, and so on. Don't try to exhaust every possibility, but rather focus on the actions that represent common steps in the process.

6) Record a summary example of your listen and act exercise.

7) Review your learning exercises related to building for 20 minutes with the community member.

8) Listen to your new recordings for 20 minutes and previous recordings for 20 minutes.

9) Prepare for the coming day's learning plan for 30 minutes.

Level 1 Daily Learning Plan 32

THINGS TO DO FOR LEARNING

1) PARTICIPANT OBSERVATION: Continue to participate in four hours of daily activities in the community.

Here are a few goals for your participant observation:

OBSERVE the common objects, positions of objects, people who are working with the objects, ways you would describe the objects, and actions that they use to work with the objects in the activities that you participate in.

LISTEN for unique sounds, syllable stress, and general pronunciation.

RESPOND by appropriately asking WHAT, WHERE, HOW, WITH WHAT, WHEN, and WHO questions in whatever second language you have in common with the community.

NOTE common daily activities and categories of activities in people's lives, as well as WHY questions you have but shouldn't ask, and so on.

2) LISTEN AND ACT WITH SPEAKING: Practice understanding terms related to common body parts (hand, ear, nose, mouth, foot, eye, neck, back, stomach, hair, and so on). Use what you've drawn previously. Respond by pointing as the community member uses a sentence like "Point to HIS nose," "Point to HIS finger," "Point to HIS head," and so on.

As the person works through the body parts, you point and say, "This is his nose," or "That is his hand." (Also see Lexicarry.)

3) LISTEN AND ACT WITH SPEAKING: Practice understanding some of the body parts of animals that are different from people (a bird such as a chicken, a four-legged animal like a dog, a snake, a fish, and so on). Use your sketches or other pictures for this exercise.

As you point to the appropriate part, again repeat in a sentence like "This is a tail," or if it isn't too hard, expand to say something like "This is the dog's tail," and so on.

4) LISTEN AND ACT: In the community where you live, you've probably observed common activities that relate to washing and cleaning. In some cases you will have noted that these kinds of activities are primarily for men or for women, so you will have to think about that as you work with this exercise.

Identify an activity that relates to washing clothes, washing a hammock, doing dishes, or doing some other common cleaning task. If the location is a river, creek, or community area, you can carry out the exercise in that place if convenient.

Let's use washing clothes as our example. You can consider aspects of the task like positions of the items (on the rock, under the water, in the bucket, and so on), the objects used in washing (bucket, soap, scrub brush, scrub board, and so on), the washing actions (getting wet, putting on soap, dipping in the water, floating, sinking, beating on rock or log, wringing out the clothes, dropping the clothes on the ground, picking them up, laying them out in the sun to dry, hanging them on the line, collecting them after dry, and so on), and descriptive phrases that tell you about the cleaning process (clean, dirty, wet, dry, soapy, soap free, and so on).

In order to practice this with the community member, first observe the whole process in the way that they do this. Take note of the common actions, objects, positions, and descriptive phrases that might apply. The community member can then begin to work with you using the common objects in a sentence like, "Show me the soap," or "Where is the brush?" Or "What is on the rock?" As you become familiar in understanding the objects and positions, the person can then begin to add in commands that relate to the associated actions, such as, "Put soap on the shirt," or "Drop the shirt on the ground."

Additionally, the person can include the descriptive words by arranging some of the items in categories according to clean, dirty, wet, dry, soapy, soap free, and so on. They can ask, "Where is the soapy shirt?" Or "Where is the clean shirt?"

5) Record a summary example of your listen and act exercise.

6) Review the listen and act exercise related to weaving with the community member for 20 minutes.

7) Listen to your recordings for 40 minutes.

8) Prepare for the coming day's learning plan for 30 minutes.

Level 1 Daily Learning Plan 33

THINGS TO DO FOR LEARNING

1) PARTICIPANT OBSERVATION: Continue to participate in four hours of daily activities in the community.

Here are a few goals for your participant observation:

OBSERVE the common objects, positions of objects, people who are working with the objects, ways you would describe the objects, and actions that they use to work with the objects in the activities that you participate in.

LISTEN for unique sounds, syllable stress, and general pronunciation.

RESPOND by appropriately asking WHAT, WHERE, HOW, WITH WHAT, WHEN, and WHO questions in whatever second language you have in common with the community.

NOTE common daily activities and categories of activities in people's lives, as well as WHY questions you have but shouldn't ask, and so on.

2) LISTEN AND ACT WITH SPEAKING: Practice understanding the body parts for people and animals, with a variety of people combinations. You can use stick pictures to help you. You should also include yourself and the community member as two of the stick figures. Basic people words that you've already learned would include words like man, woman, baby, young person, older person, and so on. Also you should use the people reference words that you learned previously, such as his, her, its, our, their, and so on. For example, the person can say, "Point to his shoulder," and you would respond. Or "Point to the baby's leg." Or "Point to the dog's tail." Go through as many combinations at random as you can handle.

As you are pointing, practice saying the body parts in a sentence. This might be challenging depending on the language. Try to use the full expression such as, "This is the baby's leg," or "This is the dog's tail."

3) LISTEN AND ACT WITH SPEAKING: Practice understanding your previous learning of actions including actions related to body positions (walking, standing, sitting, kneeling, squatting, crawling, bending over, leaning, lying down, and so on). The community member can use a sentence that is more complicated like "Point to the man who is leaning." Or if that is too difficult, begin with simple statements like, "He is crawling" and move toward the more complicated sentence type as you can follow.

As you point, you yourself try making a simple statement in keeping with what the community member is saying like "The man is leaning," or "He is crawling." (**Also see Lexicarry.**)

4) LISTEN AND ACT: Take an hour to expand your previous day's exercise to include another activity in the community related to washing and cleaning. Your 20 minutes of review for the previous day's activity can just be included as part of the hour. For example, if you focused the day before on washing clothes or a hammock, you might move on to washing dishes. This should help you to reinforce the earlier material as well as expand the exercise.

For washing dishes, you can consider aspects of the task like positions of the items (on the rock, under the water, in the bucket, and so on), the objects used in washing (bucket, soap, scrub brush, rag, and so on), the washing actions (getting wet, putting on soap, dipping in the water, scrubbing with sand, dropping the dish on the ground, picking it up, laying it out in the sun to dry, drying with a towel, collecting them after dry, and so on), and descriptive phrases that tell you about the cleaning process (clean, dirty, wet, dry, soapy, soap free, and so on).

In order to practice this with the community member, first observe the whole process in the way that they do this in *participant observation*. Take note of the common actions, objects, positions, and descriptive phrases that might apply. The person can then begin to work with you using the common objects in a sentence like, "Show me the soap," or "Where is the rag?" Or "What is in the bucket?" As you become familiar in understanding the objects and positions, they can then begin to add in commands that relate to the associated actions, such as, "Put soap on the rag," or "Drop the bowl on the ground."

Additionally, the community member can include the descriptive words by arranging some of the items in categories according to clean, dirty, wet, dry, soapy, soap free, and so on. They can ask, "Where is the soapy bowl?" Or "Where is the clean plate?"

5) Record a summary example of your listen and act exercise.

6) Listen to your new recordings for 20 minutes and previous recordings for 20 minutes.

7) Prepare for the coming day's learning plan for 30 minutes.

Level 1 Daily Learning Plan 34

THINGS TO DO FOR LEARNING

1) PARTICIPANT OBSERVATION: Continue to participate in four hours of daily activities in the community.

Here are a few goals for your participant observation:

OBSERVE the common objects, positions of objects, people who are working with the objects, ways you would describe the objects, and actions that they use to work with the objects in the activities that you participate in.

LISTEN for unique sounds, syllable stress, and general pronunciation.

RESPOND by appropriately asking WHAT, WHERE, HOW, WITH WHAT, WHEN, and WHO questions in whatever second language you have in common with the community.

NOTE common daily activities and categories of activities in people's lives, as well as WHY questions you have but shouldn't ask, and so on.

2) LISTEN AND ACT WITH SPEAKING: Using a picture of your family or a sketch, practice understanding basic terms for kinship relationships (my father, my mother, my grandfather, my grandmother, my wife, my child, my baby, my uncle, my aunt, my niece, my nephew, my father-in-law, my mother-in-law, and so on) for either you or for the community member.

As you practice pointing appropriately, repeat the expression in a sentence like, "This is my mother," or "This is my father." (**Also see Lexicarry.**)

3) LISTEN AND ACT WITH SPEAKING: Practice understanding ways of seeing and looking using house parts and house objects, as well as terms that you learned for the area around the house. Include common terms like see, look, stare, peek, watch, spy on, and so on. You might act these out in appropriate ways with the person to create scenarios for the terms.

As the community member makes a statement, you point and repeat, such as "The man is staring," or "I am watching." (**Also see Lexicarry.**)

4) LISTEN AND ACT: Take 20 minutes to review the exercises related to building and weaving. Take 40 minutes to review all that you have learned to understand regarding washing and cleaning.

5) Listen to your new recordings for 20 minutes and previous recordings for 20 minutes.

6) Prepare for the coming day's learning plan for 30 minutes.

Level 1 Daily Learning Plan 35

THINGS TO DO FOR LEARNING

1) PARTICIPANT OBSERVATION: Continue to participate in four hours of daily activities in the community.

Here are a few goals for your participant observation:

OBSERVE the common objects, positions of objects, people who are working with the objects, ways you would describe the objects, and actions that they use to work with the objects in the activities that you participate in.

LISTEN for unique sounds, syllable stress, and general pronunciation.

RESPOND by appropriately asking WHAT, WHERE, HOW, WITH WHAT, WHEN, and WHO questions in whatever second language you have in common with the community.

NOTE common daily activities and categories of activities in people's lives, as well as WHY questions you have but shouldn't ask, and so on.

2) LISTEN AND ACT WITH SPEAKING: Practice expanding your previous kinship term exercise to include the description of someone's kinship relations besides your own using your sketches. For example, the community member can say "Point to the man's mother," in which case you will first point to a sketch of a man and then the equivalent relationship on the tree. Try to include terms sufficient to cover my, your, her, his, their, and our if possible. This can be difficult, but do the best that you can, because family relationships are important.

As you listen and point, try to respond appropriately with a sentence like, "This is the man's mother." (**Also see Lexicarry.**)

3) LISTEN AND ACT WITH SPEAKING: Practice common household objects to comprehend terms for touching, such as touching, grabbing, hitting, kicking, rolling, throwing, pinching, squeezing, hugging, and so on. Begin by acting out these things with the community member only as appropriate! Include also your holding and carrying terms as you work through this exercise.

As with previous exercise, respond appropriately by repeating the command or sentence, like "Touch the book," or "Hit the chair," or "Kick the ball." (**Also see Lexicarry.**)

4) LISTEN AND ACT: For the next several learning plans, the *listen and act* learning exercise will relate to ways of obtaining food, hunting, trapping, foraging, or fishing. The settings and activities vary greatly from place to place, so you will need to think about the settings and activities most common to the community where you live.

Let's begin with an example that relates to obtaining food through buying and selling. First, during your *participant observation*, you want to go with the community member to a context where this activity takes place, such as a store or market. Take note of the common actions, objects, positions, and possible descriptive phrases.

Often it is impractical or awkward to try to practice the *listen and act* exercise in the store or market location. Instead, set up a pretend store or market scene using various of the items that you purchased or sketched when you were in the actual location.

The community member can then begin to work with you using the common objects in a sentence like, "Show me the tomato," or "Where is the onion?" Or "What is in the basket?" As you become familiar in understanding the objects and positions, the person can then begin to add in commands that relate to the associated actions, such as, "I want a tomato," or "I am buying three onions," or "I am selling two baskets."

Additionally, the person can include the descriptive words by arranging some of the items in categories according to ripe, unripe, good, bad, rotten, and so on. They can ask, "Where is the rotten tomato?" Or "Where is the good mango?"

Another good option is for you to practice your numbers by marking prices on the items and having the community member randomly ask you the prices of the items in a culturally appropriate way. You can respond by pointing to the item, or you can respond with the correct amount.

5) Record a summary example of your listen and act exercise.

6) Review your previous washing and cleaning activities for 20 minutes with the community member.

7) Listen to your new recordings for 20 minutes and previous recordings for 20 minutes.

8) Prepare for the coming day's learning plan for 30 minutes.

Level 1 Daily Learning Plan 36

THINGS TO DO FOR LEARNING

1) PARTICIPANT OBSERVATION: Continue to participate in four hours of daily activities in the community.

Here are a few goals for your participant observation:

OBSERVE the common objects, positions of objects, people who are working with the objects, ways you would describe the objects, and actions that they use to work with the objects in the activities that you participate in.

LISTEN for unique sounds, syllable stress, and general pronunciation.

RESPOND by appropriately asking WHAT, WHERE, HOW, WITH WHAT, WHEN, and WHO questions in whatever second language you have in common with the community.

NOTE common daily activities and categories of activities in people's lives, as well as WHY questions you have but shouldn't ask, and so on.

2) LISTEN AND ACT WITH SPEAKING: Use a family picture or sketch to practice combining body part words and kinship terms. For example, the community member can say, "Point to my aunt's foot," or "Point to your brother's face." Your goal is to be able to recognize the combinations successfully and point appropriately.

In addition to pointing, you yourself make an appropriate response, such as "This is my aunt's foot," or "This is my brother's face."

3) LISTEN AND ACT WITH SPEAKING: Take the opportunity to practice again with fire and cooking.

As you go through the exercise, try to repeat the commands that the person is giving you.

4) LISTEN AND ACT: Think of an activity in the community related to foraging or gathering that you have observed. (Gardening activities will be covered specifically in later plans.) For example, perhaps community members collect certain kinds of cash crops, fruit, nuts, honey, coconuts, caterpillars, larvae, and so on. With that activity in mind, draw sketches or set up a scenario where you can practice the common actions, objects, positions, and descriptive phrases that might apply to the foraging or processing activity.

For example, if the activity is picking and processing coconuts, common objects might include the coconut tree, the coconut, the fronds, the trunk of the tree, the loop used to climb the tree, the sharp stick used to peel the coconut, and so on. Common positions include on the ground, in the tree, on the way up, on the way down, and so on. Common actions include standing on the ground, climbing the tree, picking the coconuts, peeling the coconuts, drinking the liquid, eating the fruit inside, and so on. Common descriptions would include green, ripe, large, small, hard, soft, and so on.

As you've done with previous activities, practice these various options using sketches and actions, with the community member describing or commanding.

5) Record a summary example of your listen and act exercise.

6) Review your buying and selling listen and act exercise for 20 minutes with the community member.

7) Listen to your new recordings for 20 minutes and previous recordings for 20 minutes.

8) Prepare for the coming day's learning plan for 30 minutes.

Level 1 Daily Learning Plan 37

THINGS TO DO FOR LEARNING

1) PARTICIPANT OBSERVATION: Continue to participate in four hours of daily activities in the community.

Here are a few goals for your participant observation:

OBSERVE the common objects, positions of objects, people who are working with the objects, ways you would describe the objects, and actions that they use to work with the objects in the activities that you participate in.

LISTEN for unique sounds, syllable stress, and general pronunciation.

RESPOND by appropriately asking WHAT, WHERE, HOW, WITH WHAT, WHEN, and WHO questions in whatever second language you have in common with the community.

NOTE common daily activities and categories of activities in people's lives, as well as WHY questions you have but shouldn't ask, and so on.

2) LISTEN AND ACT WITH SPEAKING: Organize objects that represent a large variety of colors, incorporating options like spotted and striped as well. The community member can say, "Point to the red cup," or "Point to the blue cup," etc..

As you point, use a sentence like, "This is the red cup," or "This is the blue cup." (**Also see Lexicarry.**)

3) LISTEN AND ACT WITH SPEAKING: Organize an assortment of household and other objects that you've learned which represent adjective pair opposites (large/small, heavy/light, long/short, cold/hot, rough/smooth, tall/short, thick/thin, round/flat, and so on). The community member can use a phrase such as, "Point to the thing that is hot," or "Point to the long one." In this way try to work through the sets of adjectives in random order.

As you are pointing, you can repeat in a sentence like, "This is the long one," or "This is the thing that is hot."

4) LISTEN AND ACT: Think of another activity in the community related to foraging or gathering that you have observed (collecting certain kinds of cash crops or fruit not in the garden, nuts, honey, coconuts, caterpillars, larvae, and so on).

With that activity in mind, draw sketches or set up a scenario where you can practice the common actions, objects, positions, and descriptive phrases that might apply to the foraging or processing activity.

For example, if the activity is harvesting larvae, common objects might include the rotted tree trunk, the larvae, the tool for peeling back the bark, the leaves for putting the larvae in, the trail for getting to the location, the vines for tying the leaves, and so on. Common positions include in the tree, in the leaves, and so on. Common actions include peeling back the bark, collecting the larvae, putting the larvae in leaves, tying the leaves, putting the bundles in a basket, and so on. Common descriptions would include alive, dead, wiggling, still, bad smelling, and so on.

As you've done with previous activities, practice these various options using sketches and actions, with the community member describing or commanding.

5) Record a summary example of your listen and act exercise.

6) Review your previous day's listen and act exercise with the community member for 20 minutes.

7) Listen to your new recordings and previous recordings for 20 minutes each.

8) Prepare for the coming day's learning plan for 30 minutes.

Level 1 Daily Learning Plan 38

THINGS TO DO FOR LEARNING

1) PARTICIPANT OBSERVATION: Continue to participate in four hours of daily activities in the community.

Here are a few goals for your participant observation:

OBSERVE the common objects, positions of objects, people who are working with the objects, ways you would describe the objects, and actions that they use to work with the objects in the activities that you participate in.

LISTEN for unique sounds, syllable stress, and general pronunciation.

RESPOND by appropriately asking WHAT, WHERE, HOW, WITH WHAT, WHEN, and WHO questions in whatever second language you have in common with the community.

NOTE common daily activities and categories of activities in people's lives, as well as WHY questions you have but shouldn't ask, and so on.

2) LISTEN AND ACT WITH SPEAKING: Using objects and simple sketches, practice hearing words for throwing to, showing to, taking to, bringing to, giving to, and so on. *Listen and act* with speaking as the community member tells you, "Throw the rock to me," or "Spear the ground with the spear," "Give the basket to him," or "Take the book to the boy." If others are around, include them in the exercise as well.

As you are following the commands of the community member, repeat the commands out loud. At the end of the exercise, you can practice giving similar commands to your friend as well.

3) LISTEN AND ACT WITH SPEAKING: Using a pouring container and a cup, practice hearing terms for drinking, dumping out, spilling, and pouring different types of liquids. The community member can use commands to work through these actions with you, like "Pour me some coffee," or "Dump out the water."

Repeat the commands out loud as you are following them.

4) LISTEN AND ACT: Think of a common activity in the community related to gardening. In many places, community members will follow a process of preparing the garden, planting and caring for the garden, and harvesting the food from the garden. This will be the order that you will follow in your practice.

For this exercise, you will focus on the process of garden preparation. You should first observe and participate in the steps of preparing a garden for planting. With that activity in mind, draw sketches or set up a scenario where you can practice the common objects and actions that apply to the preparation phase of the gardening activity.

Common objects might include knives, machetes, axes, rakes, fire, sticks, leaves, branches, logs, brush, trees, vines, thorns, and so on. Common actions will include chopping, cutting brush, cutting up, falling trees, setting fire, piling up, raking, marking boundaries, and so on.

As you've done with previous activities, practice these various options using sketches and actions, with the community member describing or commanding.

5) Record a summary example of your listen and act exercise.

6) Review your previous day's listen and act exercise with the community member for 20 minutes.

7) Listen to your new recordings for 20 minutes and previous recordings for 20 minutes.

8) Prepare for the coming day's learning plan for 30 minutes.

Level 1 Daily Learning Plan 39

THINGS TO DO FOR LEARNING

1) PARTICIPANT OBSERVATION: Continue to participate in four hours of daily activities in the community.

Here are a few goals for your participant observation:

OBSERVE the common objects, positions of objects, people who are working with the objects, ways you would describe the objects, and actions that they use to work with the objects in the activities that you participate in.

LISTEN for unique sounds, syllable stress, and general pronunciation.

RESPOND by appropriately asking WHAT, WHERE, HOW, WITH WHAT, WHEN, and WHO questions in whatever second language you have in common with the community.

NOTE common daily activities and categories of activities in people's lives, as well as WHY questions you have but shouldn't ask, and so on.

2) LISTEN AND ACT WITH SPEAKING: Using the words for common food items and pictures of animals and people, practice comprehending sentences related to feeding and eating. The community member can use commands such as, "Eat the salt," or "Feed me the sweet potato." Later they can relate the food items to pictures and you can pick the appropriate picture and food. For example, they can say, "The man (or woman) is eating the mango," in which case you'd pick up the mango and indicate that the man (or woman) was eating it by pointing to them and repeating the person's statement.

3) LISTEN AND ACT WITH SPEAKING: Collect all the objects that you've learned that serve as tools or instruments for working. These should include things like broom, machete, shell, knife, fire, axe, planting tools, shovel, and so on. Practice understanding the actions that are associated with the objects by having the community member use simple commands. Be prepared for multiple terms for cutting and chopping. Include a rope or vine for terms of tying and untying. Act out the commands as they give them to you.

As you are acting, repeat the commands that the person is giving you. Toward the end of the exercise, try commanding them to act with the objects.

4) LISTEN AND ACT: Continue with the common activity in the community related to gardening.

You should first observe and participate in the steps for planting and caring for the garden. With that activity in mind, draw sketches or set up a scenario where you can practice the common objects and actions that apply to the planting and caring for phase of the gardening activity.

Common objects might include planting sticks, machetes, shovels, rakes, plows, seeds, and so on. Common actions will include cutting, plowing, marking boundaries, collecting seed, setting up garden houses, building fences, planting in various ways, weeding, and so on.

As you've done with previous activities, practice these various options using sketches and actions, with the community member describing or commanding.

5) Record a summary example of your listen and act exercise.

6) Review your previous day's listen and act exercise with the community member for 20 minutes.

7) Listen to your new recordings for 20 minutes and previous recordings for 20 minutes.

8) Prepare for the coming day's learning plan for 30 minutes.

Level 1 Daily Learning Plan 40

THINGS TO DO FOR LEARNING

1) PARTICIPANT OBSERVATION: Continue to participate in four hours of daily activities in the community.

Here are a few goals for your participant observation:

OBSERVE the common objects, positions of objects, people who are working with the objects, ways you would describe the objects, and actions that they use to work with the objects in the activities that you participate in.

LISTEN for unique sounds, syllable stress, and general pronunciation.

RESPOND by appropriately asking WHAT, WHERE, HOW, WITH WHAT, WHEN, and WHO questions in whatever second language you have in common with the community.

NOTE common daily activities and categories of activities in people's lives, as well as WHY questions you have but shouldn't ask, and so on.

2) LISTEN AND ACT WITH SPEAKING: Using sketches and known food items, have the community member practice ways to describe possession and ownership with you. Begin with something such as "Point to my knife," or "Show me your axe," in which case you'd pick up the appropriate object and point to the respective owner. Expand this exercise with sketches of people, family, and animals.

As you hear and follow the instructions of the community member, repeat the object in a sentence like, "This is your knife," or "This is my axe."

3) LISTEN AND ACT WITH SPEAKING: Using sketches and objects, practice recognizing differences in singular and plural objects. The community member can ask questions like, "Where is the stone?" or "Where are the sticks?" As you point to the appropriate objects, use a sentence like, "This is the stone," or "These are the sticks."

4) LISTEN AND ACT WITH SPEAKING: Using times during the day that you've previously learned and times on a clock, begin learning how to state times of day if applicable. The community member can mark the time on a simple clock and ask, "What time is it?" You can respond with an appropriate answer to the question.

5) LISTEN AND ACT WITH SPEAKING: Collect 55 common objects to practice understanding the numbers one to ten. Sort the objects into groups one to ten. Then the community member can say, "Point to one stone," and you point to one stone and say, "one stone." They can say, "three stones," and you point to three and say, "three stones." Do this until you can respond correctly and say to all ten numbers.

6) LISTEN AND ACT: Continue with the common activity related to gardening in the community. You should first observe and participate in the steps for harvesting produce from the garden. With that activity in mind, draw sketches or set up a scenario where you can practice the common objects and actions that apply to the harvesting phase of the gardening activity. Common objects might include machetes and other harvesting tools, vines for bundling produce, baskets for collection, and so on. Common actions will include cutting, digging, various kinds of picking or harvesting, and so on.

As you've done with previous activities, practice these various options using sketches and actions, with the community member describing or commanding.

7) Record a summary example of your listen and act exercise.

8) Review your previous day's listen and act exercise with the community member for 20 minutes.

9) Listen to your new recordings for 20 minutes and previous recordings for 20 minutes.

10) Prepare for the coming day's learning plan for 30 minutes.

Level 1 Daily Learning Plan 41

THINGS TO DO FOR LEARNING

1) PARTICIPANT OBSERVATION: Continue to participate in four hours of daily activities in the community.

Here are a few goals for your participant observation:

OBSERVE the common objects, positions of objects, people who are working with the objects, ways you would describe the objects, and actions that they use to work with the objects in the activities that you participate in.

LISTEN for unique sounds, syllable stress, and general pronunciation.

RESPOND by appropriately asking *WHAT, WHERE, HOW, WITH WHAT, WHEN,* and *WHO* questions in whatever second language you have in common with the community.

NOTE common daily activities and categories of activities in people's lives, as well as *WHY* questions you have but shouldn't ask, and so on.

2) LISTEN AND ACT WITH SPEAKING: Practice understanding terms for days of the week and time (today, tomorrow, day before, day after, and so on). Also terms for common times of day, seasons, day, month, year, and so on. An easy way to practice today, yesterday, tomorrow, the day before yesterday, and the day after tomorrow is to draw five slots on a piece of paper and put the date on the center slot. The community member can randomly say one of the five terms and you point to the appropriate slot that corresponds. You can do similar sketches for times of day, seasons, months, days of the week, and so on.

As you point or follow the command of the community member, also practice repeating the terms themselves. (**Also see Lexicarry.**)

3) LISTEN AND ACT WITH SPEAKING: Practice understanding terms related to the sky and weather using sketches and your environment, like sun, sky, moon, stars, clouds, rain, mist, fog, wind, and so on.

As you point to the appropriate pictures, practice repeating the object in a sentence like, "This is the sun," or "This is a cloud," and so on.

4) LISTEN AND ACT: In the community where you live, probably some form of hunting, trapping, or animal domestication is common. Choose an activity that reflects one of these. Again be sure to observe and participate in the activity first so that you can note objects and actions associated with it.

For example, perhaps people in the community raise pigs. Common objects for the activity might be pens, fences, food, terms for various ages of pigs, pig wallow, mud, pig droppings, a bag for taming a young pig, and so on. Common actions can include feeding, cleaning up, taming, teaching, following, rooting, eating, slaughtering, and so on.

As you've done with previous activities, practice these various options using sketches and actions, with the community member describing or commanding.

5) Record a summary example of your listen and act exercise.

6) Review your previous day's listen and act exercise with the community member for 20 minutes.

7) Listen to your new recordings for 20 minutes and previous recordings for 20 minutes.

8) Prepare for the coming day's learning plan for 30 minutes.

Level 1 Daily Learning Plan 42

THINGS TO DO FOR LEARNING

1) PARTICIPANT OBSERVATION: Continue to participate in four hours of daily activities in the community.

Here are a few goals for your participant observation:

OBSERVE the common objects, positions of objects, people who are working with the objects, ways you would describe the objects, and actions that they use to work with the objects in the activities that you participate in.

LISTEN for unique sounds, syllable stress, and general pronunciation.

RESPOND by appropriately asking WHAT, WHERE, HOW, WITH WHAT, WHEN, and WHO questions in whatever second language you have in common with the community.

NOTE common daily activities and categories of activities in people's lives, as well as WHY questions you have but shouldn't ask, and so on.

2) LISTEN AND ACT WITH SPEAKING: Use sketches or actions to review terms related to people's emotions. The community member can make statements like, "The man is angry," or "He is crying."

As you point to the appropriate picture, repeat the statement of the community member for each emotion. (**Also see Lexicarry.**)

3) LISTEN AND ACT WITH SPEAKING: Practice understanding terms for 15 or more common types of clothing if possible. As you point to the appropriate clothing item, say, "This is a shirt," or "This is a skirt." (Also see Lexicarry.)

4) LISTEN AND ACT WITH SPEAKING: Review your previous terms for colors, numbers, and adjective pair opposites, combining them with actions related to the objects and food items that you've already learned. For example, the community member can say, "Point to the two long sticks," or "Show me the three black cups" or "Give me the two sweet potatoes." Try to use the response in a sentence as you point: "These are three black cups," or "Here are the sweet potatoes."

5) LISTEN AND ACT: In the community where you live, probably some form of collecting a food source from rivers, lakes, or oceans is common. Choose an activity that reflects one of these. Again be sure to observe and participate in the activity first so that you can note objects and actions associated with it.

For example, perhaps people in the community dam up streams to poison fish. Common objects for the activity might be types of fish, crayfish, poisonous vine, the dam, stones for the dam, leaves for the dam, mud for the dam, bark for the dam, baskets for scooping the fish, spears for spearing the fish, rapids, shallows, waterfalls, waves, and so on. Common actions can include building the dam, poisoning the water, scooping the fish, following the stream, slipping on the stones, the water level rising and falling, and so on.

As you've done with previous activities, practice these various options using sketches and actions, with the community member describing or commanding.

6) Record a summary example of your listen and act exercise.

7) Review your previous day's listen and act exercise with the community member for 20 minutes.

8) Listen to your new recordings for 20 minutes and previous recordings for 20 minutes.

9) Prepare for the coming day's learning plan for 30 minutes.

Level 1 Daily Learning Plan 43

THINGS TO DO FOR LEARNING

1) PARTICIPANT OBSERVATION: Continue to participate in four hours of daily activities in the community.

Here are a few goals for your participant observation:

OBSERVE the common objects, positions of objects, people who are working with the objects, ways you would describe the objects, and actions that they use to work with the objects in the activities that you participate in.

LISTEN for unique sounds, syllable stress, and general pronunciation.

RESPOND by appropriately asking WHAT, WHERE, HOW, WITH WHAT, WHEN, and WHO questions in whatever second language you have in common with the community.

NOTE common daily activities and categories of activities in people's lives, as well as WHY questions you have but shouldn't ask, and so on.

2) LISTEN AND ACT WITH SPEAKING: Use your sketches of common words for animals to practice understanding several actions of various animals, including the common sounds that animals make as well. For example the community member can say "The cat hisses," or "The cat meows." Dogs bark and growl. Chickens scratch, cluck, and crow. Pigs root and grunt. Birds sing and fly. Fish swim and bite.

As the community member states what is happening in a picture, you follow the instructions and repeat, "The cat is hissing," or "The cat meows," and so on. (Also see Lexicarry.)

3) LISTEN AND ACT WITH SPEAKING: Using sketches and examples, practice understanding words for common bugs and creeping things in the community.

As the community member gives instructions, you point to the bug and say, "This is a centipede," or "This is a grasshopper," and so on. (Also see Lexicarry.)

4) LISTEN AND ACT WITH SPEAKING: Using sketches, review known objects with emotional states of individuals. A good way to do this is to use the action giving. The community member can state, "Give the rock to the sad man," or "Give the sweet potato to the happy man." Try to include a wide range of objects and the emotion words you've already learned. As you follow the commands of the community member, repeat the commands out loud. At the end of the exercise, you can try commanding the community member to perform some of the actions. (Also see Lexicarry.)

5) LISTEN AND ACT: For the remaining daily learning plans, your *listen and act* learning exercise is going to focus specifically on the comprehension of common questions. These would include things like WHO, WHAT, WITH WHAT, WHERE, and WHEN.

Although you have probably heard these questions in your activities over the last months, you still need practice in comprehending them well.

Here is the process for you to follow: get out your picture or sketch of common people. Also draw a quick picture that represents the idea of "today" (Try pointing to a calendar or have the written word in the language for 'today' to point to.) And then collect 10 common objects that you are already very familiar with. Finally, sketch out the village area and label the garden, house, cooking house, yard, and a couple other common places.

Explain to the community member that you are going to learn to understand common questions. Then tell the community member to begin simply with a statement and question related to a person and object or place like, "The man is in the garden. Where is the man?" You would respond by pointing to the garden. The community member would then ask a follow up question, "Who is in the garden?" You'd point to the man.

The person could then state something like, "The woman is holding a stick. Who is holding the stick?" You would respond by pointing to the woman. The community member would ask, "What is the woman holding?" You'd point to the stick.

The community member could say, "The boy is throwing a rock. What is the boy throwing?" You'd respond by pointing to the rock. The community member would say, "Who is throwing the rock?" You'd respond by pointing to the boy.

The community member could say, "The girl is cutting grass with a machete. What is the girl cutting with?" You'd respond by pointing to the machete. The community member would say, "Who is cutting with the machete?" You'd point to the girl.

The community member would say, "What is she cutting?" You'd point to the grass. The community member could say, "I am running today. When am I running?" You'd point to the picture of today. The community member could say, "Who is running?" You'd point to the community member. The community member could say, "What am I doing?" You'd act out the running action.

Try to go through this process with lots of the actors, objects and actions that you already know really well so that you can listen and respond to the variety of questions appropriately.

6) Record a summary example of your listen and act exercise.

7) Review your previous day's listen and act exercise with the community member for 20 minutes.

8) Listen to your new recordings for 20 minutes and previous recordings for 20 minutes.

9) Prepare for the coming day's learning plan for 30 minutes.

Level 1 Daily Learning Plan 44

THINGS TO DO FOR LEARNING

1) PARTICIPANT OBSERVATION: Continue to participate in four hours of daily activities in the community.

Here are a few goals for your participant observation:

OBSERVE the common objects, positions of objects, people who are working with the objects, ways you would describe the objects, and actions that they use to work with the objects in the activities that you participate in.

LISTEN for unique sounds, syllable stress, and general pronunciation.

RESPOND by appropriately asking WHAT, WHERE, HOW, WITH WHAT, WHEN, and WHO questions in whatever second language you have in common with the community.

NOTE common daily activities and categories of activities in people's lives, as well as WHY questions you have but shouldn't ask, and so on.

2) LISTEN AND ACT WITH SPEAKING: Using terms for bugs, practice understanding terms related to what these creatures do to people. For example, centipedes sting, snakes strike, wasps sting, ants bite, dogs bite, and so on. Use simple sketches.

As the community member states what is happening, point to the appropriate sketch and repeat, "The dog bites," or "The wasp stings," and so on. (Also see Lexicarry.)

3) LISTEN AND ACT WITH SPEAKING: Review your sketches of landforms and parts of rivers and waterways.

As the community member tells you to point to the various items, you do so and state, "This is a waterfall," or "This is a mountain," and so on. (Also see Lexicarry.)

4) LISTEN AND ACT WITH SPEAKING: Apply the use of color and number to a wide range of items that you collect in numbers of 10. If possible, collect five different sets of items that are the same but vary in color. For example, you can get 10 white stones and 10 black stones, 10 red leaves and 10 green leaves, 10 blue flowers and 10 yellow flowers, and so on. The community member can command you, "Give three yellow flowers to me," or "Give four red leaves to me." You can also include your sketches of people and relatives to apply this exercise to a broad range of people.

As you go through the practice, simply repeat the part of the sentence that reflects the color, number and object. For example, if the community member tells you, "Give three yellow flowers to me," you can say, "three yellow flowers."

5) LISTEN AND ACT: Focus again on the common questions WHO, WHAT, WITH WHAT, WHERE, and WHEN.

Get out your sketch of common people, your picture that represents the idea of "today," and your village area sketch. This time, though, use objects related to the fire and cooking.

Then tell the community member to begin simply with a statement and question related to a person and object or place like, "The man is blowing on the fire. What is the man doing?" You would respond by pointing to the blowing on the fire step. The community member would then ask a follow up question, "Who is blowing on the fire?" You'd point to the man. The community member would ask, "What is the man blowing on?" You'd respond by pointing to the fire.

The community member could then state something like, "The woman is cooking bananas with leaves." Who is cooking?" You would respond by pointing to the woman. The community member would ask, "What is the woman cooking?" You'd point to the banana. The community member would ask, "What is she cooking with?" You'd point to the leaves.

The community member could say, "I am roasting the sweet potato today. When am I roasting the sweet potato?" You'd respond by pointing to the picture of today. The community member would say, "Who is roasting the sweet potato?" You'd respond by pointing to the community member. The community member would say, "What am I roasting?" You'd respond by pointing to the sweet potato.

The community member could say, "You are peeling the manioc with a knife. Who is peeling the manioc?" You'd respond by pointing to yourself. The community member would say, "What are you peeling?" You'd point to the manioc. The community member would say, "What are you peeling the manioc with?" You'd point to the knife.

Try to go through this process with lots of the actors, objects and actions related to the fire and cooking so that you can listen and respond to the variety of questions appropriately.

6) Record a summary example of your listen and act exercise.

7) Listen to your new recordings for 20 minutes and previous recordings for 20 minutes.

8) Prepare for the coming day's learning plan for 30 minutes.

Level 1 Daily Learning Plan 45

THINGS TO DO FOR LEARNING

1) PARTICIPANT OBSERVATION: Continue to participate in four hours of daily activities in the community.

Here are a few goals for your participant observation:

OBSERVE the common objects, positions of objects, people who are working with the objects, ways you would describe the objects, and actions that they use to work with the objects in the activities that you participate in.

LISTEN for unique sounds, syllable stress, and general pronunciation.

RESPOND by appropriately asking WHAT, WHERE, HOW, WITH WHAT, WHEN, and WHO questions in whatever second language you have in common with the community.

NOTE common daily activities and categories of activities in people's lives, as well as WHY questions you have but shouldn't ask, and so on.

2) LISTEN AND ACT WITH SPEAKING: Use 10 of an object that you already know to practice your ordinal numbers 1 thru 10. The community member can use a sentence like, "Point to the third stone," or "Point to the seventh stone."

You point to the appropriate item and say, "This is the third stone," or "This is the seventh stone," and so on.

3) LISTEN AND ACT WITH SPEAKING: Using many or most of the objects you have learned so far and your sketches of people, family, and animals, practice understanding the action wanting. For example, the community member can say, "The dog wants a chicken," and you'd indicate the dog and chicken in the proper order. Or "I want a rock," in which case you'd give the community member a rock. Combine as many people, family, and animals as you can.

As you indicate the proper person or animal and object, repeat the sentence exactly as the community member has said it.

4) LISTEN AND ACT: Focus again on the common questions WHO, WHAT, WITH WHAT, WHERE, and WHEN.

Get out your sketch of common people, your picture that represents the idea of "today," and your village area sketch. This time, though, use objects related to the house and activity of building.

Have the community member ask many questions using the actors, objects and actions related to the house and house building.

5) Record a summary example of your listen and act exercise.

6) Listen to your new recordings for 20 minutes and previous recordings for 20 minutes.

7) Prepare for the coming day's learning plan for 30 minutes.

Level 1 Daily Learning Plan 46

In daily learning plans 46 to 50, you should try to continue learning from your earlier daily learning plans 21 to 25.

For each plan 46 to 50, try to think of two new ways to use the *listen and act* with speaking learning exercise. The *listen and act* learning exercise for each plan is already included below.

THINGS TO DO FOR LEARNING

1) PARTICIPANT OBSERVATION: Continue to participate in four hours of daily activities in the community.

Here are a few goals for your participant observation:

OBSERVE the common objects, positions of objects, people who are working with the objects, ways you would describe the objects, and actions that they use to work with the objects in the activities that you participate in.

LISTEN for unique sounds, syllable stress, and general pronunciation.

RESPOND by appropriately asking WHAT, WHERE, HOW, WITH WHAT, WHEN, and WHO questions in whatever second language you have in common with the community.

NOTE common daily activities and categories of activities in people's lives, as well as WHY questions you have but shouldn't ask, and so on.

2) LISTEN AND ACT WITH SPEAKING: Apply this learning exercise to a previous activity in the community that you have observed.

3) LISTEN AND ACT WITH SPEAKING: Apply this learning exercise to a previous activity in the community that you have observed.

4) LISTEN AND ACT: Focus again on the common questions WHO, WHAT, WITH WHAT, WHERE, and WHEN.

Get out your sketch of common people, your picture that represents the idea of "today," and your village area sketch. This time, though, use objects related to making an object, such as the weaving of a bed mat.

Have the community member ask many questions using the actors, objects and actions related to the activity.

5) Record a summary example of your listen and act exercise.

6) Listen to your new recordings for 20 minutes and previous recordings for 20 minutes.

7) Prepare for the coming day's learning plan for 30 minutes.

Level 1 Daily Learning Plan 47

THINGS TO DO FOR LEARNING

1) PARTICIPANT OBSERVATION: Continue to participate in four hours of daily activities in the community.

Here are a few goals for your participant observation:

OBSERVE the common objects, positions of objects, people who are working with the objects, ways you would describe the objects, and actions that they use to work with the objects in the activities that you participate in.

LISTEN for unique sounds, syllable stress, and general pronunciation.

RESPOND by appropriately asking WHAT, WHERE, HOW, WITH WHAT, WHEN, and WHO questions in whatever second language you have in common with the community.

NOTE common daily activities and categories of activities in people's lives, as well as WHY questions you have but shouldn't ask, and so on.

2) LISTEN AND ACT WITH SPEAKING: Apply this learning exercise to a previous activity in the community that you have observed.

3) LISTEN AND ACT WITH SPEAKING: Apply this learning exercise to a previous activity in the community that you have observed.

4) LISTEN AND ACT: Focus again on the common questions WHO, WHAT, WITH WHAT, WHERE, and WHEN.

Get out your sketch of common people, your picture that represents the idea of "today," and your village area sketch. This time, though, use objects related to washing and cleaning.

Have the community member ask many questions using the actors, objects and actions related to the activity.

5) Record a summary example of your listen and act exercise.

6) Listen to your new recordings for 20 minutes and previous recordings for 20 minutes.

7) Prepare for the coming day's learning plan for 30 minutes.

Level 1 Daily Learning Plan 48

THINGS TO DO FOR LEARNING

1) PARTICIPANT OBSERVATION: Continue to participate in four hours of daily activities in the community.

Here are a few goals for your participant observation:

OBSERVE the common objects, positions of objects, people who are working with the objects, ways you would describe the objects, and actions that they use to work with the objects in the activities that you participate in.

LISTEN for unique sounds, syllable stress, and general pronunciation.

RESPOND by appropriately asking WHAT, WHERE, HOW, WITH WHAT, WHEN, and WHO questions in whatever second language you have in common with the community.

NOTE common daily activities and categories of activities in people's lives, as well as WHY questions you have but shouldn't ask, and so on.

2) LISTEN AND ACT WITH SPEAKING: Apply this learning exercise to a previous activity in the community that you have observed.

3) LISTEN AND ACT WITH SPEAKING: Apply this learning exercise to a previous activity in the community that you have observed.

4) LISTEN AND ACT: Focus again on the common questions WHO, WHAT, WITH WHAT, WHERE, and WHEN.

Get out your sketch of common people, your picture that represents the idea of "today," and your village area sketch. This time, though, use objects related to buying and selling.

Have the community member ask many questions using the actors, objects and actions related to the activity.

5) Record a summary example of your listen and act exercise.

6) Listen to your new recordings for 20 minutes and previous recordings for 20 minutes.

7) Prepare for the coming day's learning plan for 30 minutes.

Level 1 Daily Learning Plan 49

THINGS TO DO FOR LEARNING

1) PARTICIPANT OBSERVATION: Continue to participate in four hours of daily activities in the community.

Here are a few goals for your participant observation:

OBSERVE the common objects, positions of objects, people who are working with the objects, ways you would describe the objects, and actions that they use to work with the objects in the activities that you participate in.

LISTEN for unique sounds, syllable stress, and general pronunciation.

RESPOND by appropriately asking WHAT, WHERE, HOW, WITH WHAT, WHEN, and WHO questions in whatever second language you have in common with the community.

NOTE common daily activities and categories of activities in people's lives, as well as WHY questions you have but shouldn't ask, and so on.

2) LISTEN AND ACT WITH SPEAKING: Apply this learning exercise to a previous activity in the community that you have observed.

3) LISTEN AND ACT WITH SPEAKING: Apply this learning exercise to a previous activity in the community that you have observed.

4) LISTEN AND ACT: Focus again on the common questions WHO, WHAT, WITH WHAT, WHERE, and WHEN.

Get out your sketch of common people, your picture that represents the idea of "today," and your village area sketch. This time, though, use objects related to foraging, hunting, and fishing.

Have the community member ask many questions using the actors, objects and actions related to the activity.

5) Record a summary example of your listen and act exercise.

6) Listen to your new recordings for 20 minutes and previous recordings for 20 minutes.

7) Prepare for the coming day's learning plan for 30 minutes.

Level 1 Daily Learning Plan 50

THINGS TO DO FOR LEARNING

1) PARTICIPANT OBSERVATION: Continue to participate in four hours of daily activities in the community.

Here are a few goals for your participant observation:

OBSERVE the common objects, positions of objects, people who are working with the objects, ways you would describe the objects, and actions that they use to work with the objects in the activities that you participate in.

LISTEN for unique sounds, syllable stress, and general pronunciation.

RESPOND by appropriately asking WHAT, WHERE, HOW, WITH WHAT, WHEN, and WHO questions in whatever second language you have in common with the community.

NOTE common daily activities and categories of activities in people's lives, as well as WHY questions you have but shouldn't ask, and so on.

2) LISTEN AND ACT WITH SPEAKING: Apply this learning exercise to a previous activity in the community that you have observed.

3) LISTEN AND ACT WITH SPEAKING: Apply this learning exercise to a previous activity in the community that you have observed.

4) LISTEN AND ACT: Focus again on the common questions WHO, WHAT, WITH WHAT, WHERE, and WHEN.

Get out your sketch of common people, your picture that represents the idea of "today," and your village area sketch. This time, though, use objects related to gardening.

Have the community member ask many questions using the actors, objects and actions related to the activity.

5) Record a summary example of your listen and act exercise.

6) Listen to your new recordings for 20 minutes and previous recordings for 20 minutes.

7) Prepare for the coming day's learning plan for 30 minutes.

Self-evaluation for Level 1

At the end of the daily learning plans for each level, you will work through a self-evaluation to see how much progress you've made in applying the learning exercises in your plans. In the following Level 1 self-evaluation, read each statement and mark the number that represents your current ability.

1. I have completed all 50 Level 1 daily learning plans.

1 ☐ not at all well   2 ☐ barely well   3 ☐ somewhat well   4 ☐ adequately well   5 ☐ extremely well

2. I can list forty to fifty of the most common daily activities in the community around me.

1 ☐ not at all well   2 ☐ barely well   3 ☐ somewhat well   4 ☐ adequately well   5 ☐ extremely well

3. I can greet people appropriately when I see them.

1 ☐ not at all well   2 ☐ barely well   3 ☐ somewhat well   4 ☐ adequately well   5 ☐ extremely well

4. I can say good-bye politely.

1 ☐ not at all well   2 ☐ barely well   3 ☐ somewhat well   4 ☐ adequately well   5 ☐ extremely well

5. I can thank people simply.

1 ☐ not at all well   2 ☐ barely well   3 ☐ somewhat well   4 ☐ adequately well   5 ☐ extremely well

6. I can understand and repeat words for kinds of animals (such as dog, chicken, fish, snake, bird) and people (such as men, women, boys, girls, babies, him, her, it, we, they).

1 ☐ not at all well   2 ☐ barely well   3 ☐ somewhat well   4 ☐ adequately well   5 ☐ extremely well

7. I can give and respond to common commands (such as stand up, sit down, walk, run, crawl, lie down, go, come, jump, stop, kneel, bend over, go up, go down, come up, come down).

1 ☐ not at all well   2 ☐ barely well   3 ☐ somewhat well   4 ☐ adequately well   5 ☐ extremely well

8. I can understand and repeat phrases related to cooking and the cook area, including ways to cook.

1 ☐ not at all well   2 ☐ barely well   3 ☐ somewhat well   4 ☐ adequately well   5 ☐ extremely well

9. I can understand and repeat words for items and tools in and around a common household.

1 ☐ not at all well   2 ☐ barely well   3 ☐ somewhat well   4 ☐ adequately well   5 ☐ extremely well

10. I can understand and repeat terms for the parts and rooms in common buildings.

1 ☐ not at all well   2 ☐ barely well   3 ☐ somewhat well   4 ☐ adequately well   5 ☐ extremely well

11. I can understand and repeat common placement words (such as beside, under, on, between, with, in, out, here, there).

1 ☐ not at all well   2 ☐ barely well   3 ☐ somewhat well   4 ☐ adequately well   5 ☐ extremely well

12. I can give and respond to common commands related to house parts and rooms (such as close the door, open the door, sit in the chair, go down the stairs, come up the stairs, lie on the bed, open the window, close the window).

1 ☐ not at all well   2 ☐ barely well   3 ☐ somewhat well   4 ☐ adequately well   5 ☐ extremely well

13. I can give and respond to common commands and statements for putting, taking, giving, moving, carrying, picking up, and throwing common household objects and tools.

1 ☐ not at all well   2 ☐ barely well   3 ☐ somewhat well   4 ☐ adequately well   5 ☐ extremely well

14. I can understand and repeat words for the items in the general outdoor and yard area (such as shrubs, grass, trees, flowers, path, rocks, dirt, ground).

1 ☐ not at all well   2 ☐ barely well   3 ☐ somewhat well   4 ☐ adequately well   5 ☐ extremely well

15. I can give and respond to commands for the steps of making something (such as a house or basket) that is common in the community.

1 ☐ not at all well   2 ☐ barely well   3 ☐ somewhat well   4 ☐ adequately well   5 ☐ extremely well

16. I can give and respond to commands for the actions that are associated with commonly used tools.

1 ☐ not at all well   2 ☐ barely well   3 ☐ somewhat well   4 ☐ adequately well   5 ☐ extremely well

17. I can understand and repeat words for common body parts of people and animals.

1 ☐ not at all well   2 ☐ barely well   3 ☐ somewhat well   4 ☐ adequately well   5 ☐ extremely well

18. I can understand and repeat words for common kinds of clothing.

1 ☐ not at all well   2 ☐ barely well   3 ☐ somewhat well   4 ☐ adequately well   5 ☐ extremely well

19. I can understand and repeat words and phrases related to washing and cleaning.

1 ☐ not at all well   2 ☐ barely well   3 ☐ somewhat well   4 ☐ adequately well   5 ☐ extremely well

20. I can give and respond to statements made about people and common body positions (such as walking, standing, sitting, kneeling, squatting, crawling, bending over, leaning, lying down).

1 ☐ not at all well   2 ☐ barely well   3 ☐ somewhat well   4 ☐ adequately well   5 ☐ extremely well

21. I can understand and repeat words for common family relationships for myself and others (such as father, mother, grandfather, grandmother, wife, child, baby, uncle, aunt, niece, nephew, father-in-law, mother-in-law).

1 ☐ not at all well   2 ☐ barely well   3 ☐ somewhat well   4 ☐ adequately well   5 ☐ extremely well

22. I can understand and repeat statements for seeing and looking (such as see, look, stare, peek, watch, spy on).

1 ☐ not at all well   2 ☐ barely well   3 ☐ somewhat well   4 ☐ adequately well   5 ☐ extremely well

23. I can understand and repeat statements for touching (such as touching, grabbing, hitting, kicking, rolling, throwing, pinching, squeezing, hugging).

1 ☐ not at all well   2 ☐ barely well   3 ☐ somewhat well   4 ☐ adequately well   5 ☐ extremely well

24. I can understand and repeat words and statements for buying and selling food items.

1 ☐ not at all well   2 ☐ barely well   3 ☐ somewhat well   4 ☐ adequately well   5 ☐ extremely well

25. I can understand and repeat words and statements for gardening and foraging activities.

1 ☐ not at all well   2 ☐ barely well   3 ☐ somewhat well   4 ☐ adequately well   5 ☐ extremely well

26. I can understand and repeat words and statements for adjective pair opposites (such as large/small, heavy/light, long/short, cold/hot, rough/smooth, tall/short, thick/thin, round/flat).

1 ☐ not at all well   2 ☐ barely well   3 ☐ somewhat well   4 ☐ adequately well   5 ☐ extremely well

27. I can give and respond to commands for drinking, pouring, spilling, and dumping out common liquids.

1 ☐ not at all well   2 ☐ barely well   3 ☐ somewhat well   4 ☐ adequately well   5 ☐ extremely well

28. I can understand and repeat words and phrases for eating common food items.

1 ☐ not at all well   2 ☐ barely well   3 ☐ somewhat well   4 ☐ adequately well   5 ☐ extremely well

29. I can understand and repeat words and phrases for times of the day, week, months, year, and for telling time.

1 ☐ not at all well   2 ☐ barely well   3 ☐ somewhat well   4 ☐ adequately well   5 ☐ extremely well

30. I can understand and repeat common number words, including cardinal and ordinal numbers.

1 ☐ not at all well   2 ☐ barely well   3 ☐ somewhat well   4 ☐ adequately well   5 ☐ extremely well

31. I can understand and repeat words for common color distinctions.

1 ☐ not at all well   2 ☐ barely well   3 ☐ somewhat well   4 ☐ adequately well   5 ☐ extremely well

32. I can understand and repeat words and phrases for sky and weather (such as sun, sky, moon, stars, clouds, rain, mist, fog, wind).

1 ☐ not at all well   2 ☐ barely well   3 ☐ somewhat well   4 ☐ adequately well   5 ☐ extremely well

33. I can understand and repeat words and phrases for hunting and/or animal domestication.

1 ☐ not at all well   2 ☐ barely well   3 ☐ somewhat well   4 ☐ adequately well   5 ☐ extremely well

34. I can understand and repeat words and phrases for the emotional states of people.

1 ☐ not at all well   2 ☐ barely well   3 ☐ somewhat well   4 ☐ adequately well   5 ☐ extremely well

35. I can understand and repeat words and phrases for common activities of animals and insects (such as hissing, meowing, barking, growling, swimming, biting).

1 ☐ not at all well   2 ☐ barely well   3 ☐ somewhat well   4 ☐ adequately well   5 ☐ extremely well

36. I can understand and repeat words for common landforms and parts of rivers and waterways.

1 ☐ not at all well   2 ☐ barely well   3 ☐ somewhat well   4 ☐ adequately well   5 ☐ extremely well

37. I can understand and repeat common questions using who, what, with what, where and when.

1 ☐
not at all
well

2 ☐
barely
well

3 ☐
somewhat
well

4 ☐
adequately
well

5 ☐
extremely
well

Level 2

Relating through Daily Routines

During Level 2 you will relate to others through recognizing and creating sentences in the language, through asking and answering simple questions, and through talking about what is becoming familiar to you and what you and others do each day in the community. You will be able to understand and use sentences at this level rather than just words and phrases.

This chapter gives practical guidance to your Level 2 learning. The first section of the chapter introduces the learning exercises that you will use in this level. The second section gives daily learning plans to guide you as you apply the learning exercises each day.

SECTION 1

Learning Exercises for Level 2

Learning Exercise 1: Participant observation

Participant observation is still very important to your learning in Level 2. In this level, you will focus more specifically on applying other learning exercises to the activities in which you participate and observe in the lives of others around you. In fact, your daily learning plans will reflect this in new, creative ways.

You should continue to think about specific activities that you can participate in with members of the community. As we've already noted, many categories of life experience, like gardening or cooking, can be broken down into a large number of activities that you can work with.

Unlike the time you spend with community members in other learning exercises, *participant observation* is an opportunity for you to spend time with lots of people that you might not typically associate with. Try to be friendly and engage in *participant observation* with a good representation of those who live in the community. This can serve as an excellent foundation for broad-ranging relationships with them. You will need to spend time with at least 30 local people regularly during Levels 3 and 4, so now is a good time to develop more relationships.

Remember that during your daily *participant observation* in activities in the community you should:

> **OBSERVE** what is going on around you in a purposeful way. Who is speaking to whom, what tone are they using, what activities are taking place, and what people, actions, and objects are a part of those activities?

Make an effort to listen with understanding to the language used in the activity in the community.

RESPOND by showing friendship and appreciation to others. Genuinely participate as much as you can in what is taking place. Try to act in appropriate ways, while still being yourself. Try to practice speaking appropriately in the local language as you are able.

You should continue to ask appropriate questions about WHAT, HOW, WITH WHAT, WHERE, WHEN, and WHO as you observe activities in the community.

NOTE in your *Daily Learning Plan Notebook* any questions you have and new vocabulary areas related to the activity in the community that you would like to practice later.

Also, note the common categories of community life and the specific activities that you participate in or can plan for later. You might also note questions about why people behave the way that they do. Much later in your learning you will carefully ask questions about this. You will wait until you are trusted and can converse in the new language to ask any of your why questions.

Learning Exercise 4: Working with daily routines

This new learning exercise for Level 2 will teach you how to profitably learn more from the common activities in the community that you participate in. The exercise will also explain how you can effectively use short texts related to those activities to help you learn. All of this is described and applied in the daily learning plans for Level 2.

SECTION 2

Daily Learning Plans for Level 2

With the two learning exercises for Level 2 in mind, let's move on to the daily learning plans. As much as possible, you should continue to spend 40 or more hours each week in relating to others by working through the daily learning plans for Level 2.

Your ability to understand and speak small pieces of the language will be increasing. In Level 2, you will build on the foundation of what you learned in Level 1 as you continue to participate in activities in the community. Your goal will be to focus on understanding and eventually speaking whole sentences that you yourself create based on the activities that you participate in. You will also learn to understand and ask questions about the things that you are learning in the local language.

Level 2 plans will be divided into two parts, just as they were for Level 1. The first half of the plans will help you *to understand* descriptions of daily routines and activities as community members explain them to you. You will also learn to *understand appropriate questions* regarding these activities.

The second half of the plans will help you *to begin to describe* these daily routines and processes for yourself, as well as *ask your own questions* about them. Because the daily learning plans will relate specifically to the activities in the community where you live. Examples of daily learning plans will be given that you can modify to suit the particular community in which you live. Example plans for the first and second halves of Level 2 will be given and another *example plan for the second half* of Level 2. These plans will be concrete illustrations and will give instructions for application to further plans.

If you are able to complete five daily learning plans each week you would be able to finish all 80 for level 2 in 16 weeks. If you complete four per week, it will take around 20 weeks to finish Level 2.

As you work through your daily learning plans based on your community participation, you will encounter new vocabulary items. One primary goal for each day should be to learn to comprehend about *30 new vocabulary items* through using your learning exercises.

You will use the *participant observation* learning exercise for three hours each day in your daily learning plans in Level 2. Again, often it will be challenging for you to control your time of *participant observation* each day. Even so, try to be conscious of the amount of time you'd like to spend in that learning exercise. If your *participant observation* for a day ends up extending longer than three hours, simply plan to finish whatever exercises you didn't complete for that daily plan the next day before moving on to another daily plan. For example, some common activities would be washing clothes, gardening, getting public transport, making a banking transaction, getting a haircut, cooking a local dish, etc.

In addition to *participant observation*, you will also use the *working with daily routines* learning exercise for three and a half hours each day in your Level 2 learning plans. During this time you will focus specifically on relating your learning exercises directly to your participation in activities in the community. For each daily learning plan, you will try to relate the working with daily routines learning exercise to one specific common activity in the community in which you've participated at some point in the past.

In order to learn from the activity that you've identified for each daily plan, you will apply the working with daily routines learning exercise in four different ways:

FIRST, you want to understand the steps of common routines in that activity in the community.

SECOND, you want to understand simple descriptions related to the setting for the activity.

THIRD, you want to understand common questions which could be asked about the activity.

FOURTH, you want to understand a short recorded text (3 to 8 minutes) of the community member explaining the process of the activity and another short recorded text (3 to 8 minutes) of the person describing the setting for the activity.

These four steps are explained in greater detail in the following example daily learning plan.

Daily time schedule for Level 2

For a full-time Level 2 learner, your time should break down each day as follows:

Participant observation learning exercise in activities in the community	3 hours
Working with daily routines learning exercise with community members	3 hours
Reviewing previous daily routine exercises	30 minutes
Review recorded texts yourself	1 hour
Preparing for the next daily learning plan	30 minutes
TOTAL:	8 hours

Sample Daily Learning Plan for Level 2

For each daily learning plan 1 to 40, you want to find a common activity in the community that you can experience and work with, such as the ideas above. You want to focus on activities that are daily processes and common routines. Again, try to identify the activities that are most common in the lives of those around you. Your goal is to learn to understand the descriptions and processes of those routine activities, as well as common questions that might be asked about them.

When you make your recordings with the community member each day, you may need to try a few times to record texts that are 3 to 8 minutes long for the routine steps of the activity and the description of the setting. Some community members will get the idea for doing this more quickly than others. In the case of routine steps, sometimes the community member will need to again act out the process so that they can talk through the activity to describe what they are doing at each step while you are recording. If possible, try not to get a story about what happened in the past, but rather a step-by-step description about what is happening in the present as they go through the steps.

Here is an example plan of how you could use the common activity of washing the clothes in a creek or river in a Level 2 learning plan.

EXAMPLE

THINGS TO DO FOR LEARNING PLAN

1) PARTICIPANT OBSERVATION:

OBSERVE the common objects, positions of objects, people who are working with the objects, ways you would describe the objects, and actions that they use to work with the objects in the activities that you participate in.

LISTEN for unique sounds, syllable stress, and general pronunciation, as well as words and expressions that you are already familiar with.

RESPOND by appropriately asking *what, where, how, with what, when,* and *who* questions in whatever second language you have in common with the community. Use as many of the words and phrases that you are now familiar with as you can.

NOTE common daily activities and categories of activities in people's lives, as well as *why* questions you have but shouldn't ask, and so on.

2) WORKING WITH DAILY ROUTINES 1 — STEPS OF COMMON ROUTINE:

THINK of a common routine in an activity in the community that you have already participated in multiple times. For example, let's return to the routine of washing clothes in a creek or river.

Visit that setting with the community member and refer back to your sketches of the activity. Have that person review the actors, objects, positions, actions, and descriptive phrases associated with that activity using the *listen and act* while speaking learning exercise. This should only take 15 to 20 minutes.

Next, have the community member go through the steps of the process of washing the clothes, while at the same time describing the process of what they are doing out loud for you. Much of what they are saying should be familiar to you because it is based on foundational material that you have already learned to understand in previous activities. If the first time through is very difficult for you to follow, try having the helper talk through the steps again slowly for you a second time. If the helper ends up giving an extremely short version of the process, you can think of some of the steps that you have observed to give suggestions as to what else might be included.

Then you should follow the instructions of the community member as you go through the steps of washing the clothes in order yourself. You may want to do this twice. You should begin to become familiar with the process order and sentences used to describe the steps.

After that, explain to the community member that you'd like for them to tell you to do steps out of order, and you'll try to follow their instructions. They can begin with two random steps, and add more random steps as you are able to respond correctly by doing the appropriate action. Although it may seem strange at first, the community member needs to understand the reason why you want them to give commands out of process order, so that you can recognize the step and respond appropriately. Go through this until you are able to respond quickly to all the steps as the community member relates them to you.

Finally, have the community member reenact and describe the process of what they are doing one final time so that you can record a text of the whole process in order. Ideally the text should be between 3 to 8 minutes long, though may extend a little longer.

3) WORKING WITH DAILY ROUTINES 2 — SIMPLE DESCRIPTION OF THE SETTING:

Now explain to the community member that you are going to move on to explaining the setting where you are working. For example, in the context of the river and washing clothes, you want the community member to give you a simple description of the river, the weather at the time, the surrounding environment, including the colors and objects, and so on. This can be difficult at first because the community member may not be used to describing their environment or activities in this way. But do the best that you can. As the community member gains experience doing this for you, he will find this exercise easier and easier.

The community member can describe more than one setting or aspect for you (the river, the weather, the clothes, and so on), but each description should be fairly short (3 to 8 minutes). You may find it helpful to give an example to the community member of the kind of description you are looking for in a common second language, although you want to approach this sensitively and appropriately.

As you feel that the descriptions of the settings are helpful and mostly understandable, record text examples of what the community member describes.

4) WORKING WITH DAILY ROUTINES 3 — TEXTS OF COMMON ROUTINE STEPS AND SETTING DESCRIPTION:

Having recorded your texts, sit with the community member and listen to your texts for both the common routine steps for washing clothes as well as the descriptions of the setting.

Go carefully through each text recording to stop the recording and identify any words or pieces that you do not understand as they come up. The community member can explain these words and connectors to you. You should listen to each text with the community member several times through in this way, trying intently to understand everything that is being said, and repeatedly having the community member clarify the unclear segments for you. You may want to make some written notes, but don't rely too much on these at this stage. Your goal in going over the texts like this is to make them fully understandable when you listen to the texts later yourself.

5) WORKING WITH DAILY ROUTINES 4 — QUESTIONS RELATED TO THE SETTING AND ROUTINE:

Spend about 30 minutes trying to understand common questions related to the setting and routine. These would include *WHO, WHAT, WITH WHAT, WHERE,* and *WHEN.*

You can use a process similar to the one that you followed previously. Get out your sketch of common people and a picture that represents the idea of "today." Also plan to use the objects, setting, and sketches of the washing clothes activity.

Then tell the community member to begin simply with a statement and question related to a person and object or place like, "The man is washing clothes at the river. Where is the man washing clothes?" You would respond by pointing to the river. The community member would then ask a follow up question, "Who is washing the clothes?" You'd point to the man. If you are able, you can also begin to actually give simple answers to the questions as the community member is asking them.

The community member could then state something like, "The woman is holding the soap. Who is holding the soap?" You would respond by pointing to the woman. The community member would ask, "What is the woman holding?" You'd point to the soap.

The community member could say, "The boy is rinsing the shirt. What is the boy rinsing?" You'd respond by pointing to the shirt. The community member would say, "Who is rinsing the shirt?" You'd respond by pointing to the boy.

The community member could say, "The girl is washing the clothes with soap. What is the girl washing with?" You'd respond by pointing to the soap. The community member would say, "Who is washing with the soap?" You'd point to the girl. The community member would say, "What is she washing?" You'd point to the clothes.

The community member could say, "He is washing clothes today. When is he washing clothes?" You'd point to the picture of today. The community member could say, "Who is washing clothes?" You'd point to the community member. The community member could say, "What is he doing?" You'd imitate the action of washing clothes.

Try to go through this process with lots of the actors, objects and actions that are present in the scene so that you can listen and respond to the variety of questions appropriately. You can also begin to give short answers to the questions as you feel you are able to do so.

6) Each day on your own you should take 30 minutes to listen to your working with daily routines texts from that day. You will also listen to your previous working with daily routines texts for 30 minutes.

7) Prepare tomorrow's daily learning plan.

Ideas for common daily activities for Level 2 learning

The following are some common activities that learners have used for their Level 2 learning - they may help you to get some ideas for Level 2 activities in your own community.

- Getting money out of an ATM.
- Buying food and eating at a fast-food restaurant.
- Making rice in a rice-cooker.
- Getting a driver's license.
- Taking a tour.
- Going to the doctor or hospital.
- Walking or driving directions from point A to point B.
- Getting a motorcycle booked in for mechanical service.
- Mailing a letter at the Post Office.
- Going shopping at the supermarket.
- Making tea.
- Early morning exercises in the park.
- Waiting for and riding on the bus or train.
- Buying a book at the bookstore.
- Getting money from the teller at the bank.
- Checking mobile phone balance and refilling money on the account.
- Arriving at church and specific parts of the church service.
- Checking what is happening on the cultural scene - how to do this - finding out about concerts, plays, movies, etc.
- Using any electronic equipment for it's purpose - DVD, Computer, Printer, etc.
- Getting connected to the Internet or phone.
- How to use a search engine to get information.
- Getting a haircut.
- Renewal of a rental contract.
- Process of eating at a restaurant with a menu, waiters, etc.
- Buying fruit and vegetables at the market.
- Planting a garden crop.
- Washing clothes at the river.
- Harvesting rice or sweet potato.
- Making a basket.
- Cooking a meal on a fire.
- Making a grass roofing panel for a house.
- Hiking from one village to another.
- Hunting wild pigs.
- Making a trap for birds.
- Checking or participating in local leisure activities (hiking, biking, theme parks, beach, picnic, golf, movies, etc.)
- Carrying out household repairs.
- Moving to a new home.
- Looking after a pet.
- Playing a local game - cards, checkers.
- Playing a musical instrument.
- Attending a funeral.
- Attending a class at university.
- Driving and parking a car.
- Teaching a class at a university.
- Shopping for clothes.
- Taking a taxi.
- Getting gas (or petrol).
- Attending a wedding.
- Going to a dragon boat race.
- Paying the electricity or water bill.
- Visiting a temple.
- Taking children to school in the morning.
- Cooking a simple dish

Procedure for using videos during Level 2

Many learners have found that video is a very helpful learning tool during Level 2 activities. You can make videos for each of the daily routines, which will help you to learn and review and can also be shared with others.

Making the videos

The video you make will have four parts:

1) The first part is the original video clip of the daily routine activity.

Start with a 3-5 minute video of a routine that you have observed in *participant observation* time.

Edit the video so that the steps in it are as clear as possible. If someone is doing one activity in it for too long, edit just a few seconds of it into the video and then put in a transition to the next step in the activity.

Ask a community member to describe exactly what they see happening - encourage them to give simple narration without commentary, like opinions, reasons, etc. Record what they say or dub it over this part of the video.

2) The second part includes still pictures of the setting.

After the video of the daily routine, put in a divider that says "picture #1" so you know that there is a still photo coming up with the setting description.

Take a still out of the video or take an actual photo at the location where you took the video. Make the still last for around 4 minutes on the video to give the community member time to make a description later when you are recording on to it.

If you are including two pictures of the setting, do another divider that says "picture #2" and do the same as you did with the first picture. Try to pick one from a different angle or with a different person in it than the first picture.

Ask the community member to describe the setting; including objects and people, weather, etc. Encourage them to describe rather than just giving an inventory of the objects. Record what they say or dub it over this part of the video.

3) The third part includes the step-by-step description of very simple "instructions" on how the routine was done. This should be around 5-6 steps.

After the still pictures, make a divider that says 'step by step' on it. This divider can be 4 minutes long so that the community member can record the simple steps over it [voice-over recording]. You could have the local person write these down first to help them keep it simple and clear. The steps should be one sentence only.

4) The last part is the questions where the community member will give some appropriate or common questions that might be asked in the situation, along with the answers.

Ask the community member to record questions having to do with the scenario (they could write them down first). For example, you could ask them what questions they would ask the person doing this routine in the video if they were there. Your goal is to try to get natural questions.

Try to record 4-5 questions with answers. It will end up like a short conversation.

Using the videos for learning and review

After the community member does the recordings, and your video is complete, go back through each section, pausing after each phrase, and have him or her repeat what they said. Ask about any of the words you don't know and write them down in a notebook, along with a simple definition. This will end up being a short glossary to reference when you review the video on your own later. Your goal in going over the recordings like this is to make them fully understandable when you hear them later yourself.

After you get through the whole video ask the community member to record one simple sentence using each of the new words, preferably about a different subject so that you can hear the words used in a different context.

You can use the same videos to talk with a number of different people, and see what their reactions are or if they have any other comments. Your goal is to eventually be able to talk about similar scenes in daily life in the same way that a local person would, and to understand how they feel or what they know about what is going on in that scene. It will help you in your conversational skills if you practice talking with a number of people about the same daily activities. You can share your videos with other learners as well.

Simple video procedure

If your video editing skills or equipment are not quite up to the level required for the above procedure, you can simplify it by just taking a video of a daily routine event, and have a community member describe and comment on the scene, perhaps pausing at an interesting still shot and having them describe it for you. You could then use the resulting recordings for further review, questions, or new vocabulary. It might help to watch the video once through with the local person first, and then turn down the sound and have them watch it again while describing in their own words what is going on - and this is the text you would record.

Level 2 Daily Learning Plans 1 to 40

This is a set of instructions that will help you with plans 1 to 40. The instructions and steps are already included. You need to select your activity in the community, and think about how you will apply the instructions and steps to that activity.

As you plan for each daily learning plan 1 to 40, write in your *Daily Learning Plan Notebook* the plan number and what activity in the community you will cover, as well as who will help you. You should also record any categories of life experience or daily routine activities that you'd be hoping to experience in the days ahead. You can use this same page of printed instructions for daily learning plans 1 to 40 in that way.

THINGS TO DO FOR LEARNING PLANS 1 TO 40

1) PARTICIPANT OBSERVATION:

OBSERVE the common objects, positions of objects, people who are working with the objects, ways you would describe the objects, and actions that they use to work with the objects in the activities that you participate in.

LISTEN for unique sounds, syllable stress, and general pronunciation, as well as words and expressions that you are already familiar with.

RESPOND by appropriately asking WHAT, WHERE, HOW, WITH WHAT, WHEN, and WHO questions in whatever second language you have in common with the community. Use as many of the words and phrases that you are now familiar with as you can.

NOTE common daily activities and categories of activities in people's lives, as well as WHY questions you have but shouldn't ask, and so on.

2) WORKING WITH DAILY ROUTINES 1 — STEPS OF COMMON ROUTINE:

Think of common routine in an activity in the community:

Visit that setting with the community member and refer back to your sketches of the activity. Have that person review the actors, objects, positions, actions, and descriptive phrases associated with that activity using the *listen and act* while speaking learning exercise. This should only take 15 to 20 minutes.

Next, have the person go through the steps of the process, while at the same time describing the process of what they are doing out loud for you. Do this two times.

Then you should follow the instructions of the community member as you go through the steps of washing the clothes in order yourself. Do this two times.

Have the community member tell you to do steps out of order, and you'll try to follow their instructions. They can begin with two random steps, and add more random steps as you are able to respond correctly by doing the appropriate action. Go through this until you are able to respond quickly to all the steps as the community member relates them to you.

Finally, have the community member reenact and describe the process of what they are doing one final time so that you can record a text of the whole process in order. Ideally the text should be between 3 to 8 minutes long, though may extend a little longer.

3) WORKING WITH DAILY ROUTINES 2 — SIMPLE DESCRIPTION OF THE SETTING:

Now explain to the community member that you are going to move on to them explaining the setting where you are working.

The community member can describe more than one setting or aspect for you (the river, the weather, the clothes, and so on), but each description should be fairly short (3 to 8 minutes).

Record text examples of what the community member describes.

4) WORKING WITH DAILY ROUTINES 3 — TEXTS OF COMMON ROUTINE STEPS AND SETTING DESCRIPTION:

Having recorded your texts, sit with the community member and listen to your texts for both the common routine steps as well as the descriptions of the setting.

Go carefully through each text recording to stop the recording and identify any words or pieces that you do not understand as they come up. The community member can explain these words and connectors to you. You should listen to each text with the community member several times through in this way, trying intently to understand everything that is being said, and repeatedly having the community member clarify the unclear segments for you. Your goal in going over the texts like this is to make them fully understandable when you listen to the texts later yourself.

5) WORKING WITH DAILY ROUTINES 4 — QUESTIONS RELATED TO THE SETTING AND ROUTINE:

Spend about 30 minutes trying to understand common questions related to the setting and routine. These would include WHO, WHAT, WITH WHAT, WHERE, and WHEN.

You can use a process similar to the one that you followed previously. Get out your sketch of common people and a picture that represents the idea of "today." Also plan to use the objects, setting, and sketches of the routine activity that you are working with.

Have the community member ask lots of questions using the actors, objects and actions that are present in the scene so that you can listen and respond to the variety of questions appropriately. You can also begin to give short answers to the questions as you feel you are able to do so.

6) Each day on your own you should take 30 minutes to listen to your working with daily routines texts from that day. You will also listen to your previous working with daily routines texts for 30 minutes as well.

7) Prepare tomorrow's daily learning plan.

Level 2 Daily Learning Plans 41 to 80

For each daily learning plan 41 to 80, you will be reviewing your previous daily learning plans 1 to 40 related to common activities in the community. This time your goal is to revisit those plans, only this time to learn to speak about the descriptions and processes of those routine activities, as well as to ask common questions about them.

For each plan 41 to 80, it may be helpful for you to try to meet with the same individual who helped you with the plan related to that activity in plans 1 to 40. If that is not possible, do your best to apply the plan with someone different.

At this point you will also want to designate a blank notebook as your *Text Notebook.* You will use this notebook to write down some of the texts that you will record. The explanation for this process is described in the example below.

EXAMPLE

THINGS TO DO FOR LEARNING PLAN

1) PARTICIPANT OBSERVATION:

OBSERVE the common objects, positions of objects, people who are working with the objects, ways you would describe the objects, and actions that they use to work with the objects in the activities that you participate in.

LISTEN for unique sounds, syllable stress, and general pronunciation, as well as words and expressions that you are already familiar with.

RESPOND by appropriately asking WHAT, WHERE, HOW, WITH WHAT, WHEN, and WHO questions in whatever second language you have in common with the community. Use as many of the words and phrases that you are now familiar with as you can.

NOTE common daily activities and categories of activities in people's lives, as well as WHY questions you have but shouldn't ask, and so on.

2) WORKING WITH DAILY ROUTINES 1 — STEPS OF COMMON ROUTINE:

Go back to daily learning plan 1 to review the activity for that plan. For example, return to the routine of washing clothes in a creek or river.

Visit that setting again with the community member and refer back to your sketches of the activity. Have the community member quickly review the actors, objects, positions, actions, and descriptive phrases associated with that activity using the *listen and act* while speaking learning exercise.

Next, have the community member go through the steps of the process of washing the clothes, while at the same time describing the process of what they are doing out loud for you as a review.

Then you should follow the instructions of the community member as you go through the steps of washing the clothes in order yourself. You might go through this exercise several times.

As you go through the steps in this way, you yourself explain out loud what it is that you are doing in each step. For example, if the community member tells you, "Pick up the shirt," you would pick it up and say, "I am picking up the shirt."

After that, explain to the community member that you'd like for them to tell you to do steps out of order, and you'll try to follow their instructions. They can begin with two random steps, and add more random steps as you are able to respond correctly by doing the appropriate action. Go through this until you are able to respond quickly to all the steps as the community member relates them to you.

As you are going through the steps, tell the community member what you are doing at each step. For example, if the community member tells you, "Rinse the pants," you follow the instruction and say at the same time, "I am rinsing the pants."

3) WORKING WITH DAILY ROUTINES 2 - SIMPLE DESCRIPTION OF THE SETTING:

Move on to the common descriptions of the setting that you have heard from the community member. For example, in the context of the river and washing clothes, the community member might have given you a simple description of the river, the weather at the time, the surrounding environment, including the colors and objects, and so on.

The community member can describe one setting or aspect for you (the river, the weather, the clothes, and so on), sentence by sentence. You try repeating the sentences as the community member describes them.

As you are able, you yourself try to give short descriptions of the various aspects of the setting similar to the way that the community member is doing this. Try to give 3 to 5 sentences of description if possible.

4) WORKING WITH DAILY ROUTINES 3 — TEXTS OF COMMON ROUTINE STEPS AND SETTING DESCRIPTION:

Sit with the community member and listen to your texts from daily learning plans 1 to 40 that relate to the activity for that day for both the common routine steps for washing clothes as well as the descriptions of the setting. These texts should already be familiar to you since you recorded them some time ago in plans 1 to 40 and have heard them multiple times since then.

Clarify any words or connectors in those texts that are still unfamiliar to you.

Select one of your recordings and transcribe the text using whatever phonetic alphabet or orthography that is available. You can do this step after your time with the community member.

Gloss (define the meaning) any words or connectors in the texts that are still unclear to you by talking about the meanings of these with the community member.

5) WORKING WITH DAILY ROUTINES 4 — QUESTIONS RELATED TO THE SETTING AND ROUTINE:

Spend about 30 minutes trying to ask common questions related to the setting and activity that you are working with. These would include WHO, WHAT, WITH WHAT, WHERE, and WHEN.

You can use a process for asking questions similar to the one that you followed previously. Get out your sketch of common people and a picture that represents the idea of "today." Also plan to use the objects, setting, and sketches of the washing clothes activity.

Then begin simply by making a statement and asking a question related to a person and object or place like, "The man is washing clothes at the river. Where is the man washing clothes?" The community member would respond appropriately. Then ask a follow up question, "Who is washing the clothes?" The community member would respond.

You could then state something like, "The woman is holding the soap. Who is holding the soap?" The community member would respond. You would ask, "What is the woman holding?" The community member would respond.

You could say, "The boy is rinsing the shirt. What is the boy rinsing?" You would ask, "Who is rinsing the shirt?"

You could say, "The girl is washing the clothes with soap. What is the girl washing with?" You would ask, "Who is washing with the soap?" You would say, "What is she washing?"

You could say, "I am washing clothes today. When am I washing clothes?" You could say, "Who is washing clothes?" You could say, "What am I doing?"

Try to ask lots of questions about the actors, objects and actions that are present in the setting.

6) Each day on your own you should take 30 minutes to listen to your working with daily routines texts from that day. You will also listen to your previous working with daily routines texts for 30 minutes as well.

7) Prepare tomorrow's daily learning plan.

Level 2 Daily Learning Plans 41 to 80

This is a set of instructions that will help you with plans 41 to 80. The instructions and steps are already included. You need to select your activity in the community, and think about how you will apply the instructions and steps to that activity. If possible, have the same person help you in plans 41 to 80 who helped you in the plan that corresponds to that same activity in plans 1 to 40.

As you plan for each daily learning plan 41 to 80, write in your *Daily Learning Plan Notebook* the plan number and what activity you will cover, as well as who will help you. You should also record any categories of life experience or daily routine activities that you'd be hoping to experience in the days ahead. You can use this same page of instructions for daily learning plans 1 to 40 in that way.

THINGS TO DO FOR LEARNING PLANS 41 TO 80

1) PARTICIPANT OBSERVATION:

OBSERVE the common objects, positions of objects, people who are working with the objects, ways you would describe the objects, and actions that they use to work with the objects in the activities that you participate in.

LISTEN for unique sounds, syllable stress, and general pronunciation, as well as words and expressions that you are already familiar with.

RESPOND by appropriately asking WHAT, WHERE, HOW, WITH WHAT, WHEN, and WHO questions in whatever second language you have in common with the community. Use as many of the words and phrases that you are now familiar with as you can.

NOTE common daily activities and categories of activities in people's lives, as well as WHY questions you have but shouldn't ask, and so on.

2) WORKING WITH DAILY ROUTINES 1 — STEPS OF COMMON ROUTINE:

Go back to your earlier daily learning plan to review the activity for that plan.

Visit that setting again with the community member and refer back to your sketches of the activity. Have the community member quickly review the actors, objects, positions, actions, and descriptive phrases associated with that activity using the *listen and act* while speaking learning exercise.

Next, have the community member go through the steps of the process, while at the same time describing the process of what they are doing out loud for you as a review.

Then you should follow the instructions of the community member as you go through the steps in order yourself. You might go through this exercise several times.

As you go through the steps in this way, you yourself explain out loud what it is that you are doing in each step.

After that, explain to the community member that you'd like for them to tell you to do steps out of order, and you'll try to follow their instructions. They can begin with two random steps, and add more random steps as you are able to respond correctly by doing the appropriate action. Go through this until you are able to respond quickly to all the steps as the community member relates them to you.

As you are going through the steps of the activity, tell the community member what you are doing at each step.

3) WORKING WITH DAILY ROUTINES 2 — SIMPLE DESCRIPTION OF THE SETTING:

Move on to the common descriptions of the setting that you have heard from the community member.

The community member can describe one setting or aspect for you, sentence by sentence. You try repeating the sentences as the community member describes them.

As you are able, you yourself try to give short descriptions of the various aspects of the setting similar to the way that the community member is doing this. Try to give 3 to 5 sentences of description if possible.

4) WORKING WITH DAILY ROUTINES 3 — TEXTS OF COMMON ROUTINE STEPS AND SETTING DESCRIPTION:

Sit with the community member and listen to your texts from daily learning plans 1 to 40 that relate to the activity for that day for both the common routine steps for washing clothes as well as the descriptions of the setting. These texts should already be familiar to you since you recorded them some time ago in plans 1 to 40 and have heard them multiple times since then.

Clarify any words or connectors in the texts that are unfamiliar to you.

Select one of your recordings and transcribe the text using whatever phonetic alphabet or orthography that is available. Leave two blank lines between each line of text.

In the space between lines of text, write meanings for any words or connectors that are still unclear to you as you go over the texts with the community member.

5) WORKING WITH DAILY ROUTINES 4 — QUESTIONS RELATED TO THE SETTING AND ROUTINE:

Spend about 30 minutes trying to ask common questions related to the setting and activity that you are working with. These would include WHO, WHAT, WITH WHAT, WHERE, and WHEN.

You can use a process for asking questions similar to the one that you followed previously. Get out your sketch of common people and a picture that represents the idea of "today." Also plan to use the objects, setting, and sketches of the activity.

Try to ask lots of questions about the actors, objects and actions that are present in the setting.

6) Each day on your own you should take 30 minutes to listen to your working with daily routines texts from that day. You will also listen to your previous working with daily routines texts for 30 minutes as well.

7) Prepare tomorrow's daily learning plan.

Self-evaluation for Level 2

In the following Level 2 self-evaluation, read each statement and mark the number that represents your current ability. For statements 1 to 40, first go back through your daily learning plans and write the activity in the blank that you participated in for each daily plan. Then estimate your ability using the example statements at the top of each page.

I have completed all 80 Level 2 daily learning plans.

1 ☐	2 ☐	3 ☐	4 ☐	5 ☐
not at all well	barely well	somewhat well	adequately well	extremely well

I can understand a short explanation of the steps and setting for washing the clothes, and can briefly state the steps and describe the setting myself. I can also ask and answer who, what, with what, where, and when questions related to this activity.

1 ☐	2 ☐	3 ☐	4 ☐	5 ☐
not at all well	barely well	somewhat well	adequately well	extremely well

1. ....

1 ☐	2 ☐	3 ☐	4 ☐	5 ☐
not at all well	barely well	somewhat well	adequately well	extremely well

2. ....

1 ☐	2 ☐	3 ☐	4 ☐	5 ☐
not at all well	barely well	somewhat well	adequately well	extremely well

3. ....

1 ☐	2 ☐	3 ☐	4 ☐	5 ☐
not at all well	barely well	somewhat well	adequately well	extremely well

4. ....

1 ☐	2 ☐	3 ☐	4 ☐	5 ☐
not at all well	barely well	somewhat well	adequately well	extremely well

5. ....

1 ☐	2 ☐	3 ☐	4 ☐	5 ☐
not at all well	barely well	somewhat well	adequately well	extremely well

6. ....

1 ☐	2 ☐	3 ☐	4 ☐	5 ☐
not at all well	barely well	somewhat well	adequately well	extremely well

7. ....

1 ☐	2 ☐	3 ☐	4 ☐	5 ☐
not at all well	barely well	somewhat well	adequately well	extremely well

8. ....

1 ☐	2 ☐	3 ☐	4 ☐	5 ☐
not at all well	barely well	somewhat well	adequately well	extremely well

9. ....

1 ☐	2 ☐	3 ☐	4 ☐	5 ☐
not at all well	barely well	somewhat well	adequately well	extremely well

10. ....

1 ☐	2 ☐	3 ☐	4 ☐	5 ☐
not at all well	barely well	somewhat well	adequately well	extremely well

11. ....

1 ☐	2 ☐	3 ☐	4 ☐	5 ☐
not at all well	barely well	somewhat well	adequately well	extremely well

12. ....

1 ☐	2 ☐	3 ☐	4 ☐	5 ☐
not at all well	barely well	somewhat well	adequately well	extremely well

13. ....

1 ☐	2 ☐	3 ☐	4 ☐	5 ☐
not at all well	barely well	somewhat well	adequately well	extremely well

14. ....

1 ☐	2 ☐	3 ☐	4 ☐	5 ☐
not at all well	barely well	somewhat well	adequately well	extremely well

15. ....

1 ☐	2 ☐	3 ☐	4 ☐	5 ☐
not at all well	barely well	somewhat well	adequately well	extremely well

16. ....

1 ☐	2 ☐	3 ☐	4 ☐	5 ☐
not at all well	barely well	somewhat well	adequately well	extremely well

17. ....

1 ☐	2 ☐	3 ☐	4 ☐	5 ☐
not at all well	barely well	somewhat well	adequately well	extremely well

18. ....

1 ☐	2 ☐	3 ☐	4 ☐	5 ☐
not at all well	barely well	somewhat well	adequately well	extremely well

19. ....

1 ☐	2 ☐	3 ☐	4 ☐	5 ☐
not at all well	barely well	somewhat well	adequately well	extremely well

20. ....

1 ☐	2 ☐	3 ☐	4 ☐	5 ☐
not at all well	barely well	somewhat well	adequately well	extremely well

21. ....

1 ☐	2 ☐	3 ☐	4 ☐	5 ☐
not at all well	barely well	somewhat well	adequately well	extremely well

22. ....

1 ☐	2 ☐	3 ☐	4 ☐	5 ☐
not at all well	barely well	somewhat well	adequately well	extremely well

23. ....

1 ☐	2 ☐	3 ☐	4 ☐	5 ☐
not at all well	barely well	somewhat well	adequately well	extremely well

24. ....

1 ☐	2 ☐	3 ☐	4 ☐	5 ☐
not at all well	barely well	somewhat well	adequately well	extremely well

25. ....

1 ☐	2 ☐	3 ☐	4 ☐	5 ☐
not at all well	barely well	somewhat well	adequately well	extremely well

26. ....

1 ☐	2 ☐	3 ☐	4 ☐	5 ☐
not at all well	barely well	somewhat well	adequately well	extremely well

27. ....

1 ☐	2 ☐	3 ☐	4 ☐	5 ☐
not at all well	barely well	somewhat well	adequately well	extremely well

28. ....

1 ☐	2 ☐	3 ☐	4 ☐	5 ☐
not at all well	barely well	somewhat well	adequately well	extremely well

29. ....

1 ☐	2 ☐	3 ☐	4 ☐	5 ☐
not at all well	barely well	somewhat well	adequately well	extremely well

30. ....

1 ☐   2 ☐   3 ☐   4 ☐   5 ☐

not at all   barely   somewhat   adequately   extremely

well   well   well   well   well

31. ....

1 ☐   2 ☐   3 ☐   4 ☐   5 ☐

not at all   barely   somewhat   adequately   extremely

well   well   well   well   well

32. ....

1 ☐   2 ☐   3 ☐   4 ☐   5 ☐

not at all   barely   somewhat   adequately   extremely

well   well   well   well   well

33. ....

1 ☐   2 ☐   3 ☐   4 ☐   5 ☐

not at all   barely   somewhat   adequately   extremely

well   well   well   well   well

34. ....

1 ☐   2 ☐   3 ☐   4 ☐   5 ☐

not at all   barely   somewhat   adequately   extremely

well   well   well   well   well

35. ....

1 ☐   2 ☐   3 ☐   4 ☐   5 ☐

not at all   barely   somewhat   adequately   extremely

well   well   well   well   well

36. ....

1 ☐   2 ☐   3 ☐   4 ☐   5 ☐

not at all   barely   somewhat   adequately   extremely

well   well   well   well   well

37. ....

1 ☐   2 ☐   3 ☐   4 ☐   5 ☐

not at all   barely   somewhat   adequately   extremely

well   well   well   well   well

38. ....

1 ☐   2 ☐   3 ☐   4 ☐   5 ☐

not at all   barely   somewhat   adequately   extremely

well   well   well   well   well

39. ....

1 ☐   2 ☐   3 ☐   4 ☐   5 ☐

not at all   barely   somewhat   adequately   extremely

well   well   well   well   well

40. ....

1 ☐   2 ☐   3 ☐   4 ☐   5 ☐

not at all   barely   somewhat   adequately   extremely

well   well   well   well   well

Level 3

Relating through Sharing Life Stories

During Level 3 you will relate to others through explaining, comparing, and describing things that already happened, are happening, or will happen later. At this level you will be able to understand and speak in paragraphs instead of just single sentences. You can handle situations that have something unexpected that comes up that you have to resolve, and you can now talk about lots of the life experience that you and others have had.

This chapter gives practical guidance to your Level 3 learning. The first section of the chapter introduces the learning exercises that you will use in this level. The second section gives daily learning plans to guide you as you apply the learning exercises each day.

If you have a second language in common with the community that you've been using to help you up to this point, this is the level where you will stop speaking that language and only communicate in the local language. This is challenging at first, but don't let the challenge keep you from taking this important step.

At the latest, complete the transition to the local language by the end of week four of your level three learning. This will give you a month to first establish a good routine in the daily learning plans for Level 3 before you stop using the second language.

Four life perspectives to think about in Level 3

As you have related to others around you in the last seven to eight months, your attention has been primarily focused on learning about their outward behavior. This is important, because engaging in the lives of others at the level of how they behave is an important and necessary first step to building good relationships with them.

But as you move forward, you will want to begin thinking about some other areas in addition to observable behavior. You want to begin thinking about WHY people behave in the way that that they do. What are their motivations for behavior? What do they appreciate and prioritize in their lives? What are their underlying beliefs about life?

These kinds of questions are so important because as you look forward to later communicating deeply with them, you need to understand the ways that their thinking about life will be impacted by the things that you want to share. You also want to later apply concepts to their lives in ways that are relevant to them, but that also confront incorrect motivations and beliefs about life.

Your desire to understand people this deeply may feel HUGE and OVERWHELMING to you at this point. How would you ever know what the factors are that cause people to behave in the way that they do? How would you know what they appreciate and prioritize in life? How do you discover their underlying beliefs about life?

While getting to know people this well is challenging, it is not impossible. You will take another step toward this level of understanding by considering four different life perspectives. These perspectives can help direct your participation in the lives of others in Level 3. The perspectives will help you to begin thinking through the aspects of people's lives that go beyond their behavior to their beliefs and motivations.

Here are the four life perspectives that can help you as you observe life activities and talk with others about those activities in Level 3:

1) What communication is taking place in the activity?

2) How is group or individual identity playing out in the activity?

3) What rules for living are being expressed in the activity?

4) What relationships are evident in the activity?

Each of the four life perspectives will include questions for you to consider. These questions are written in detail below. We provide these questions to help stimulate your thinking as you spend time with others in Level 3.

What communication is taking place?

What relationships are evident?

How is identity playing out?

What rules for living are being expressed?

So how should you best use the four life perspectives in Level 3?

We realize that at this point in your ability to communicate, you WON'T be asking these questions directly to community members. You certainly SHOULD NOT ever ask these questions to others in a second language.

Your goal, however, is to begin to think about these questions in light of what you see and experience as you participate in the lives of those around you. You won't draw conclusions about beliefs and motivations, but will begin to consider the possibilities for good answers based on the behavior patterns of others.

Life Perspectives Notebook

So what should you do? First, you should set up a *Life Perspectives Notebook* for yourself. You can do that in this way. Buy a notebook that has 150 blank pages, or buy several notebooks that add up to 150 pages. Number all the pages in the notebook front and back, one number for every side of every page. You can also document your *Life Perspectives Notebook* electronically.

On the top of the first page, write down:

Life perspective 1) What communication is taking place?

Then just underneath that still on the top of the page, write down the subheading:

AVENUES AND METHODS OF COMMUNICATION, as well as the first question under that heading,

i) "Notice verbal and non-verbal communication around you. Do you hear continuous verbal interaction or long periods of silence? How do eyes, face, tilt of head, hands, posture, space, time, pitch and tone of voice seem to be used to convey meaning?"

Now skip the back of that page plus one complete blank page front and back. Write down the next question:

ii) on the top of the next page. (This will be the top of page number 5 if you number all the pages front and back.)

Now skip the back of that page plus one complete blank page front and back. Write the next question:

iii) on the top of the next blank page. (This will be page number 9 if you number all the pages front and back.)

Continue this through your notebook until you have written down all the questions for all four life perspectives.

Now that you have set up your *Life Perspectives Notebook*, you will read through the life perspectives questions at least once a week to remind yourself of these four life perspectives. Read through one complete life perspective each day, and really consider what you have observed in the behavior of others that relates to that perspective. To help you with this exercise, you can keep a copy of the complete list of life perspectives questions below in your notebook.

As you read through the questions for one of the four perspectives each day, consider what you don't understand yet about the thinking of those around you. What behaviors can you think of that would give insight into these questions? Remember that you aren't identifying motivation for people's behavior. You probably won't accurately understand very much about their deep-seated beliefs about life. But first thinking about observable behavior according to these four perspectives will help you to begin focusing your attention toward your longer term goals and objectives. So for now, write down examples of activities and behaviors that give insight into the answers to these questions in your *Life Perspectives Notebook*. As you move into Level 4, you will use expanded questions to think further about the beliefs that motivate behavior.

Questions for you to consider for the four life perspectives in Level 3

1) What COMMUNICATION is taking place in the activity?

Observe people in conversation, listening for volume, tone and stress in their speech, noticing gestures and the social distance maintained. Also notice what people do and don't talk about and what information is important to have and listen to.

Here are some questions related to **communication** for you to think about.

A) AVENUES AND METHODS OF COMMUNICATION

1. Notice verbal and non-verbal communication around you. Do you hear continuous verbal interaction or long periods of silence? How do eyes, face, tilt of head, hands, posture, space, time, pitch and tone of voice seem to be used to convey meaning?

2. Are you beginning to notice the use of more than one language or dialect in the community? If so, when do people tend to use other languages?

3. Is there much communication coming from outside the society in the form of visitors or media sources?

4. Do you notice others interacting with spiritual beings or spending time praying in any way?

5. What do you notice about literacy in the community? How many people can read and in what languages? Are materials for reading available to them? Do they attend schools?

B) LEVELS OF COMMUNICATION

1. Do you notice changes in people's speech when they are talking to people they know versus those they don't know? To their elders versus their peers? To friends versus strangers? To family members versus others outside the family?

2. Do all people interact with all others with the same freedom? Is everyone expected to talk, or is there a spokesperson (within families or larger groups)?

C) EFFECTIVE AND INEFFECTIVE COMMUNICATION

1. Who do people really seem to listen to? What are the situations where you notice that others are really listening? What about situations where they are not listening? How do they show that they are listening?

2. Do people make it clear when they haven't understood something from another person, or do they just pretend to have done so anyway? How do people show that they don't understand?

D) TRUTH

1. Have you noticed general areas where people show that they believe some things to definitely be true and some things to definitely be false? What kinds of things are definitely true? What kinds of things are definitely false?

2. How do people deal with new information that comes to them? What if that information contradicts what they already believe to be true? Do they act like both things can be true at the same time or are they intent on resolving the contradiction?

3. Are there formal times for teaching? Informal times?

2) How is group or individual IDENTITY playing out in the activity?

Notice how the status, age, and sex of individuals affects their overall behavior within the society. Notice the boundaries and roles of individuals both within and outside the society.

Here are some questions related to identity for you to think about.

A) INDIVIDUALISM AND COMMUNITY

1. Does an individual make decisions on their own? Are group beliefs and decisions accepted by all? Is individual action socially encouraged?

2. Do you see evidence that people compete with one another? Are they generally cooperative or non-cooperative?

3. What would they see as group identifying factors? Are some criteria more important than others?

4. What is the group proud of? What do they consider a 'scandal', a 'tragedy'? What do they complain about? What are they ashamed of?

B) BOUNDARIES

1. What are the boundaries of their perception of who is 'one of them' and who isn't? When is someone seen as an outsider? When is someone accepted into the society? What is their reaction to your culture, education, personality, customs?

2. What do they see as their position in wider society? How do they identify themselves to outsiders?

3. How do they view those of other races and cultures, like you, for example?

C) ROLES

1. Do people have roles that are assigned at birth? Can those roles change? Are they assigned, and by whom? Are they defined by personality, birth order, family line, imposed by government, schools, church?

2. Are roles shifting or evolving within the society? Have the expectations for certain roles changed?

3. What is your real or expected role?

3) What RULES FOR LIVING are being expressed in the activity?

Notice the rules for living in the community around you. Notice when these rules are broken and how broken rules are enforced or not enforced.

Here are some questions related to **rules for living** for you to think about.

A) HARMONY

1. What is considered polite behavior and what embarrasses people? How do people deal with embarrassment?

2. What is expected and what is enforced? Do people bend the rules? What do they expect of you and of one another in relationship to the rules of society?

3. What systems are in place to provide harmony within the society? Do the control systems have to do with internal social and religious controls or outside political controls? Do they involve both? Are there other forms of control that you notice?

B) AUTHORITY

1. Who has authority to tell others what to do and how is it expressed? Within families? Within other social groups?

2. In which areas do people give over the responsibility to others for making decisions?

3. Does it seem like the society members all have equal authority, or are some more dominant than others?

4. Do most people follow the rules? What are the consequences if they do not?

C) RESPONSIBILITY

1. What are the tasks or obligations an individual is expected to do in a group? What are those they are expected to do by themself? How do responsibilities divide between ages and sexes?

2. What responsibilities do people demonstrate to one another? To groups outside the society? To the spiritual world?

3. How do others respond when someone fails to live up to their responsibility?

D) TIME

1. Do people seem to be conscious of time and keeping time commitments? What are the repercussions for failing to keep an appointment? How is this handled?

2. Are there definite times assigned to activities for fun and those which are work? Do you notice how people feel about wasting time? Do people tend to work quickly to finish tasks, or is the pace often slow? In group tasks, do all work together or in shifts?

3. Are you noticing seasons and patterns for different common activities in the lives of individuals, families, and groups?

4. Do different age groups and sexes use their time differently? If so, how?

E) PRIVACY

1. How is space used in the community? Do people seem to want a certain amount of space for themselves? Do they mark space with physical boundaries?

2. Do people spend much time by themselves, or do they act mostly in groups?

3. Do individuals or families have a high or low degree of privacy? Are houses and living spaces open to the view and to visits by others? How often?

F) SECURITY

1. What do people seem to be afraid of? How are these fears communicated and resolved?

2. What are the sources of security that you notice? Possibilities might include special knowledge, jobs, education, specific relationships, government, religious or secular organizations.

3. What makes people feel insecure? Possibilities might include sickness, uncertainty, loss, weakness, childlessness, divorce, being parentless, or poverty.

G) MOTIVATION/AGENDAS

1. Do people seem interested in gaining prestige, physical comfort, financial gain, learning and improving individually or as a society, being a role model for others, or enjoying power and influence?

2. Which goals are shared and openly talked about? What are some goals that people might only mention confidentially?

3. Who is seen as being successful?

4. Do people pursue comfortable lives, exciting lives, family security, freedom, happiness, national security, pleasure, social recognition, true friendship?

H) ENCULTURATION

1. What are common topics of conversation?

2. How do people describe their group identity? Do they talk about this often in a proud way, or are they ashamed of who they are as a group?

3. What do people respect as the behavior of a good woman? Good man? Good son or daughter? Good friend? Good relative? Good father or mother?

4. Do you notice change in the rules of society? What is causing this change?

I) ORIGIN OF BELIEFS/FOUNDATIONS FOR ETHICS

1. What do people say are the reasons for their rules? Do they have myths or other religious stories about these rules? Do they participate in formal religious activities that teach these rules?

2. Do they act as if they have high regard for nature around them?

3. Do they have views of starting and ending points for history? Where do they say that humans and animals, as well as the created world, came from?

4) What RELATIONSHIPS are evident in the activity?

Notice levels of curiosity, bluntness or subtlety, and showing appreciation for others. Notice patterns of formal and informal relationships. Notice good and bad relationships.

Here are some questions related to relationships for you to think about.

A) RELATIONSHIP INTERACTION

1. Who interacts with whom? When? How?

2. When do people spend time together? Doing what? Is anyone excluded?

3. Do all members interact with equal freedom?

4. Who touches whom and how? On what occasions?

5. Who visits whom and where?

6. When, where and how do people interact, socialize, converse, eat together, meet, organize events, chat, gather?

B) LEVELS AND TYPES OF RELATIONSHIPS WITHIN THE SOCIETY

1. What are the distinct social groups evident within the society?

2. What are the relationships between individuals of the same or different age, gender, social status, family groups?

3. How many close relationships does a person develop and with whom? What are their obligations to one another in gift exchange, authority, respect, language?

C) RELATIONSHIPS WITH THOSE OUTSIDE THE SOCIETY

1. How do people relate to outsiders?

2. Who do they fear, socialize with, scorn, suspect, accept from outside the society?

D) FORMING AND BREAKING OF RELATIONSHIPS

1. Do you notice any consequences for being on bad terms with another person? How are these usually resolved?

2. Do you notice public confrontations over relationship differences?

E) RELATIONSHIPS BETWEEN THE PHYSICAL AND THE SPIRITUAL WORLD

1. Are there individual or group times of communing with spiritual beings? What are the rules of behavior in these contexts?

2. Do you notice specific practices in people's lives that might have to do with their respecting or fearing taboos and spirit beings?

3. Are there people who are dedicated in a special way to the task of relating to spiritual beings? How are they identified?

SECTION 1

Learning Exercises for Level 3

Learning Exercise 1: Participant observation

As you have done in earlier levels, you will continue to use the *participant observation* learning exercise in Level 3 as well. You will apply this learning exercise for one hour in each daily learning plan.

By this point you have spent many, many hours participating in the lives of members of the local community over the last seven to eight months. During that time you have observed a large number of their common routines and activities, and you have spent lots of time learning specifically to communicate about many of those routine activities.

At this level, you should be thinking through the categories of life experience of those around you to identify the "gaps" in your participation with them. Specifically, you should plan to participate in activities in the community that you've not yet participated in. Go back through your previous *participant observation* notes in your *Daily Learning Plan Notebook* to help you identify what some of these activities might be.

During your daily *participant observation* activities in the community in Level 3 you should:

OBSERVE what is going on around you in a purposeful way. Observe the way that people behave and relate to each other. Think about the four life perspectives previously introduced.

Continue to make an effort to listen with understanding to all that you are hearing as you participate.

RESPOND by speaking appropriately in the local language. Ask questions in the local language about WHAT, HOW, WITH WHAT, WHERE, WHEN, and WHO during your participation. You can use previous level learning exercises to help you with unfamiliar process steps and vocabulary areas as you apply *participant observation*.

Continue to note any questions you have as you observe the behavior of others about WHY people behave and interact the way that they do. How does the behavior of others compare to what you would do if you were in that situation? What do you think the cause of some of those different responses might be? Try to note these questions in your *Life Perspectives Notebook* in the areas of the perspectives where they apply best.

Learning Exercise 5: Sharing life stories

This is a new learning exercise that will teach you how to profitably learn more from the stories of the lives of others. You will use this exercise to share about your life experience as well. This learning exercise will also show how you can effectively use recorded texts of those life stories to help you learn. All of this is described and applied in the daily learning plans below.

Don't fall into the trap of thinking that *sharing life stories* is an exercise that is separate from your participation in the lives of community members. Really it is just another form of participation in relationships with others! Try to find ways to practice this exercise in natural ways when you are spending time with others as they engage in normal life activities. In that sense you are creating space for lots of informal *participant observation* while you apply the *sharing life stories* exercise.

SECTION 2

Daily Learning Plans for Level 3

With the two learning exercises for Level 3 in mind, let's move on to the daily learning plans. As much as possible, you should continue to spend 40 or more hours each week in relating to others by working through the daily learning plans for Level 3.

Your ability to understand and speak in sentences in the language is now developing. In Level 3, you will build on this foundation of what you learned in previous levels. Your goal will be to focus on understanding and eventually speaking whole paragraphs related to the life experience of yourself and others.

We will divide the daily learning plans for Level 3 into sections similar to Level 2. The earlier plans will help you to understand life stories as community members relate them to you. The later plans will help you to begin to tell stories yourself, both about the experience of others as well as your own life experience.

We will give examples of daily learning plans that you can use to fit the life experience of those around you and your own life experience. These plans will provide instructions to guide you through each week.

Your overall goal will be to participate in 100 daily learning plans for Level 3. Hopefully you can complete five daily learning plans each week. This would enable you to finish all 100 of the daily learning plans for Level 3 in 20 weeks or so. If you complete four per week, you will be finished Level 3 in around 25 weeks.

As you work through your daily learning plans, you will encounter new vocabulary items. Many of these vocabulary items will relate to understanding stories about things that have happened at different times in the past or will happen in future. Also, you'll be exposed to terminology that helps you understand more complicated ways of talking about life experience. While you won't have a specific daily vocabulary goal at this level, you will certainly be exposed to lots of new words every day in this way.

As previously mentioned, you will use the *participant observation* learning exercise for one hour each day in your daily learning plans in Level 3. Remember to focus your attention on categories and activities in the lives of community members that you still haven't experienced. During your *participant observation*, you can apply learning exercises from earlier levels to routine processes and vocabulary areas that you'd like to learn more from.

In addition to *participant observation*, you will also use the *sharing life stories* learning exercise for five hours each day in your Level 3 learning plans. This is because you want to spend most of your time listening to others as they share stories with you about their lives.

Four hours is a LOT of time each day. It is unreasonable to expect that you will be able to spend four hours with a single person every day in your *sharing life stories* learning exercise. You should try to include lots of others in helping you to learn at this level. This is a great way to get to know them. The daily learning plans for Level 3 will be divided into parts to help you involve more than one person each day.

You will apply the *sharing life stories* learning exercise in two ways during the first eight weeks of Level 3.

WEEKS 1 TO 4: In the first four weeks of daily learning plans, you will listen to stories of activities in the community that you have participated in. Community members will tell about these activities in the past and in the future.

WEEKS 5 TO 8: In the second four weeks of daily learning plans, you will revisit the explanations of activities in the community from your daily learning plans in weeks 1 to 4. You will practice using the past and future to tell stories about these activities yourself.

In the second part of the Level 3 daily learning plans, you will apply the *sharing life stories* learning exercise to general and specific life stories from those in the community, as well as to your own life stories.

WEEKS 9 TO 14: In weeks 9 to 14 of daily learning plans, you will move on to listening to the general and specific life stories of those in the community. You will again want to hear stories about the past, as well as about future planning. Community members will compare and contrast life experiences, and will talk about situations where things didn't go as planned because something unexpected occurred.

WEEKS 15 TO 17: In weeks 15 to 17, you will revisit the general and specific life stories that you have heard from others in the community. You will try to repeat back the stories that you have heard to those who have told them to you, including past experiences and future plans, compare and contrast, and unexpected complications.

WEEKS 18 TO 20: In weeks 18 to 20, you will try to tell your own life experience stories to others following the many examples that you have already heard.

As you apply the *sharing life stories* learning exercises each day, you will also take time to review recordings and to reflect on what you have heard.

There are daily learning plan instructions on the following pages so that you can see how to apply the learning exercises each day in Level 3.

Daily time schedule for Level 3 (learning plans 1-40)

For a full-time Level 3 learner, your time should break down each day as follows for daily learning plans 1 to 40:

Participant observation learning exercise in activities in the community	1 hour
Sharing life stories learning exercise with community members	4 hours
Writing out a sharing life stories text yourself	1 hour
Review recorded texts yourself	30 minutes
Reading and reflection on the four life perspectives	1 hour
Preparing for the next daily learning plan	30 minutes
TOTAL	8 hours

Level 3 Daily Learning Plans 1 to 20

In your daily learning plans for the first four weeks of Level 3, you will return to common daily activities in the community to learn how to understand stories about these activities. You should plan to work with two people for each daily learning plan. One of the easiest ways to plan for each day is to follow the order of routine activities that you used for your relating through daily routines exercise in your Level 2 plans.

You would do this by thinking of an individual with whom you can talk about the activity that you applied in *Level 2 Daily Learning Plan 1*. Perhaps you can get help from the same person who helped you with that plan before. You would spend two hours with that individual talking about the activity in the recent past and near future.

You would then think of another individual with whom you could talk about the activity that you applied in *Level 2 Daily Learning Plan 2*. Perhaps you can get help from the same person who helped you with that plan before. You would spend another two hours with the person talking about that activity in the distant past and distant future.

You would then need to choose one of the texts to write out. If necessary, get help from a community member in doing this.

Here is an example of how you can apply this process:

EXAMPLE

THINGS TO DO FOR LEARNING PLAN

1) PARTICIPANT OBSERVATION:

Here are a few goals for your participant observation for the coming weeks.

OBSERVE and listen by evaluating what you experience in light of the questions for the four life perspectives in the introduction to this chapter.

RESPOND by appropriately asking WHAT, WHERE, HOW, WITH WHAT, WHEN, and WHO questions. Also speak as much as you are able.

NOTE any thoughts or questions related to the four life perspectives as well as other WHY questions you have but shouldn't ask, and so on.

2) SHARING LIFE STORIES 1 — TALKING ABOUT ROUTINE ACTIVITIES IN THE PAST AND FUTURE (2 HOURS):

Sharing life stories — talking about the recent past

Replay your previous recording for a community member in which he explained the steps to you of a common daily routine process. You should also play the recording for the community member of the descriptions of the setting that you'd recorded in relationship to that activity. Let's use our washing clothes routine from *Daily Learning Plan 1* in Level 2 as an example.

After you've replayed the washing clothes process recording and the descriptions recording, explain to the community member that you would like for them to tell you the process as a story of what *you* did recently. Have them tell the story as if you'd just done this activity in the recent past, like yesterday or the day before. They should also include some of the descriptive material from the setting as part of the story for you. They can tell the story as if he were present and witnessed you doing this activity.

After the community member has worked out a story that includes many of the steps of the process that you'd remembered as well as some setting description, record them telling the story. You might need to help remind them of some of the steps of the process and descriptions of the setting to make the story longer (8 to 15 minutes). Again, they should tell the story as if *you* had just done the activity recently. Depending on the steps of the process and the descriptions, the story could begin like:

"Yesterday you and I went to the river so that you could wash your clothes. The sun was shining brightly and it was very hot out. You went to the deep spot in the river where all the rocks are and where the water runs swiftly. You stood in the water up to your knees. You had a bucket of dirty clothes with you, as well as some soap and a scrub brush.

You first took one blue shirt out of the bucket and dipped that piece of clothing in the water. The shirt was really dirty because you had worked hard in it the day before. So you put soap on the shirt, then picked up the scrub brush and scrubbed the shirt. You then ..."

The story would continue to the end of the description and process steps. If the community member enjoys adding more to the stories, that is good as well. Just be sure that the majority of what is added is understandable.

After your recording is complete, listen through your recording with the community member. If there are parts of the story you don't understand, stop the recording and have the community member explain those sections of the story to you.

Sharing life stories — talking about the near future

Now explain to the community member that you would like for them to tell you the same story, but instead tell the story as if *THEY* will be doing that activity tomorrow or the next day. They can include as much description and detail from the first account as seems natural to him.

After the community member has worked out a story that includes many of the steps of the process that you'd remembered, record an example. You might need to first prompt them with some of the steps of the process to make the story longer (8 to 15 minutes). Depending on what is natural to include when talking about the future, the story could begin like:

"Tomorrow, if it is a nice day, I will go to the river to wash my clothes. If it is raining I probably won't go. I will go to the spot that is deep where all the rocks are. The water runs well there. I'll take along with me my bucket of dirty clothes, as well as soap and a scrub brush.

When I get there, I'll get in and take a shirt out. I'll dip the shirt in the water, then I'll put soap on it and scrub it with the scrub brush. I'll then ..."

The story would continue to the end of the description and process steps.

After your recording is complete, listen through your recording with the community member. If there are parts of the story you don't understand, stop the recording and have the community member explain those sections of the story to you.

3) SHARING LIFE STORIES 2 — TALKING ABOUT ROUTINE ACTIVITIES IN THE PAST AND FUTURE (2 HOURS):

Sharing life stories — talking about the more distant past

Follow a similar process as that which you've just followed in your first exercises. This time take your activity in the community from *Daily Learning Plan 2* in Level 2. Replay your previous recording for a community member in which he related the steps to you of that common daily routine process. You should also play the recording for the community member of the descriptions of the setting that you'd recorded in relationship to that activity.

After you've replayed the process recording and the descriptions recording, explain to the community member that you would like for them to tell you the process as a story of what another person (of the same gender) did some months ago. They should also include some of the descriptive material from the setting as part of the story for you. You can tell the community member that they can tell the story as if they were present and witnessed this activity taking place.

After the community member has worked out a story that includes many of the steps of the process that you'd remembered as well as some setting description, record them telling the story. You might need to remind them of some of the steps of the process and descriptions of the setting to make the story longer (8 to 15 minutes). Again, they should tell the story as if another person (of the same gender) had done the activity several months ago and that he was present at the time. Depending on the steps of the process and the descriptions, the story could begin like:

"Several months ago John decided to cook some manioc on the fire in his cooking house. He first had to start the fire, as there were just dead ashes. He used matches and some paper to do that. He then made the fire really hot by adding lots of wood from his overhead wood rack. Then he blew on the fire and waited a few minutes until there were some glowing coals. While he was waiting, he used his knife to peel the skin off the manioc root that he was going to roast.

"When the fire was ready, John carefully set the manioc on the fire. He used the fire tongs to keep turning it every several minutes so that the manioc wouldn't burn. The cooking house was smoky and hot by then.

When the manioc was black all over, John got the clam shell and scraped the whole piece of manioc with it. Then he ..."

The story would continue to the end of the description and process steps. If the community member enjoys adding to the stories that is good as well. Just be sure that the majority of what is added is understandable to you.

After your recording is complete, listen through your recording with the community member. If there are parts of the story you don't understand, stop the recording and have the community member explain those sections of the story to you.

Sharing life stories — talking about the more distant future

Now explain to the community member that you would like for them to tell you the same story, but instead tell the story as if a person, of the opposite gender, will be doing that activity several months from now. They can include as much description and detail from the first account as seems natural to them. They could, for example, tell the story as if their spouse were doing the activity and that they were present at the time.

After the community member has worked out a story that includes many of the steps of the process that you'd remembered, record an example. You might need to first prompt them with some of the steps of the process to make the story longer (8 to 15 minutes). The story would be very much like the first only it will be talking about the opposite gender doing the activity several months from now, instead of the other, having done the activity several months ago.

After your recording is complete, listen through your recording with the community member. If there are words in the story you don't understand, stop the recording and have the community member explain those sections of the story to you.

4) SHARING LIFE STORIES 3 — WRITING OUT A LIFE STORY TEXT (1 HOUR)

Write one of the four stories down in your *Text Notebook* using a phonetic alphabet or whatever orthography is already available in that language. Leave three blank lines between each line of text that you write out. As you come across words in the story that you don't understand, see if a community member can explain those to you.

Don't plan to write out more than one text each day from each activity. For the first day, write out your first activity text for that day. On your second day, write out the second text for your activities for that day. On the third day, write out your third text for your activities for that day. On the fourth day, write out your fourth text for the activities for that day.

5) Listen to your *sharing life stories* texts from that day for about 30 minutes.

6) Read and reflect on one of the four life perspectives for an hour, taking notes in your *Life Perspectives Notebook.*

7) Prepare tomorrow's daily learning plan.

Level 3 Daily Learning Plans 1 to 20

This is a set of instructions that you can use for plans 1 to 20. The instructions and steps are already included. In your *Daily Learning Plan Notebook*, write down the plan number, what two activities you will cover, what two individuals you will talk to, and which text you recorded for each day. You can use this same set of instructions for daily learning plans 1 to 20 in that way.

THINGS TO DO FOR LEARNING PLANS 1 TO 20

1) PARTICIPANT OBSERVATION:

OBSERVE and listen by evaluating what you experience in light of the questions for the four life perspectives in the introduction to this chapter.

RESPOND by appropriately asking *WHAT, WHERE, HOW, WITH WHAT, WHEN,* and *WHO* questions. Also speak as much as you are able.

NOTE any thoughts or questions related to the four life perspectives as well as other *WHY* questions you have but shouldn't ask, and so on.

2) SHARING LIFE STORIES 1 — TALKING ABOUT ROUTINE ACTIVITIES IN THE PAST AND FUTURE (2 HOURS):

Sharing life stories — talking about the recent past

Replay your recordings for a community member from your previous daily learning plan in Level 2. Play the recording in which the community member explained the steps to you of a common daily routine process. You should also play the recording for the community member of the descriptions of the setting that you'd recorded in relationship to that activity.

After you've replayed the process recording and the descriptions recording, explain to the community member that you would like for them to tell you the process as a story of what *you* did recently. Have them tell the story as if you'd just done this activity in the recent past, like yesterday or the day before. They should also include some of the descriptive material from the setting as part of the story for you. They can tell the story as if they were present and witnessed you doing this activity.

After the community member has worked out a story that includes many of the steps of the process that you'd remembered as well as some setting description, record them telling the story. You might need to help remind them of some of the steps of the process and descriptions of the setting to make the story longer (8 to 15 minutes). Again, they should tell the story as if *you* had just done the activity recently.

If the community member enjoys adding more details to the stories, that is good as well. Just be sure that the majority of what is added is understandable to you.

After your recording is complete, listen through your recording with the community member. If there are parts of the story you don't understand, stop the recording and have the community member explain those sections of the story to you.

Sharing life stories — talking about the near future

Now explain to the community member that you would like for them to tell you the same story, but instead tell the story as if THEY will be doing that activity tomorrow or the next day. They can include as much description and detail from the first account as seems natural to them.

After the community member has worked out a story that includes many of the steps of the process that you'd remembered, record an example. You might need to first prompt them with some of the steps of the process to make the story longer (8 to 15 minutes).

After your recording is complete, listen through your recording with the community member. If there are parts of the story you don't understand, stop the recording and have the community member explain those sections of the story to you.

3) SHARING LIFE STORIES 2 — TALKING ABOUT ROUTINE ACTIVITIES IN THE PAST AND FUTURE (2 HOURS):

Sharing life stories — talking about the more distant past

Follow a similar process as that which you've just followed in your first exercises. This time take your activity in the community from the next daily learning plan in Level 2. Replay your previous recording for a community member in which the community member related the steps to you of that common daily routine process. You should also play the recording for the community member of the descriptions of the setting that you'd recorded in relationship to that activity.

After you've replayed the process recording and the descriptions recording, explain to the community member that you would like for them to tell you the process as a story of what another person (of the same gender) did some months ago. They should also include some of the descriptive material from the setting as part of the story for you. You can tell the community member that they can tell the story as if they was present and witnessed this activity taking place.

After the community member has worked out a story that includes many of the steps of the process that you'd remembered as well as some setting description, record them telling the story. You might need to remind them of some of the steps of the process and descriptions of the setting to make the story longer (8 to 15 minutes). Again, they should tell the story as if another person (of the same gender) had done the activity several months ago and that they were present at the time.

If the community member enjoys adding to the stories that is good as well. Just be sure that the majority of what is added is understandable to you.

After your recording is complete, listen through your recording with the community member. If there are parts of the story you don't understand, stop the recording and have the community member explain those sections of the story to you.

Sharing life stories — talking about the more distant future

Now explain to the community member that you would like for them to tell you the same story, but instead tell the story as if a person, of the opposite gender, will be doing that activity several months from now. They can include as much description and detail from the first account as seems natural to them. They could, for example, tell the story as if their spouse were doing the activity and that they were present at the time.

After the community member has worked out a story that includes many of the steps of the process that you'd remembered, record an example. You might need to first prompt them with some of the steps of the process to make the story longer (8 to 15 minutes). The story would be very much like the first only it would be talking about a person of the opposite gender doing the activity several months from now, instead of the other, having done the activity several months ago.

After your recording is complete, listen through your recording with the community member. If there are words in the story you don't understand, stop the recording and have the community member explain those sections of the story to you.

4) SHARING LIFE STORIES 3 — WRITING OUT A LIFE STORY TEXT (1 HOUR)

Write one of the four stories down in your *Text Notebook* using a phonetic alphabet or whatever orthography is already available in that language. Leave three blank lines between each line of text that you write out. As you come across words in the story that you don't understand, see if a community member can explain those to you.

Don't plan to write out more than one text each day from each activity. For the first day, write out your first activity text for that day. On your second day, write out the second text for your activities for that day. On the third day, write out your third text for your activities for that day. On the fourth day, write out your fourth text for the activities for that day.

5) Each day on your own you should listen to your *sharing life stories* texts from that day for about 30 minutes.

6) Read and reflect on one of the four life perspectives for an hour, taking notes in your *Life Perspectives Notebook*.

7) Prepare tomorrow's daily learning plan.

Level 3 Daily Learning Plans 21 to 40

In your daily learning plans for the next four weeks of Level 3, you will review the stories that you've heard over the last four weeks related to common daily activities. Once again you will work with two different activities for each daily learning plan.

If you haven't already done so, now is the time when you need to stop using a common second language and only speak in the local language with community members.

This is a set of instructions that you can use for plans 21 to 40. The instructions and steps are already included. In your *Daily Learning Plan Notebook*, write down the plan number, what two activities you will cover, what two individuals you will talk to, and which text you recorded for each day. You can use this same set of instructions for daily learning plans 21 to 40 in that way.

THINGS TO DO FOR LEARNING PLANS 21 TO 40

1) PARTICIPANT OBSERVATION:

OBSERVE and listen by evaluating what you experience in light of the questions for the four life perspectives in the introduction to this chapter.

RESPOND by appropriately asking *WHAT, WHERE, HOW, WITH WHAT, WHEN*, and *WHO* questions. Also speak as much as you are able.

NOTE any thoughts or questions related to the four life perspectives as well as other *WHY* questions you have but shouldn't ask, and so on.

2) SHARING LIFE STORIES 1 — TALKING ABOUT ROUTINE ACTIVITIES IN THE PAST AND FUTURE (2 HOURS):

Sharing life stories—talking about the recent past

Replay your recordings for a community member from one of your previous daily learning plans 1 to 20. Play the recording in which the community member explained the steps to you of a common daily routine process. You should also play the recording for the community member of the descriptions of the setting that you'd recorded in relationship to that activity.

After you've replayed the process recording and the descriptions recording, explain to the community member that you would like to try to repeat the process as a story of what *you* did recently. Tell the story as if you'd just done this activity in the recent past, like yesterday or the day before. You should try to also include some of the descriptive material from the setting as part of the story in a similar way as the community member did.

After your retelling is complete, talk with the community member about the parts of what you've said that aren't clear to them. Sometimes the community member will try to help or correct you while you are talking, which is okay. But if possible, try to save the conversation about improvements until the end of the exercise.

Sharing life stories — talking about the near future

Now explain to the community member that you would like to tell them the same story, but instead tell the story as if *THEY* will be doing that activity tomorrow or the next day. You can include as much description and detail from the first account as seems natural to you. You might want to first listen through the recording with the community member to refresh your memory on the content.

After your retelling is complete, talk with the community member about the parts of what you've said that aren't clear to them. Sometimes the community member will try to help or correct you while you are talking, which is okay. But if possible, try to save the conversation about improvements until the end of the exercise.

3) SHARING LIFE STORIES 2 — TALKING ABOUT ROUTINE ACTIVITIES IN THE PAST AND FUTURE (2 HOURS):

Sharing life stories—talking about the more distant past

Follow a similar process as that which you've just followed in your first exercises. This time take your activity in the community from the next daily learning plan in Level 2. Replay your previous recording for a community member in which they related the steps to you of that common daily routine process. You should also play the recording for the community member of the descriptions of the setting that you'd recorded in relationship to that activity.

After you've replayed the process recording and the descriptions recording, tell the community member the process as a story of what another person (of the same gender) did some months ago similar to your recording.

After your retelling is complete, talk with the community member about the parts of what you've said that aren't clear to them. Sometimes the community member will try to help or correct you while you are talking, which is okay. But if possible, try to save the conversation about improvements until the end of the exercise.

Sharing life stories — talking about the more distant future

Now explain to the community member that you would like to tell them the same story, but instead you will tell the story as if a person, of the opposite gender, will be doing that activity several months from now. Listen to your previous recording to refresh your memory on the details in the text example that you have.

Tell the story as best you can, inlcuding as many details as possible.

After your retelling is complete, talk with the community member about the parts of what you've said that aren't clear to them. Sometimes the community member will try to help or correct you while you are talking, which is okay. But if possible, try to save the conversation about improvements until the end of the exercise.

4) SHARING LIFE STORIES 3 — WRITING OUT A LIFE STORY TEXT (1 HOUR)

Write one of the four stories down in your *Text Notebook* that you haven't yet written down from plans 1 to 20 using a phonetic alphabet or whatever orthography is already available in that language. Leave three blank lines between each line of text that you write out. As you come across words in the story that you don't understand, see if a community member can explain those to you.

Don't plan to write out more than one text each day from each activity.

5) Each day on your own you should listen to your sharing life stories texts from that day for about 30 minutes.

6) Read and reflect on one of the four life perspectives for an hour, taking notes in your *Life Perspectives Notebook.*

7) Prepare tomorrow's daily learning plan.

Level 3 Daily Learning Plans 41 to 70

In this group of daily learning plans, you will transition from stories of daily activities to the life stories of community members through question and answer times. You will ask questions so as to HEAR stories from their lives that explain, compare, and describe things that already happened, are happening, or will happen later. You will also ask about situations in their lives that had something unexpected that came up that they had to resolve.

One of the benefits of the daily learning plans 41 to 70 is that you can use these plans to get to know lots of people in the community to a greater depth than before. For that reason, you should begin thinking of as many as 30 different people that you can spend time with to learn more about their lives over the next six weeks.

Since four hours is a lot of time, you should consider trying to work with two individuals for each day's *sharing life stories* exercises. For this reason the sharing life stories exercises in the daily learning plans are divided into two parts.

As an example of how you can do this in daily learning plans 41 to 70, the first part of the *sharing life stories* exercise is called *explaining life overview and describing future plans*. This first part can be applied in one conversation with one person for two hours on the first day. The second part of the *sharing life stories* exercise in each daily plan is called *handling unusual situations and comparing life experiences*. You could talk about this second part with a second person that same day for two hours.

Once you have completed the explaining life overview and describing future plans with someone, you can then work with that same person on another day to go through handling unusual situations and comparing life experiences. In this way you can cycle through the exercises with different community members so you don't keep one person too long on any one day.

If possible, try to use the *sharing life stories* exercises with people of different ages, as well as with both men and women as is appropriate and possible. One way to do this is to visit husbands and wives together with your own husband or wife present.

Conversation Notebook

Before you begin plans 41 to 70, you need to set up a *Conversation Notebook*. This notebook will list all the individuals that you talk to and the dates that you talked with them, as well as which of the two parts of the *sharing life stories* exercise you applied on each day. This will help you to keep track of which people you talked to and what you can still talk to them about later.

In order to set up the Conversation Notebook, you should first number all the pages in the notebook front and back. The first time that you have a conversation, write the name of the person and date at the top of the first page. Record information from your conversation there. When you come back to talk to that same person another day, simply return to that name, write the date under your notes from before, and continue on with notes for that speaker. Between each speaker, leave five blank sides of paper. In other words, the name of the first speaker will be on page 1, the name of the second on page 6, the name of the third on page 11, the name of the fourth on page 16, and so on. You can set up an electronic Conversation Notebook if that is easier for you.

Daily time schedule for Level 3 (learning plans 41-85)

For a full-time level 3 learner, your time should break down each day as follows for daily learning plans 41 to 85:

Participant observation learning exercise in activities in the community	1 hour
Sharing life stories learning exercise with community members	4 hours
Writing and reviewing recorded texts yourself	1 hour 30 mins
Reading and reflection on the four life perspectives	1 hour
Preparing for the next daily learning plan	30 minutes
TOTAL:	8 hours

Level 3 Daily Learning Plans 41 to 70

This is a set of instructions that you can use for plans 41 to 70. The instructions and steps are already included. In your *Daily Learning Plan Notebook*, write down the plan number and what individuals you plan to spend time talking with for each plan. You can use this same set of instructions for daily learning plans 41 to 70 in that way.

THINGS TO DO FOR LEARNING PLANS 41 TO 70

1) PARTICIPANT OBSERVATION:

OBSERVE and listen by evaluating what you experience in light of the questions for the four life perspectives in the introduction to this chapter.

RESPOND by appropriately asking *WHAT, WHERE, HOW, WITH WHAT, WHEN,* and *WHO* questions. Also speak as much as you are able.

NOTE any thoughts or questions related to the four life perspectives as well as other *WHY* questions you have but shouldn't ask, and so on.

2) SHARING LIFE STORIES 1 — EXPLAINING LIFE OVERVIEW AND DESCRIBING FUTURE PLANS:

Identify an individual with whom you can spend two hours. This should be a person that you know and have a relationship with through previous opportunities to interact. This shouldn't be a formal or uncomfortable process, so make sure the person is comfortable and at ease based on your relationship with that person.

Begin by asking casual and appropriate questions about how things are going for the individual. What are they up to that day? Are they busy right now? Do they have time to talk? Can you talk with them as they work? Be sensitive to the conversation opportunities that are convenient and appropriate for others. It is a good idea to prearrange conversations with community members who are willing to spend time with you.

Explain briefly to the person that you want to hear some stories about their life. Tell them that you might make some notes as they are talking to help you remember what is said.

Ask the person to give you an overview of their life. Where were they born? Where are they from? What do they remember about their life growing up? What was life like for them at that time? Can they tell you the story of their life up to the present? Can the person describe their family to you? How do they spend their time now? What their daily life is like today? Remember that you will often need to ask questions to keep others talking. Show interest and be thinking of ways to encourage the speaker to continue.

Ask about the future plans of the individual. Here are a few examples of the kinds of questions you might ask:

"What do you think you will do after we are done here?"

"Do you think you will make any trips or do any specific jobs or projects later this month or year? Where might you go and what will you do?"

"Do you have any big thoughts about your life in the future? What would you like to do that you aren't already doing?"

As the person talks, make notes in your *Daily Learning Plan Notebook* of:

The main facts and details from the person's life overview

Unusual situations in the person's life that you can return to later

- Exciting, difficult, memorable, or life changing events
- Experiences that person has had that seem unique to them
- Complicated situations that took the person by surprise

Parts of the story that are really confusing to you that you can clarify later

Any questions that you have about the person's life that you can return to with follow up questions later

3) SHARING LIFE STORIES 2 — HANDLING UNUSUAL SITUATIONS AND COMPARING LIFE EXPERIENCES:

Identify a person you have previously spoken with that you can talk to for two hours. Glance through your notes to follow up with questions related to situations in that person's life that were unusual in some way. What made the situation unusual? How did the individual handle the situation? Here are a few examples of the kinds of questions you might ask:

"You said when I talked with you before that on your trip to the beach your friend was stung by a stingray. That must have been really bad! What did you do?"

"You said before that when you were young you were fearful of being attacked by an enemy village. Do you remember a situation when that actually happened? Tell me about that a little."

"You said before that you were really excited the first time that you went out to town. Do you remember what happened? Explain that to me."

Think about events that the person has described to you that the person can compare. Think of some questions to ask about those events. Here are a few examples of the kinds of questions you might ask:

"You said just a minute ago that life is different today than it was when you were little? What is so different now? What has changed?"

"You said that you once took a trip to the coast to see the ocean. Do you like the coast or the village better? What do you like better about each place?"

"You said that you once lived out in town for two months. Was life there better or worse than here? What did you like about it? What did you not like about it?"

4) RECORDING AND WRITING DOWN A SHARING LIFE STORIES TEXT:

As you are going through the exercises above, record an interesting example text from one of the two people. Try to record a variety of text types each week, including two life overviews texts, one future plans text, one unusual situations text, and one comparing life experiences text. If possible, the text should be no longer than 30 minutes so that you will have time to process the whole thing.

Once the story is recorded, write the text down in your *Text Notebook*, leaving three blank lines between each line of text. After you do this, carefully clarify any words in the story that you don't understand fully with a community member.

5) Each day on your own you should listen to your sharing life stories texts from that day for about 30 minutes.

6) Read and reflect on one of the four life perspectives for an hour. Make observation notes in your *Life Perspectives Notebook* from your conversations for the day that give insight into possible examples for the life perspective questions.

7) Prepare tomorrow's daily learning plan.

Level 3 Daily Learning Plans 71 to 85

As you apply plans 71 to 85, you will work with individuals that you've heard life stories from in previous plans 41 to 70. Your goal will be to retell their life stories to them in a similar way to which they've told them to you.

Your *sharing life stories* exercises will be divided into three parts, though you may only want to plan to work with two people for each plan. You could apply the first part with one person for two hours, then the other two parts with another person for three hours.

Remember that you will be trying to follow the examples of telling stories that you have heard over the last six weeks, though you will make many mistakes in the process of doing so. This is natural and isn't something to be afraid of or worry about. Be open to correction and input from those who are listening. Be aware of the signs from them that they don't understand what you are saying so that they can help you to be clearer.

Level 3 Daily Learning Plans 71 to 85

This is a set of instructions that you can use for plans 71 to 85. The instructions and steps are already included. In your *Daily Learning Plan Notebook*, write down the plan number and what individuals you plan to spend time talking with. You can use this same set of instructions for daily learning plans 71 to 85 in that way.

THINGS TO DO FOR LEARNING PLANS 71 TO 85

1) PARTICIPANT OBSERVATION:

OBSERVE and listen by evaluating what you experience in light of the questions for the four life perspectives in the introduction to this chapter.

RESPOND by appropriately asking WHAT, WHERE, HOW, WITH WHAT, WHEN, and WHO questions. Also speak as much as you are able.

NOTE any thoughts or questions related to the four life perspectives as well as other WHY questions you have but shouldn't ask, and so on.

2) SHARING LIFE STORIES 1 — EXPLAINING LIFE OVERVIEW AND DESCRIBING FUTURE PLANS (2 HOURS):

Identify an individual who has shared their life experience with you that you can talk with for two hours. Go back to the notes and recordings that apply to that individual so that you can familiarize yourself with their life overview and future plans. You will need to spend a half hour preparing in this way before you meet with the person.

Meet with the person and begin the conversation by asking casual and appropriate questions about how things are going for the individual. What are they up to that day? Are they busy right now? Do they have time to talk? Can you talk with them as they work? Be sensitive to the conversation opportunities that are convenient and appropriate for others. If possible, prearrange conversations beforehand.

Explain briefly to the person that you want to retell their life overview to them. Tell them that you would like for them to help you to remember the details that you might have forgotten.

Do your best to retell the life overview that the person previous shared with you. Include also any future plans that the person talked about.

When you are done, ask the person for input. Was the story clear? Where did you make mistakes or how could you have said things differently? Can the person retell those parts correctly so that you can hear the proper version?

3) SHARING LIFE STORIES 2 — HANDLING UNUSUAL SITUATIONS (1 HOUR 30 MINUTES):

Identify a person you have previously spoken with that you can talk to for another hour and a half.

Go through your notes and recordings for a half hour on your own first to prepare.

Retell a story of an unusual situation that the person was involved in. Explain what made the situation unusual, what happened, and how the individual handled the situation.

When you are done, ask the person for input. Was the story clear? Which parts did you mess up? Can the person retell those parts right so that you can hear the corrections?

If you have time left, ask the person if they can think of other unusual situations that they have experienced that they can tell you about.

4) SHARING LIFE STORIES 3 — COMPARING LIFE EXPERIENCES (1 HOUR 30 MINUTES):

Identify a person you have previously spoken with that you can talk to for another hour and a half.

Go through your notes and recordings for a half hour on your own first to prepare.

Think about events that the person has described to you that the person compared. Try to retell the compared events in the same way that the person did.

When you are done, ask the person for input. Was the story clear? Which parts did you mess up? Can the person retell those parts right so that you can hear the corrections?

If you have time left over, see if there are other comparisons that the speaker can think of that they can tell you about.

5) Read and reflect on one of the four life perspectives for an hour. Make observation notes in your *Life Perspectives Notebook* from your conversations for the day that give insight into possible answers to the life perspective questions.

6) Prepare tomorrow's daily learning plan.

Level 3 Daily Learning Plans 86 to 100

In daily learning plans 86 to 100 you will try to tell stories from your own life following the examples that you have heard from others. We will divide the sharing life stories exercises into two parts so that you can share about your life with two different individuals each day. Try not to tell the same life stories to the same people more than once. This means that in three weeks of plans, you will tell your life stories to at least fifteen different people.

Your life stories will be different from those you have heard from others because your life and situation are based on another place and set of experiences. Even so, this is a good exercise for you to work through. As you speak, be creative and try to relate your life stories to the things that you know about their lives as much as you can. There will be no *participant observation* exercises included in this set of plans.

Daily time schedule for Level 3 (learning plans 86-100)

For a full-time Level 3 learner, your time should break down each day as follows for daily learning plans 86 to 100:

Sharing life stories learning exercise with community members	6 hours
Reviewing recorded texts yourself	1 hour
Reading and reflection on the four life perspectives	1 hour
Preparing for the next daily learning plan	30 minutes
TOTAL	8 hours 30 minutes

Level 3 Daily Learning Plans 86 to 100

This is a set of instructions that you can use for plans 86 to 100. The instructions and steps are already included. In your *Daily Learning Plan Notebook*, write down the plan number and what individuals you plan to spend time talking with. You can use this same set of instructions for daily learning plans 86 to 100 in that way.

THINGS TO DO FOR LEARNING PLANS 86 TO 100

1) SHARING LIFE STORIES 1 — EXPLAINING LIFE OVERVIEW AND DESCRIBING FUTURE PLANS (3 HOURS):

Spend a half hour on your own to note down an outline of what you'd like to say about your life overview and future plans. Don't try to write this out word for word, just the main ideas. You might even try to practice this to yourself. Tell where you were born and where you are from. Relate what you can about your life growing up. Tell what life was like for you at that time. Try briefly telling the story of your life up to the present. Describe your family to the person. Explain how you spend your time now and what your daily life is like today.

Identify an individual with whom you can spend two and a half hours. This should be a person that you know and have a relationship with through previous opportunities to interact. This shouldn't be a formal or uncomfortable process, so make sure the person is comfortable and at ease based on your relationship with that person.

Meet with that person and explain briefly that you want to tell some stories about your life to them. Tell them that you are still learning so will need their help in the parts of the stories that are hard for you.

If the person asks questions while you are talking, respond to the questions. If at all possible, try to make the time as natural and conversational as possible. If the person wants to relate a similar story or interject their own experience, don't worry. Just try to eventually return back to your storytelling in appropriate ways.

After you have given the overview of your life to the person based on your outline, ask them if they understood what you have communicated. Ask them to retell the overview to you. Follow along in your outline to identify gaps. If there are certain ways that you haven't communicated clearly, ask questions about that, and listen to the way that person makes that part of the story clearer. See how much of the overview they have heard and understood.

After that is finished, tell the person a little about your future plans for the day, for the month, and in the months ahead. When you are done, see what the person has understood. Ask the person to retell anything that you could have made clearer.

Once this is completed, ask that person if they can tell you your life overview and future plans so that you can record that as an example to listen to. You will repeat this recording exercise once a week for the next three weeks. Choose a speaker to record each week who is good at retelling the details of the story.

2) SHARING LIFE STORIES 2 — HANDLING UNUSUAL SITUATIONS (1 HOUR 30 MINUTES):

Spend a half hour each day thinking through two situations in your life that were unusual or unexpected. Write some notes to help you prepare to tell those two stories. Examples include:

    Exciting, difficult, memorable, or life changing events

    Experiences that you have had that are unique to you

    Complicated situations that took you by surprise

Identify a person you have previously spoken with that you can talk to for an hour about this. Tell the person that you'd like to talk with them to tell a couple of stories from your experience.

Tell the first of the two stories. Monitor the person to see if they are understanding what you are saying.

When you are finished, ask the person to retell the story to you. See what details he or she does and doesn't include. Ask them about the details that they didn't include. Were those clear? How could you have said them better?

Move on to the second story and go through the same process.

When you are done, choose one of the two stories and have the person tell the story back to you so that you can record it as an example. Try to record a different example story each day to listen to later.

3) SHARING LIFE STORIES 3 — COMPARING LIFE EXPERIENCES (1 HOUR 30 MINUTES):

Spend a half hour thinking about how your life experience (or those who live where you are from) compares to the experience of those around you. For each day, think of one good example of how this life experience is the same as those around you, and one example of how this life experience is different. Remember that you aren't criticizing your life or their life, just explaining how they are the same or different. Take notes so that you can remember what to say. Include examples and details.

Meet with an individual and explain that you want to talk about your life experience so that they can help you.

Start by explaining again where you are from. Mention that in some ways life is the same in that place, and in some ways it is very different. Talk as long as you can about why this is so. Give details and examples to explain what exactly you are talking about.

After you are finished, ask the person if they understood. Can they retell what you've explained to them? How might your explanation be clearer?

When you've clarified the details of the comparison, try to record an example of the person repeating what you've said.

4) Each day on your own you should listen to your sharing life stories texts from that day for an hour.

5) Read and reflect on one of the four life perspectives for an hour. Make observation notes in your *Life Perspectives Notebook* from your conversations for the day that give insight into possible answers to the life perspective questions.

6) Prepare tomorrow's daily learning plan.

Self-evaluation for Level 3

In the following Level 3 self-evaluation, read each statement and mark the number that represents your current ability.

1. I have completed all 100 Level 3 daily learning plans.

1 ☐	2 ☐	3 ☐	4 ☐	5 ☐
not at all well	barely well	somewhat well	adequately well	extremely well

2. I have read through the four life perspectives questions many times. I can give a summary of each perspective and briefly explain the areas that are covered by that perspective. I can also give examples of activities in the community that apply to each area.

1 ☐	2 ☐	3 ☐	4 ☐	5 ☐
not at all well	barely well	somewhat well	adequately well	extremely well

3. I can understand and retell short stories in the past and future related to thirty to forty common activities in the community.

1 ☐	2 ☐	3 ☐	4 ☐	5 ☐
not at all well	barely well	somewhat well	adequately well	extremely well

4. I can understand and briefly retell the general life stories of twenty to thirty people in the community.

1 ☐	2 ☐	3 ☐	4 ☐	5 ☐
not at all well	barely well	somewhat well	adequately well	extremely well

5. I can understand and briefly retell stories of how twenty to thirty people in the community dealt with unusual situations in their lives—situations that were exciting, difficult, complicated, or stressful.

1 ☐	2 ☐	3 ☐	4 ☐	5 ☐
not at all well	barely well	somewhat well	adequately well	extremely well

6. I can understand and briefly compare and contrast situations in the life experience of twenty to thirty people in the community.

1 ☐	2 ☐	3 ☐	4 ☐	5 ☐
not at all well	barely well	somewhat well	adequately well	extremely well

7. I can understand and briefly retell the future plans of twenty to thirty people in the community.

1 ☐	2 ☐	3 ☐	4 ☐	5 ☐
not at all well	barely well	somewhat well	adequately well	extremely well

8. I can give an overview of my own life.

1 ☐
not at all
well

2 ☐
barely
well

3 ☐
somewhat
well

4 ☐
adequately
well

5 ☐
extremely
well

9. I can tell stories of how I dealt with unusual situations in my life—situations that were exciting, difficult, complicated, or stressful.

1 ☐
not at all
well

2 ☐
barely
well

3 ☐
somewhat
well

4 ☐
adequately
well

5 ☐
extremely
well

10. I can briefly compare and contrast situations from my life experience.

1 ☐
not at all
well

2 ☐
barely
well

3 ☐
somewhat
well

4 ☐
adequately
well

5 ☐
extremely
well

11. I can describe my future plans and goals.

1 ☐
not at all
well

2 ☐
barely
well

3 ☐
somewhat
well

4 ☐
adequately
well

5 ☐
extremely
well

Level 4

Relating through Lifeview Conversation

Level 4 is the final level of culture and language learning, during which you will learn to understand and talk about the beliefs that motivate the behavior of those with whom you are building relationships. You will be able to understand their opinions as well as support your own opinions about these kinds of topics. You will also talk about events and ideas that are potential but that haven't happened. You will be able to connect paragraphs together to form long texts in your conversation. You can talk about the bigger issues in the world and you can also find ways to talk about concepts that are new to you but that you want to describe.

This chapter gives practical guidance to your Level 4 learning. The first section of the chapter introduces the new *learning exercise* that you will use in this level. The second section gives *daily learning plans* to guide you as you apply the learning exercise each day.

Your proficiency goal for this level

You are at a very important point in your growing relationships with others in the local community. For that reason, you need to understand what your overall goal is for completing this final level of learning. Here are a few thoughts for you to consider.

Proficiency in another language and culture relates to how you can actually function in life situations in the local community. As a functioning member of the community you have a clear purpose for being in the community and a message to communicate with others. In order to achieve these purposes, you have spent the last year/s understanding the lives of those around you so that you can integrate and relate well to them in their living environment.

While you will always be someone from another place and culture, in Level 4 exercises, your goal is to become someone who understands and acts in appropriate ways in spite of your place and language of origin — not always drawing attention to yourself, consciously or unconsciously.

As you've already seen, getting to a point of interacting this way in the host culture does not happen all at once. Becoming a typical community member in this setting is a gradual process. So what does this final goal look like for you?

One important area to consider is your ability to communicate about everyday life events. You've spent a lot of time learning to do that in Level 3. You can now discuss everyday occurrences with your neighbors or acquaintances and even strangers. Though you can manage this pretty well at this point, quite often the conversations of others are still beyond your understanding, since the community members around you will enter into cultural domains you are not familiar with.

As you work through Level 4 plans and find yourself in these kinds of conversations and situations, you will grow to recognize the areas of culture and conversation that are new to you. You will learn to cope by asking the appropriate questions to learn and participate as much as possible in the conversation in spite of your limitations. Your comprehension and vocabulary will be stretched, but this will simply give you further opportunities to learn to understand more.

In Level 4 exercises your ability will grow to talk about your future plans and what might happen if unforeseen circumstances arise. This might still be difficult for you in certain situations, but you should be able to eventually do this, especially in cultural areas that you have become very familiar with.

Another important point is that you have been learning over the last year to begin to build deep friendships with those around you. This is based on the time you have spent getting to know their daily activities and life stories in the context of the local language and culture.

In Level 4 exercises you will grow in knowing how to pursue those friendships effectively if the other person shows interest. This involves knowing and understanding the beliefs and motivations in the life of that person in a real, experiential way. Such relationships will include the ability to talk about life issues that affect that person and the circumstances that they are going through.

The fact is that in spite of your efforts to fit in, living in a foreign culture like this presents many instances where you can unintentionally offend others. In Level 4 exercises, you will learn to better recognize when this has happened, and you will know who might be able to help you figure out what has happened and what you should do. In this way you can learn to follow the appropriate actions for reconciliation.

As is the case in all communities, different members will hold differing views and opinions. They will have reasons for this, of course, and will express those reasons, even defend them. You likewise will want to learn to give your opinions appropriately and explain the reasons why you hold those beliefs. This kind of interaction will prove important for any future goals and objectives you might have. In Level 4 exercises you will learn the foundational skills that will prepare you to later do these things.

Even though you should see this kind of overall ability as your goal when you finish Level 4 learning plans, you must realize that you will still be far from 'native-like' in your speech and interactions at that point. You may even have some pronunciation issues to keep dealing with. Your speech will be far from perfect or even grammatically correct at all times.

Although you won't have consistent patterns of error in your speaking, you will still confuse grammatical features in the language from time to time. This will particularly be the case when you get into cultural domains you are not familiar with. Your use of subtleties in discourse, body language, tone of voice, and other non-linguistic cues might be lacking to a great degree at times. But in your overall interactions, these shortcomings will not have a great affect on your ability to be a part of normal life, nor will they confuse your listeners to any significant degree.

Exploring the four life perspectives in Level 4

What should you focus on in the coming months in preparing for working toward this kind of proficiency? You've now spent more than a year in this new living environment. You've gotten to know lots of people and have observed and learned to talk about their daily lives and life experience. You've learned to get around pretty well in the language and culture around you.

Over the last five months, you've been reading through the questions related to the four life perspectives once a week, and you've been thinking about what you do and do not know about these perspectives. You've made notes of behaviors and questions in your *Life Perspectives Notebook* about these things.

In your Level 4 exercises, you will further explore these four life perspectives as you talk with community members. You want to know what people actually describe as their motivation for behavior in the community. What do people appreciate and prioritize in their lives? What are their underlying beliefs about life? How do the beliefs that people claim actually measure up to what they typically do?

How will you explore the four life perspectives in Level 4?

We realize that right now in your ability to communicate, you are moving toward being able to discuss topics from the four life perspectives with others, but you cannot do so yet. Your goal, then, will be to continue on from what you've learned in your sharing life stories exercise of relationship building. Later in this level, you should be able to explore the life perspectives more freely with community members through discussion questions. Then you can compare their answers to their behavior to draw conclusions for yourself about their underlying beliefs.

So what should you do? You've already written down the previous life perspectives questions from Level 3 in your *Life Perspectives Notebook*. Now you can go back through the notebook and add the new questions in italics that expand on those questions in the following list. Simply write the italicized additions to each question underneath whatever observations you have already written down for that question in your notebook. You should have plenty of space since you've left blank pages between each question previously. Or, alternatively, add these questions into your electronic document.

Additional questions for you to consider for the four life perspectives in Level 4

1) What COMMUNICATION is taking place?

Observe people in conversation, listening for volume, tone and stress in their speech, noticing gestures and the social distance maintained. Also notice what people do and don't talk about and what information is important to have and listen to.

Here are some questions related to communication for you to think about. The expanded questions for Level 4 are in italics.

A) AVENUES AND METHODS OF COMMUNICATION

1. Notice verbal and non-verbal communication around you. Do you hear continuous verbal interaction or long periods of silence? How do eyes, face, tilt of head, hands, posture, space, time, pitch and tone of voice seem to be used to convey meaning? *Are you able to detect the attitudes and feelings of others through their non-verbal communication? In what ways?*

2. Do you notice the use of more than one language or dialect in the community? If so, when do people tend to use other languages or dialects? *Why do you think that is the case? What attitudes toward language varieties are being displayed by this behavior?*

What might this tell you about what people believe about the languages?

3. Is there much communication coming from outside the society in the form of visitors or media sources? *What are the general attitudes of older people toward incoming sources of information? The attitudes of younger people?*

4. Do you notice others interacting with spiritual beings or spending time praying in any way? *What sorts of beliefs about spiritual beings have you learned about? What priority do people place on this process of communication with spiritual beings?*

5. What do you notice about literacy in the community? How many people can read and in what languages? Are materials for reading available to them? Do they attend schools? *How high of a priority does attending school seem in the community? What does this tell you about the priority of education and outside learning?*

B) LEVELS OF COMMUNICATION

1. Do you notice changes in people's speech when they are talking to people they know versus those they don't know? To their elders versus their peers? To friends versus strangers? To family members versus others outside the family? *What attitudes are being expressed through such speaking changes? What beliefs about family and hospitality can you identify?*

2. Do all people interact with all others with the same freedom? Are there any avoidance relationships within relatives? Is everyone expected to talk, or is there a main spokesperson (within families or larger groups)? *What beliefs are being expressed by the way people interact in these relationships?*

C) EFFECTIVE AND INEFFECTIVE COMMUNICATION

1. Who do people really seem to listen to? What are the situations where you notice that others are really listening? What about situations where they are not listening? How do they show that they are listening? *What are the kinds of information and the kinds of people that community members prioritize enough to listen to? What motivates their appreciation of those individuals and that information?*

2. Do people make it clear when they haven't understood something from another person, or do they just pretend to have done so anyway? How do people show that they don't understand? *What information is valuable enough to people that they will be sure to try to understand and will make it clear in the appropriate way if they don't?*

D) TRUTH

1. Have you noticed general areas where people show that they believe some things to definitely be true and some things to definitely be false? What kinds of things are definitely true? What kinds of things are definitely false? *How do people decide to believe something as true? What makes them conclude that something must be or is likely false?*

2. How do people deal with new information that comes to them? What if that information contradicts what they already believe to be true? Do they act like both things can be true at the same time or are they intent on resolving the contradiction? *What is the best way to present new information so that the listeners believe it to be something true and important?*

3. Are there formal times for teaching? Informal times? *What are people's attitudes toward teaching times, either formal or informal? How much do they prioritize these things?*

2) How is group or individual IDENTITY playing out?

Notice how the status, age, and sex of individuals affects their overall behavior within the society. Notice the boundaries and roles of individuals both within and outside the society.

Here are some questions related to **identity** for you to think about. The expanded questions for Level 4 are in italics.

A) INDIVIDUALISM AND COMMUNITY

1. Does an individual make decisions on their own? Are group beliefs and decisions accepted by all? Is individual action socially encouraged? *What are people's attitudes toward individual versus group action? What are the consequences for individuals just making their own decisions?*

2. Do you see evidence that people compete with one another? Are they generally co-operative or non-cooperative? *What is people's attitude toward competition? How are competitive individuals viewed by the rest of society? What belief seems to be motivating these attitudes?*

3. What would they see as group identifying factors? Are some criteria more important than others? *How do they believe that being a part of the group in this way will be a help to them? What are people's attitudes towards those in the group who don't heed these markers in their behavior? What do they believe will be the consequences for that?*

4. What is the group proud of? What do they consider a 'scandal', a 'tragedy'? What do they complain about? What are they ashamed of? *What are the consequences for shameful behavior? What motivates people to involve themselves in scandals or tragedies?*

B) BOUNDARIES

1. What are the boundaries of their perception of who is 'one of them' and who isn't? When is someone seen as an outsider? When is someone accepted into the society? What is their reaction to your culture, education, personality, customs? *Are you considered an outsider or insider? Why or why not? Do people appreciate the contributions of those on the outside?*

2. What do they see as their position in wider society? How do they identify themselves to outsiders? *What attitudes do people display in this process? Are they defensive? Critical? Complimentary?*

3. How do they view those of other races and cultures, like you, for example? *What is people's general attitude towards other races and cultures? What motivates their attitudes? Are other races and cultures just as valuable as they are in their eyes? Why or why not?*

C) ROLES

1. Do people have roles that are assigned at birth? Can those roles change? Are they assigned, and by whom? Are they defined by personality, birth order, family line, imposed by government, schools, church? *What are people's attitudes toward their societal roles? Are some roles more valuable that others? Do they see certain individuals as worth more than others?*

2. Are roles shifting or evolving within the society? Have the expectations for certain roles changed? *What are some of the attitudes or consequences of role changes? Are role changes appreciated in the society, or do people generally feel these things were best left alone?*

3. What is your real or expected role? *What appreciation do people show for your role among them at this time? What do they believe that your role is leading to?*

3) What rules for LIVING are being expressed?

Notice the rules for living in the community around you. Notice when these rules are broken and how broken rules are enforced or not enforced.

Here are some questions related to rules for **living** for you to think about. The expanded questions for Level 4 are in italics.

A) HARMONY

1. What is considered polite behavior and what embarrasses people? How do people deal with embarrassment? *Do people appreciate confrontational information? What is their attitude toward messengers who are confrontational or who bring embarrassment to others?*

2. What is expected and what is enforced? Do people bend the rules? What do they expect of you and of one another in relationship to the rules of society? *What are people's attitudes toward rule followers and rule breakers? What do people believe about inviting blessing when rules are followed? What about inviting disaster when they are not?*

3. What systems are in place to provide harmony within the society? Do the control systems have to do with internal social and religious controls or outside political controls? Do they involve both? Are there other forms of control that you notice? *Do people appreciate the systems of control or resent them? Which ones do they appreciate and which do they resent? Why?*

B) AUTHORITY

1. Who has authority to tell others what to do and how is it expressed? Within families? Within other social groups? *What are people's attitudes towards authority figures? Are they respectful to them? Do they appreciate their authority? Where do they believe that this authority comes from? Do they follow their instructions? With what kinds of attitudes? What are the consequences for not heeding?*

2. In which areas do people give over the responsibility to others for making decisions? *What gives others the right to make decisions for the group? Where does that authority come from? Do people respect these decision makers? Do they heed the instructions? With what kinds of attitude?*

3. Does it seem like the society members all have equal authority, or are some more dominant than others? *What do people appreciate in those who are more dominant? What makes them so?*

4. Do most people follow the rules? What are the consequences if they do not? *What are people's attitudes toward obedience, conformity, and agreement? Do they feel that others should generally conform and just follow the rules? Why or why not?*

C) RESPONSIBILITY

1. What are the tasks or obligations an individual is expected to do in a group? What are those they are expected to do by themself? How do responsibilities divide between ages and sexes? *What are people's attitudes toward those who don't live up to their responsibilities?*

2. What responsibilities do people demonstrate to one another? To groups outside the society? To the spiritual world? *What attitudes and beliefs are demonstrated in these activities? What do people believe about the consequences for failing to fulfill these responsibilities, both to spirit beings as well as to each other?*

3. How do others respond when someone fails to live up to their responsibility? *What are their attitudes towards irresponsible people? Do they appreciate responsibility in others? Do they believe that this is important?*

D) TIME

1. Do people seem to be conscious of time and keeping time commitments? What are the repercussions for failing to keep an appointment? How is this handled? *What are people's attitudes towards time and time commitments? Is time appreciated as a resource?*

2. Are there definite times assigned to activities for fun and those which are work? Do you notice how people feel about wasting time? Do people tend to work quickly to finish tasks, or is the pace often slow? In group tasks, do all work together or in shifts? *Do people appreciate individual effort? Do the appreciate group effort? Do they believe that more is accomplished one way or the other? How so?*

3. Are you noticing seasons and patterns for different common activities in the lives of individuals, families, and groups? *What motivates people to follow these patterns of activity?*

4. Do different age groups and sexes use their time differently? If so, how? *What are the reasons why people use time differently? What beliefs about age groups and different sexes cause this to occur?*

E) PRIVACY

1. How is space used in the community? Do people seem to want a certain amount of space for themselves? Do they mark space with physical boundaries? *Do people appreciate personal space? What attitudes do they display when space is invaded?*

2. Do people spend much time by themselves, or do they act mostly in groups? *What beliefs are being displayed by the way that people spend their time alone or in groups?*

3. Do individuals or families have a high or low degree of privacy? Are houses and living spaces open to the view and to visits by others? How often? *What attitudes are displayed in the way that people respond to privacy and visitors? What beliefs are associated with these responses?*

F) SECURITY

1. What do people seem to be afraid of? How are these fears communicated and resolved? *What are people's attitudes toward these sources of fear? What are their beliefs about the causes of fear?*

2. What are the sources of security that you notice? Possibilities might include special

knowledge, jobs, education, specific relationships, government, religious or secular organizations. *What appreciation do people place on personal security? Do they actively seek it as a high priority? What do they believe about those who achieve security versus those who do not? What are the obligations of those with security toward those who do not have it? What are their beliefs about the causes?*

3. What makes people feel insecure? Possibilities might include sickness, uncertainty, loss, weakness, childlessness, divorce, being parentless, or poverty. *What are people's attitudes toward those who are in insecure positions? What are their beliefs about the causes of insecurity? Who is responsible to help?*

G) MOTIVATION/AGENDAS

1. Do people seem interested in gaining prestige, physical comfort, financial gain, learning and improving individually or as a society, being a role model for others, or enjoying power and influence? *What are people's attitudes toward those who have gained power and influence? What are the obligations of those with power and influence toward others in the group?*

2. Which goals are shared and openly talked about? What are some goals that people might only mention confidentially? *What are people's attitudes toward holding and pursuing long-term goals for life? If people hide goals and objectives, what motivates them to do so?*

3. Who is seen as being successful? *Why are they seen as successful? What are the attitudes of others toward them? Do people believe that success is a good thing?*

4. Do people pursue comfortable lives, exciting lives, family security, freedom, happiness, national security, pleasure, social recognition, true friendship? *What kind of life do people think is most important? Why do they think so?*

H) ENCULTURATION

1. What are common topics of conversation? *What motivates people to talk about these things?*

2. How do people describe their group identity? Do they talk about this often in a proud way, or are they ashamed of who they are as a group? *What attitudes and beliefs are expressed in the way that people talk and think about themselves? What are their reference points for feeling this way (other groups, societies, spiritual beings, and so on)?*

3. What do people respect as the behavior of a good woman? Good man? Good son or daughter? Good friend? Good relative? Good father or mother? *What are their attitudes toward those who don't fulfill these kinds of obligations? What beliefs are demonstrated about these people in the way that others set up rules for what constitutes 'good' behavior from them?*

4. Do you notice change in the rules of society? What is causing this change? *What are people's attitudes toward this kind of change? Does it cause distress to others or do they appreciate the change?*

I) ORIGIN OF BELIEFS/FOUNDATIONS FOR ETHICS

1. What do people say are the reasons for their rules? Do they have myths or other religious stories about these rules? Do they participate in formal religious activities that teach these rules? *What are people's attitudes toward their rules? Do they reverence them*

or resent them? Do they appreciate them enough to consistently hear the teaching of the rules by others? Do people consistently follow the rules that they know about? What areas in their system of rules seem ambiguous?

2. Do they act as if they have high regard for nature around them? *What are people's attitudes toward the created order? Do they believe in preservation and caretaking, or do they take and use at will? Do they look to the future in the process of how they treat the created order?*

3. Do they have views of starting and ending points for history? Where do they say that humans and animals, as well as the created world, came from? *What are people's attitudes toward history? Do they identify certain stories or events in their history that have strongly shaped what they believe? Do they believe that history is moving in a particular direction or is it just running in meaningless circles?*

4) What RELATIONSHIPS are evident?

Notice levels of curiosity, bluntness or subtlety, and showing appreciation for others. Notice patterns of formal and informal relationships. Notice good and bad relationships.

Here are some questions related to relationships for you to think about. The expanded questions for Level 4 are in italics.

A) RELATIONSHIP INTERACTION

1. Who interacts with whom? When? How? *To what degree is this based on their kinship relationships?*

2. When do people spend time together? Doing what? Is anyone excluded? *What does this demonstrate about their appreciation for time spent together? What about attitudes toward those who don't participate?*

3. Do all members interact with equal freedom? *What motivates people to interact with equal freedom or not to do so? What beliefs are motivating this interaction?*

4. Who touches whom and how? On what occasions? *What attitudes are displayed through physical contact? Is physical contact appreciated as a means of showing affection?*

5. Who visits whom and where? *What priority is placed on visiting others? What attitudes do people show when the responsibilities and rules for visiting aren't followed? What do they believe or assume about those who don't visit them?*

6. When, where and how do people interact, socialize, converse, eat together, meet, organize events, chat, gather? *What priority is placed on group gathering and interaction? Do people believe these activities are important? For what reasons?*

B) LEVELS AND TYPES OF RELATIONSHIPS WITHIN THE SOCIETY

1. What are the distinct social groups evident within the society? *What are people's attitudes toward social groupings? Are some groups appreciated more than others? What does this communicate about the overall worth of human beings collectively?*

2. What are the relationships between individuals of the same or different age, gender, social status, family groups? *What relationships are appreciated as most important?*

3. How many close relationships does a person develop and with whom? What are their obligations to one another in gift exchange, authority, respect, language? *What motivates people to develop close relationships with others? What are their attitudes towards the obligations of maintaining these relationships? What do they believe will occur if the relationships are not maintained?*

C) RELATIONSHIPS WITH THOSE OUTSIDE THE SOCIETY

1. How do people relate to outsiders? *What are people's attitudes toward outsiders? Do they prioritize hospitality towards them? What do they believe will happen if they don't show hospitality?*

2. Who do they fear, socialize with, scorn, suspect, accept from outside the society? *How do people show their attitudes towards these things? What beliefs are displayed in this process?*

D) FORMING AND BREAKING OF RELATIONSHIPS

1. Do you notice any consequences for being on bad terms with another person? How are these usually resolved? *How do people demonstrate that they are on bad terms with another person? What motivates these disagreements? How high of a priority is placed on reconciliation?*

2. Do you notice public confrontations over relationship differences? *What attitudes do people have about public confrontation? Do they prioritize private reconciliation more?*

E) RELATIONSHIPS BETWEEN THE PHYSICAL AND THE SPIRITUAL WORLD

1. Are there individual or group times of communing with spiritual beings? What are the rules of behavior in these contexts? *How much do people prioritize times of interacting with the spirit world? What beliefs motivate them to do so? What is the consequence for not taking this seriously?*

2. Do you notice specific practices in people's lives that might have to do with their respecting or fearing taboos and spirit beings? *What priority do they place on consistently following these practices? What do they say about the times when the practices don't produce the desired outcome?*

3. Are there people who are dedicated in a special way to the task of relating to spiritual beings? How are they identified? *What are people's attitudes towards these people? Are they highly respected in society? What powers are attributed to them? What kinds of things are believed to occur if they are disrespected?*

For the first eight weeks of daily learning plans for Level 4, you will read through and think about one of these life perspectives each day as you did in Level 3. Think about what you don't yet know or understand about the italicized questions in the lives of community members. In your *Life Perspectives Notebook*, WRITE DOWN for each question any behaviors and additional questions that you can think of to help you later explore this area. In order to help you, keep a printed copy of this revised list of life perspectives questions in your *Life Perspectives Notebook.*

In the second part of the daily learning plans for Level 4, you will begin to include the life perspectives topics into your conversations with community members. Further discussion questions are included later in this chapter to help you to explore these topics. As you explore the life perspectives at that point, you will make observation notes about the beliefs of community members that seem to be motivating their behavior based on your conversations with them.

SECTION ONE

Learning Exercises for Level 4

Learning Exercise 6 : Lifeview conversation

Your primary learning exercise for Level 4 is a conversational exercise for helping you explore the four life perspectives. The variations of this exercise are described in the following daily learning plans.

SECTION TWO

Daily Learning Plans for Level 4

The daily learning plans for Level 4 are outlined for you in the next few pages. You will notice that you will spend almost all of your time in conversation, in reviewing conversation, and in reflecting on conversation.

Your overall goal will be to participate in 100 daily learning plans for Level 3. Hopefully you can complete five daily learning plans each week. This would enable you to finish all 100 of the daily learning plans for Level 4 in 20 weeks or so.

Level 4 Daily Learning Plans 1 to 20

In the first 20 Level 4 daily learning plans you will return to the real life stories from your conversations in Level 3. Your goal is to ask more questions to HEAR examples of community members talking about broader lifeview issues that affect them, supporting their opinions about these topics, and discussing potential ideas or events that haven't happened. You will ask further questions to prompt discussion about unfamiliar situations that you can talk through together as well.

In order to think of topics for your *lifeview conversations* exercises, you will begin with the activities that you are familiar with from your notes and recordings of your Level 3 conversations. Remember, any activity has the potential to be a conversation topic!

We will use several examples to give you a basic framework for how you might take sample activities and ask questions to engage in these kinds of conversations. As a general rule, you should prepare three activities and questions for each activity for each daily learning plan. Each day you will talk to two individuals for two hours using the same set of activities with questions for both people. However, make sure to plan three DIFFERENT activities with questions to talk about for the next daily plan.

The key to this exercise is for you to ask good questions that relate to the life experience of the community members so that they will talk to you in Level 4 ways. For this reason you must take the time to think of good topics and questions in the local language before you begin each day.

Even with well-prepared questions in the local language, you will find that some people are more hesitant to talk about life in these ways than others, which is okay. Just keep in mind that each conversation is an opportunity to get to know that person better.

Remember, you have been developing close relationships for the past year to arrive at this point. This is critical, because you must EARN THE RIGHT to ask questions like this through your relationships with others. Be careful that you understand how these questions will impact each person with whom you are talking. Ask yourself first, "Will the person be offended by this topic or question? How might I adjust my questions to try to be sure that doesn't happen? How can I tell when I should stop talking about this because the person is uncomfortable?" You must learn to sensitively ask questions so you can help your friends feel comfortable in these conversations without feeling pressured or offended by you. This means that you have to learn to read others well and to realize that they are also reading you.

One of the primary ways that you can offend others is by showing a critical or judgmental attitude of their opinions and ideas. At this point, you want to simply hear all that they have to say and NOT give your opinion, not even in your body language! Your opportunity to give your opinions will come later.

Applying the lifeview conversations learning exercise

Here are some general steps for you to follow when you ask questions using the lifeview conversations learning exercise. You will apply this pattern many, many times over the coming months, so it is good for you to understand it well. You should practice the steps in your own language with people from your own community so that you have the process well in mind before you try in a second language.

1. First, identify a person to talk to. Make sure that the person can relate to the three activities you want to discuss. You will need to look through your Conversation Note-

book and review the notes and recordings that relate to that individual to help you with this. Have your recorder ready as well.

2. Spend a few minutes just talking with the person about how they are doing. Explain to the person that you want to learn more about how they talk and think about several activities. Can they help you? What are they up to that day?

3. Now turn on your recorder to begin recording the conversation. Move on to the first of the three activities that you have already identified. Set the stage for your conversation by asking about the person's life experience in relationship to this activity.

   You can also comment on what you've observed regarding how and when this activity takes place. Real examples based on your own observations and experience help you to ask relevant questions. They also serve to keep the conversation moving. See what the community member thinks of your examples and observations. Take the opportunity to ask further general questions about whatever you still don't know about the activity.

   For example, you may be living in a community where many people make gardens. You could establish the context by saying something like, "I know that many people make gardens in this community. I've gone out myself and helped in that process, so have a pretty good idea of the steps. I also know that most people have several gardens. How many do you have? How do you decide how many to make and where to make them?"

   Maybe one of your general questions is, "One question I've had but still don't know, perhaps you can help me. If a person makes a garden in a place, do they always have rights to that spot for the future?"

4. Once the person is engaging with you and has answered your general questions, you can ask a follow up question to try to relate that person's experience with the activity to the experience of others around them. One good approach is to ask the person to identify the benefits or difficulties associated with the activity. For example, in gardening you could ask about the difficulties: "What are some of the greatest difficulties that people encounter in gardening? What kinds of things keep gardens from being productive? How is gardening difficult?"

   The person might not know how to answer, so you may have to prompt them a little based on what you already know. They might respond by talking about land shortage, drought, stealing, domesticated animals ruining gardens, wild parrots eating the crops, enemy attacks keeping them from being able to garden, not doing the right protective incantations, others not following the proper behaviors at the right times, and so on. You may find that you don't understand some of the person's reply, though you should be familiar with much of this already due to your personal experience with the activity. For the statements that are unfamiliar to you, try to get further information from the person so that you can understand more about that. You could also ask about gardening benefits. For example, "What are some of the benefits from gardening? What kinds of things make gardens productive? Do you enjoy this activity? What do you enjoy about it?"

5. Once the person has described some of the benefits and difficulties, make a note of them, because each one gives you a further conversation topic. What are the reasons for and results from the difficulties and benefits? Who is responsible and who bears the consequences? For example, "You just mentioned that domesticated animals ruin lots of gardens. What are the reasons for and results from that? What are the results of that happening? Who is responsible?"

171

Work your way through the list of benefits and difficulties to find out the person's opinion of the reasons and results in this way.

6. After you have worked through the causes and solutions and have heard the person's opinion about these things, ask a couple of questions to show the opposite of the person's opinion to see if the person will defend their opinion. Use a generic phrase that talks about 'what they say' or what you've 'heard' from others about this issue. Avoid directly identifying yourself or the speakers who hold those opinions so as not to cause offense. Also be careful that you don't come across as argumentative.

   For example, "You mention that the animal owners are responsible when their animals mess up gardens. Also, though, I've heard some people say that the main problem is actually that the owners aren't building good fences to keep the animals out of their gardens. What do you think about that?"

7. Next try to ask the person about a situation related to the topic that isn't actually real or hasn't happened but that you'd like for them to speculate about. What do they think will help avoid the difficulties and add to the benefits? For example, "If you had the opportunity to speak with a group of community members about how they should take care of their domesticated animals, what would you tell them? What advice would you offer?" Another good question is to ask, "What would a person do to avoid difficulty and ensure that their gardening will be successful?" Or "What do you think makes a good gardener?"

8. Finally, ask about any unfamiliar contexts that the person might know something about related to this topic. Does he or she know anything about gardening in any other places? How do people do things in that other setting that they are aware of? What is their opinion of that way of doing things?

Once you've exhausted an activity, move on to the second of your three activities for conversation. You will be trying to spend two hours in conversation with each person, so don't be afraid to continue with a topic for close to an hour. You'd begin your second activity at step three from the steps outlined previously:

1. Move on to the second of the activities that you have a ready identified. Set the stage for your conversation by asking about the person's life experience in relationship to this activity.

   You can also comment on what you've observed regarding who and when this activity takes place. Real examples based on your own observations and experience help you to ask relevant questions. They also serve to keep the conversation moving. See what the community member thinks of your examples and observations. Take the opportunity to ask further general questions about whatever you still don't know about the activity.

   For example, you could establish the new activity related to outside employment by saying something like, "I remember you telling me the other day that your relative now has a job at that company located up the road. Is he still working there? What was his name again? How is he doing, have you seen him lately?"

2. Once the person has answered your general questions, you can ask a follow up question to try to relate that person's experience to the experience of others around them.

Ask questions about the benefits or difficulties associated with the activity. For example, in outside employment you could ask, "What are some of the advantages that your relative has working outside the community like that? What kinds of things are difficult for him? Why do you think he is working there?" The person might reply right away that their relative's daily life is easier now, that he has money, that he doesn't have to do so much manual labor, has higher prestige, and so on. They might also note the difficulties that their relative also has to deal with constant requests for things from others in their family and that they have to regularly send money back to them, that they can't be a part of the regular religious life of the local community and that they are under lots of pressure in the workplace. The relative also has a less healthy life for his children, since they tend to get into more trouble in that outside living situation.

3. Once the person has described some of the benefits and difficulties, make a note of them as further conversation topics. What are the reasons for and results from the difficulties and benefits? Who is responsible and who bears the consequences? For example, "You said that your relative's daily life is easier. In what kinds of ways?" Or "You said that your relative deals with constant requests from his family members back home for money. Why do they ask? Is the money not all theirs since they earned it? How does he or she respond to them? Is there a way for then to say no to the family members? If they do, how do they think of them?"

Work your way through the list of difficulties to find out the person's opinion of the reasons in this way.

4. After you have worked through the causes and solutions and have heard the person's opinion about these things, ask a couple of questions to show the opposite of the person's opinion to see if the person will defend their opinion. For example, "You mention that in general you think it is best for people not to live outside the community to work. Also, though, I've heard some people say that if no one ever works outside the community, then the whole community suffers from lack of prestige, knowledge, and income. What do you think of that idea?"

5. Next try to ask the person about a situation related to the activity that isn't actually real or hasn't happened but that you'd like for them to speculate about. What do they think would help avoid the difficulties and add to the benefits? For example, "If you had the chance to talk with your relative about all of this, what would you tell them? What advice would you offer?" Another good question is to ask, "What should your relative do to avoid difficulty and ensure that their life in that context will be successful?" Or "What do you think makes a good employee?"

6. Finally, ask about any unfamiliar contexts that the person might know something about related to this activity. Does he or she know anything about employment in any other places? How do people do things in that other setting that they are aware of? What is their opinion of that way of doing things?

Now you can move on to your third activity. Again, you'll go to step three of the process:

1. Set the stage for your conversation by asking about the person's life experience in relationship to this activity.

You can also comment on what you've observed regarding who and when this activity takes place. Real examples based on your own observations and experience help you to ask relevant questions. They also serve to keep the conversation moving.

See what the community member thinks of your examples and observations. Take the opportunity to ask further general questions about whatever you still don't know about the activity.

For example, you could talk about soccer: "I know that you play soccer quite often. Do you like the game? When did you play last? What position do you play?" You might take the opportunity to familiarize yourself with a few terms from the game that are unknown to you as well.

2. Ask questions about the benefits or difficulties. For example, in soccer you could ask, "Why do you play soccer? Can you think of any benefits to playing? Are there any difficulties that arise because of the game?"

The person might say that they really enjoy the exercise, and feels like soccer gives them a break from their daily working life. They also might talk about the fact that teamwork and unity are good things. They might also note difficulties. One could be that some people play soccer too much, and neglect their families and responsibilities as a result. They have seen cases where fighting breaks out as a result of a game. They have noticed that some of the players use soccer as a way to mistreat others, playing dirty and buying off referees during tournaments. Also, the teams sometimes get together after the games and waste money and time getting drunk.

3. What are the reasons for and results from the difficulties and benefits? Who is responsible and who bears the consequences? What brings these difficulties or benefits about? For example, "You said that you like to get exercise by playing. Is this one of the best ways you can do that?" Or "You said that some of the teams end up fighting after the games. Why do you think that is happening? What tends to be the result? Who is responsible?"

4. After you have worked through the causes and solutions and have heard the person's opinion about these things, ask a couple of questions to show the opposite of the person's opinion to see if the person will defend their opinion. For example, "Some people say that we should never play games like soccer, that we should just work to get our exercise. What do you think about that?"

5. Next try to ask the person about a situation that isn't actually real or hasn't happened but that you'd like for them to speculate about. What do they think will help avoid the difficulties and add to the benefits? For example, "If you had the chance to talk with your team about how to avoid the difficulties of the game, what would you tell them? What advice would you offer?" Another good question is to ask, "What should your team do to avoid difficulty and ensure that you will be successful?" Or "What do you think makes a good player or a good coach?"

6. Finally, ask about any unfamiliar contexts that the person might know something about related to this topic. Does he or she know anything about games in any other places? How do people do things in that other setting that they are aware of? What is their opinion of that way of doing things?

Using text in Level 4 exercises

The recordings of your texts at this level will be very long, as much as two hours for each recording. You won't have time to listen to them all, so don't try to do so. After you record your two conversations for the day, choose one or the other to listen to. Try to listen to the one that seems to provide the best information.

As you listen to the recording for two hours each day, make notes in your *Conversation Notebook*. Note down any further questions that you'd like to ask and any interesting observations that you've made.

After you listen to the recording, reflect on the four life perspectives for an hour. Use your *Life Perspectives Notebook* to note anything from the two conversations for the day that lends support to or serves as an example for any of the questions.

Daily time schedule for Level 4 (learning plans 1-20)

For a full-time learner using daily learning plans 1 to 20, your time should break down each day as follows:

Lifeview conversation exercise with two community members	4 hours
Review recorded lifeview conversation texts yourself	2 hours
Read and reflect on the four life perspectives	1 hour
Preparing for the next daily learning plan	1 hour
TOTAL:	8 hours

Level 4 Daily Learning Plans 1 to 20

This is a set of instructions that you can follow for your first 20 daily learning plans for Level 4. You should note the names of the individuals you plan to talk to each day in your *Daily Learning Plan Notebook*. You should also write out the questions that you will ask for each activity in that notebook.

THINGS TO DO FOR LEARNING PLANS 1 TO 20

1) Identify an individual and think of three activities. (Apply steps 2 to 8 to each of the three activities.)

Activity 1-

Activity2-

Activity 3-

2) Spend a few minutes just talking with the person.

3) Set the stage for your conversation by asking about the person's life experience in one of the activities. Ask other general questions you have.

4) Ask the person to identify the benefits and difficulties of the activity.

5) What are the reasons for and results from the difficulties and benefits? Who is responsible and who bears the consequences?

6) Ask questions that show the opposite of the person's opinion and allow them to respond.

7) Ask the person to speculate about what they think would help avoid the difficulties and add to the benefits. This would include events related to the topic that haven't happened but that they'd like to see take place, advice they would give to others about the activity, or how others could make the activity more successful.

8) Ask about unfamiliar contexts related to the activity that the person might know something about. What is their opinion of that context?

9) Each day on your own you should listen to one of your two lifeview conversation texts from that day for two hours. Make notes for yourself in your *Life Perspectives Notebook* of any important or relevant thoughts or questions.

10) Read and reflect on one of the four life perspectives for an hour. Make observation notes in your *Life Perspectives Notebook* from your conversations for the day that give insight into the life perspective questions.

11) Prepare tomorrow's daily learning plan.

Level 4 Daily Learning Plans 21 to 40

In the next 20 daily learning plans, you will continue on with the *lifeview conversations* exercise, only you will use the conversation opportunities to begin to support your opinions, discuss broader lifeview issues that affect you, and talk about potential ideas or events that haven't happened. You will also begin discussing unfamiliar situations with the community member.

You will do this by using the same question framework that we've introduced in the previous 20 plans. This time you will specifically use the conversations that you've recorded and listened to each day in plans 1 to 20 as models to follow.

In order to prepare for each daily learning plan 21 to 40, listen to the recording again of a specific previous conversation with a community member and read any notes that you have taken about that conversation. Take more notes in your *Conversation Notebook* to create an outline of the conversation with the key points that the person made as answers to your questions.

Plan to meet with the same individual again, only this time you will try to follow the *lifeview conversations* question framework to repeat back to them many of the thoughts and ideas that they have previously expressed to you. You can repeat these thoughts and ideas back as if you were that person and the ideas were your own.

In any areas where your attempts to restate the thoughts of the other person aren't clear, ask if the person can repeat their thoughts back again so that you can hear the best way to talk about that idea.

In addition to going back through the conversation with a community member, each week you will also choose a part of one of your previously recorded conversation texts to write out. Spend up to two hours each day working with the text yourself, writing it out in your *Text Notebook* and looking at the ways that the person manages to make their points and defend their thoughts and opinions. Leave three blank lines between each line of text so that you can note any words or phrases that you don't understand.

In order to choose a part of text to write down for each of the five weekdays, follow the question framework that we are using for the *lifeview conversations exercise*. Choose an activity that you talked about with the person that serves as a good example for you to write down.

DAY 1 - Write out a text where the person talked about the benefits and difficulties of one of the activities.

DAY 2 - Using the same topic of conversation from Day 1, write out the text where the person gives their opinions about the causes and solutions for the benefits and difficulties associated with the activity.

DAY 3 - Using the same conversation, write out the text where the person defends their opinion because you have given the opposite opinion.

DAY 4 - Using the same conversation, write out the text where the person speculates about something related to the topic that hasn't happened but that they would like to see take place, advice they would give to others about the activity, or how others could make the activity more successful.

DAY 5 - Using the same conversation, write out the text where the person talks about unfamiliar contexts related to the activity that they know something about.

Daily time schedule for Level 4 (learning plans 21-40)

For a full-time learner using daily learning plans 21 to 40, your time should break down each day as follows:

Lifeview conversation exercise with a community member	2 hours 30 minutes
Writing out texts of previous conversations	2 hours
Read and reflect on the four life perspectives	1 hour
Review recorded lifeview conversation texts and notes to prepare for the next daily learning plan	2 hours 30 minutes
TOTAL:	8 hours

Level 4 Daily Learning Plans 21 to 40

This is a set of instructions that you can follow for your daily learning plans 21 to 40 for Level 4.

THINGS TO DO FOR LEARNING PLANS 21 TO 40

1) Return to your notes and recordings from a conversation in learning plans 1 to 20. Tell the individual that you'd like to try to repeat their earlier thoughts so that you can learn how to do these things correctly.

(You will repeat steps 2 to 6 with each of the three activities that you talked about with that person before.)

2) Remind the person of one of the activities that you'd previously discussed with them. Give the person's opinion about the benefits and difficulties of the activity.

3) Tell about the reasons for and results from the difficulties and benefits. Explain who is responsible and who bears the consequences.

4) Make a statement that shows the opposite of the person's opinion and respond to the statement.

5) Speculate about what they think would help avoid the difficulties and add to the benefits. This would include events related to the topic that haven't happened but that they'd like to see take place, advice they would give to others about the activity, or how others could make the activity more successful.

6) Talk about unfamiliar contexts related to the activity that the person knows something about. Give their opinion of that context.

7) Each day write out a lifeview conversation text from that day for two hours.

8) Read and reflect on one of the four life perspectives for an hour. Make observation notes in your *Life Perspectives Notebook* from your conversations for the day that give insight into possible answers to the life perspective questions.

9) Review your recorded lifeview conversation texts and notes yourself to prepare for the next daily learning plan for 2 hours 30 minutes.

Level 4 Daily Learning Plans 41 to 100

In the last 60 daily learning plans, we will continue on with the lifeview conversations exercise. In these plans, however, you'll be asking specific questions related to the four life perspectives so that you can engage with community members about these issues. In each conversation your goal is to hear what the community member has to say about these topics, but also to share your observations and opinions to see if the person wants to offer a different point of view. In that way you will be having a conversation about the life perspectives topics rather than just asking and listening.

For each daily learning plan, first write down the plan number and plan topic in your *Daily Learning Plan Notebook*. Then follow the examples given below to also write out in your notebook the framework questions and examples that you will use to talk through this topic with two different individuals.

Don't forget to also include three hours each day for listening and reflecting on the recordings of your conversations. Make notes in your *Life Perspectives Notebook* as you do this. Also you will need to spend time each day preparing for the next day.

Daily time schedule for Level 4 (learning plans 41-100)

For a full-time learner using daily learning plans 41 to 100, your time should break down each day as follows:

Lifeview conversation exercise with two community members	4 hours
Listen and reflect on the conversations and make notes in your Life Perspectives Notebook	3 hours
Plan for the next day's plan	1 hour
TOTAL:	8 hours

Discussion questions day-by-day

You will once again be using the lifeview conversations question framework that you've already practiced in earlier Level 4 plans to talk to two different people each day for two hours each. Here is the basic framework:

1. Spend a few minutes just talking with the person.

2. Set the stage for the conversation by asking about the person's life experience in relationship to the life perspective topic. Ask further questions that you have about the topic at this time.
   You will prepare to do this by reviewing the observations related to that life perspective that you've previously made in your *Life Perspectives Notebook*. You should have example activities in the community that you can relate the questions to in this way.

3. Ask the person to identify the benefits and difficulties of the topic. What are the reasons for and results from the difficulties and benefits? Who is responsible and who bears the consequences?

4. Ask questions that show the opposite of the person's opinion and allow them to respond.

5. Ask the person what they think would help avoid the difficulties and add to the benefits. This would include events related to the topic that haven't happened but that they'd like to see take place, advice they would give to others about the topic, or how others could make the topic more successful.

6. Ask about unfamiliar contexts related to the topic that the person might know something about. What is their opinion of that context?

Here is a list of the life perspectives topics day-by-day with example questions from the *life-view conversations* question framework to stimulate your planning. You should find that almost every topic can be applied in some way to your setting. However, you will have to write your own questions based on the activities and circumstances in the community where you live. Write out your question framework with the specific questions you will ask in your *Daily Learning Plan Notebook* as you prepare for each day.

Remember that most people have never thought about or reflected on their lives in the kinds of ways described in these topics. This means that they won't understand and will not be able to have conversations about these topics without concrete examples that you have observed and can tie your questions to in specific ways. You must think about this and plan carefully before you begin your exercises each day. If the topics don't generate conversation, the fault is almost always poor questions and poor preparation, not the topic or the community member! For that reason, the questions below are only given as examples as you think and plan for yourself to write your own questions based on your own experience and observations in the community.

You may find that some topics are too big to cover in a single daily plan. In this case you can make a note of what you aren't able to cover and use those topics when you write your own plans toward the end of Level 4. You should also think of other life perspectives topics that are important in the community where you live that you can also note down to return to later.

Remember, you will be applying the life perspectives topics in a conversational format. For each step of the conversation process, first ask the community member for their thoughts and opinions on that step. When they have told you what they think, you then tell them your observations and ask what they thinks about those. Do they feel that your observations are accurate? Do they agree with your opinion or do they feel differently? Make sure that you present your opinions in a way that doesn't come across as critical or judgmental. Show appreciation for the other person's thoughts and opinions.

Sometimes you will find that answers to certain questions spill over into other areas and address other of your planned questions. This is fine, since your purpose is to hear the person's opinions in all of these things in a natural way. Don't worry if your plan for the conversation gets changed around or reordered. Focus on listening well and responding graciously. Try to cover all the areas associated with the question framework anyway, without needlessly asking questions that the person already answered in another way or at another time earlier in the conversation.

Level 4 Daily Learning Plan 41

The ways that languages are used in the community and the attitudes of community members toward those languages

1) Spend a few minutes just talking with the person.

2) Set the stage for the conversation by asking about the person's life experience in relationship to the life perspectives topic. Ask other general questions.

Ask about the person's experience in relationship to language use. For example, maybe you've noticed that people in this community tend to speak more than one language. Has the community member heard other languages besides the one that you are talking in? Do they know another language? If so, which ones?

You can give other examples of what you've observed regarding how and when the other languages are used. It is important for you to have already made these kinds of observations yourself to keep the conversation moving and to have real examples to relate your questions to. See what the community member thinks of your examples and observations.

Ask general questions: Does the person enjoy speaking their language? What language would they say that they knows best? Are they ever embarrassed by speaking their own language? How about when they are around others who are from the wider society? Do they want their children to learn the language? What language is most important for them to learn? What language would be best for them to learn to read and write in? Do they see that the children are learning more of a second language than their parents did? Do men speak more of the second language than the women do or vice-versa?

3) Ask the person to identify the benefits and difficulties of the topic. What are the reasons for and results from the difficulties and benefits? Who is responsible and who bears the consequences?

What does the community member tend to use the various languages for? What do others in the community use the languages for? Do they think that knowing more than one language is a good thing? What are some of the helpful aspects of knowing another language? What are some of the downsides of having more than one language in this community?

What complications does the community member think come with multiple languages in the community? Why is knowing more than one language beneficial? Why does it matter if people lose their language? Why is it important for the kids to learn the local language? What is the result if they do not? What is the result if children do not learn the majority language? Who is responsible and who bears the consequences for this difficulty or benefit?

You can also talk about what you've noticed about how others in the local community are helped or hindered by using more than one language from what you've observed. Remember not to try to teach people what they should be thinking or pass judgment on their ideas, but just try to encourage conversation. Ask the person again for their opinion of what you are saying.

4) Ask questions that show the opposite of the person's opinion and allow them to respond.

Perhaps you've heard some people say that learning a second language, especially the majority one, is causing the language to die in this community. They have said that knowing that second language is a good thing, so how would they respond to that kind of thought?

5) Ask the person what they think would help avoid the difficulties and add to the benefits. This would include events related to the topic that haven't happened but that they'd like to see take place, advice they would give to others about the topic, or how others could make the topic more successful.

> If learning other languages is a good thing and helpful for education and other purposes, what can be done to see that this increases?

> How can the community more consistently deal with the difficulties that they have mentioned?

> What would they like to see eventually with regard to the way languages are used in this community?

> What advice would the community member give to children, young people, and adults about their behavior in this area? To the more traditional community members? To the less traditional?

> What makes a person a good speaker of a second language? What kinds of things can a good speaker do?

6) Ask about unfamiliar contexts related to the activity that the person might know something about. What is their opinion of that context?

> Do they know of other places where people speak more than one language? Have them tell you about those situations and what their opinion is of them.

Level 4 Daily Learning Plan 42

The attitudes of community members toward information coming in from outside the community as well as their attitudes toward outside influence and societal change

1) Spend a few minutes just talking with the person.

2) Set the stage for the conversation by asking about the person's life experience in relationship to the life perspectives topic. Ask other general questions.

Perhaps you've noticed that certain people like buying newspapers and listening to the radio to hear about the world and country. You've also seen that nowadays people are starting to get televisions to watch DVDs. Are these things that the community member does as well?

You can give other examples of what you've observed regarding who and when these things take place. Real examples based on your own observations and experience help you to ask relevant questions. They also serve to keep the conversation moving. See what the community member thinks of your examples and observations.

Ask general questions: For example, What groups of people tend to participate in these activities the most? Do they think they are understanding much of what they are seeing and hearing, since most of that is in a second language?

3) Ask the person to identify the benefits and difficulties of the topic. What are the reasons for and results from the difficulties and benefits? Who is responsible and who bears the consequences?

Do they think that these forms of outside influence are a good thing? Why do they think that people want to participate in them? Do these outside sources of information cause any problems? What kind of problems do they see? Does participation affect their attitudes and behavior in any way?

Why do they think that listening to the radio or reading the newspaper is a good thing? How do people benefit? Who is responsible and who reaps this benefit?

Why do they say that watching television and DVDs seems to waste lots of time and changes traditional practice? Who is responsible and who bears the consequences for this happening?

You can also talk about what you've noticed about how others in the local community are helped or hindered in this area from what you've observed. Remember not to try to teach people what they should be thinking or pass judgment on their ideas, but just try to encourage conversation. Ask the person again for their opinion of what you are saying.

For example, perhaps you've noticed that while others listen to the radio for news, many times they misunderstand the reports because of the language barrier so actually are passing on misinformation.

4) Ask questions that show the opposite of the person's opinion and allow them to respond.

Perhaps you've heard some people say that the outside influences like this prepare the community to be more of a part of the larger society in a productive way. But the community member said that they tend to think that's not really true. What would they say to a person who thinks that way?

5) Ask the person what they think would help avoid the difficulties and add to the benefits. This would include events related to the topic that haven't happened but that they'd like to see take place, advice they would give to others about the topic, or how others could make the topic more successful.

What would they like to see eventually with regard to the way outside information sources come into this community?

What advice would the community member give to children, young people, and adults about their behavior in this area? To the more traditional community members? To the less traditional?

What makes a person a well-informed citizen? What kinds of things should a good citizen stay aware of?

6) Ask about unfamiliar contexts related to the activity that the person might know something about. What is their opinion of that context?

Do they know of other places where outside information has really affected the society? Have them tell you about those situations and what their opinion is of them.

Level 4 Daily Learning Plan 43

The value of formal learning and education to community members, including literacy

1) Spend a few minutes just talking with the person.

2) Set the stage for the conversation by asking about the person's life experience in relationship to the life perspectives topic. Ask other general questions.

> Perhaps you've noticed that people seem to think that education is a good thing here, and that parents work really hard to pay tuition fees for public schooling for their children. Did the community member have a chance to go to school themself or send their children (if they have any)? How about their spouse (if they have one)?

> *You can give other examples of what you've observed regarding who and when these things take place. Real examples based on your own observations and experience help you to ask relevant questions. They also serve to keep the conversation moving. See what the community member thinks of your examples and observations.*

> Ask general questions: For example, is the cost of tuition really high? Where do the kids get their books, uniforms, and school supplies? How does the school system really work? What is the school calendar like for school and holidays?

3) Ask the person to identify the benefits and difficulties of the topic. What are the reasons for and results from the difficulties and benefits? Who is responsible and who bears the consequences?

> Does the community member think that education for children is a good thing? Why do parents want education for their children? What are the benefits? Does this cause any problems, do they think? What kind of problems do they see? Does participation affect the attitudes and behavior of the children in any way?

> Why do they think that education is a good thing? What is the result of a good education? Who is responsible for promoting and maintaining this attitude? Who bears the consequences if this doesn't happen?

> If the community member thinks that school materials are hard to come by and tuition charges are too high, why is this the case? What is the result? Who is responsible and who bears the consequences?

> *You can also talk about what you've noticed about how others in the local community are helped or hindered in this area from what you've observed. Remember not to try to teach people what they should be thinking or pass judgment on their ideas, but just try to encourage conversation. Ask the person again for their opinion of what you are saying.*

> For example you've noticed that while children go to school and some get to the university level, the jobs afterward are rarely helpful to the needs of the community, because they are posted in far away places.

4) Ask questions that show the opposite of the person's opinion and allow them to respond.

> Perhaps you've heard some people say that school is just a waste of time and not a help to the local community. Others say that parents pay for tuition and act as if this is important, but really they just promote the education of their children to get money from them later when they get jobs in town. What do they think about that?

5) Ask the person what they think would help avoid the difficulties and add to the benefits. This would include events related to the topic that haven't happened but that they'd like to see take place, advice they would give to others about the topic, or how others could make the topic more successful.

> How can the community be more involved in seeing education promoted? What about the government?

> What would they like to see eventually with regard to education of children?

> What advice would the community member give to children, young people, and adults about their behavior in this area? To the more traditional community members? To the less traditional?

> What makes a person a good student? What about a good parent of a student?

6) Ask about unfamiliar contexts related to the activity that the person might know something about. What is their opinion of that context?

> Do they know of other places where people receive educations? Have them tell you about those situations and what their opinion is of them.

Level 4 Daily Learning Plan 44

Avoidance relationships in the society, as well as the overall degree and freedom of interaction between different relatives or family members in society

1) Spend a few minutes just talking with the person.

2) Set the stage for the conversation by asking about the person's life experience in relationship to the life perspectives topic. Ask other general questions.

Perhaps you've noticed that people interact with each other really freely in general in the community, but that certain relationships are more important than others. Does the community member think of certain relatives as more important than others for certain things? Which ones? Perhaps you've also seen that married men rarely, if ever, talk with their mother-in-laws. Is that true? How about the relationship that fathers have with their children? They don't really seem to do a lot of interacting with them.

You can give other examples of what you've observed regarding who and when these things take place. Real examples based on your own observations and experience help you to ask relevant questions. They also serve to keep the conversation moving. See what the community member thinks of your examples and observations.

Ask general questions: For example, maybe you've heard from others that brothers sometimes give their children to their brothers to raise. Is that true? When does that usually happen? Do other people do this besides just brothers or sisters?

3) Ask the person to identify the benefits and difficulties of the topic. What are the reasons for and results from the difficulties and benefits? Who is responsible and who bears the consequences?

Why does the community member think that people avoid their in-laws? What do they find helpful about the idea of people doing this? Are there any difficulties that arise as a result of not doing that? Who is responsible for the problems and who bears the consequences?

Why do people raise the children of others? What benefits come from raising the children of others in their opinion? Are there difficulties that they can think of that arise in these situations? Who is responsible for the problems and who bears the consequences?

What are some of the difficulties that come from the relationships to their uncles that they are especially close to? What are the benefits to them for these relationships?

How does raising the children of others create hardship for the adoptive family? Who is responsible and who bears the consequences for that problem?

Perhaps they said that uncles often force their relatives to take their advice on the marriage partners for their children and they don't like that. Why is that a problem? What is the result? Who is responsible and who bears the consequences?

Perhaps they said that it is often awkward to try to avoid their mother-in-law, especially when they are eating in close proximity or meeting her on the trail, and so on. Why is that awkward? What is the result? Who is responsible and who bears the consequences?

You can also talk about what you've noticed about how others in the local community are helped or hindered in this area from what you've observed. Remember not to try to teach people what they should be thinking or pass judgment on their ideas, but just try to encourage conversation. Ask the person again for their opinion of what you are saying.

4) Ask questions that show the opposite of the person's opinion and allow them to respond.

Perhaps you've heard some people say that the tradition of avoiding one's mother-in-law is something that is from the past that needs to be done away with. What do they think of that idea? What would they say to a person that says that?

5) Ask the person what they think would help avoid the difficulties and add to the benefits. This would include events related to the topic that haven't happened but that they'd like to see take place, advice they would give to others about the topic, or how others could make the topic more successful.

What would they like to see take place in the relationship that they have with their uncles with regard to the marriage of their children?

Would they like to see anything changed in their in-law relationships? If so, what would that be?

What advice would the community member give to children, young people, and adults about their behavior in this area? To the more traditional community members? To the less traditional?

What makes a person a good uncle? What about a good father, son-in-law, or mother-in-law?

6) Ask about unfamiliar contexts related to the activity that the person might know something about. What is their opinion of that context?

Do they know of other places where people relate to others differently? Have them tell you about those situations and what their opinion is of them.

Level 4 Daily Learning Plan 45

Formal and informal sources of information, including what kind of information and people that others listen to and how to present information so that others believe it to be true and important, as well as how people handle instances of contradictory information

1) Spend a few minutes just talking with the person.

2) Set the stage for the conversation by asking about the person's life experience in relationship to the life perspectives topic. Ask other general questions.

> Perhaps you've noticed that there are different ways to communicate information to others, and different levels to which people give importance to that information. For example, some information seems to be communicated early in the mornings by elders to the younger men as they are just awaking but all still in the common sleeping house. Also, the local government council member from the community sets up times of meetings to pass on government expectations. Then there are the religious men who pass on their insights from dreams and interaction with the spirits. Maybe you've also noticed that a lot of information comes and goes as just rumor in the community. Are there any other major ways that the community member can think of when people learn new things? What might those be?

> *You can give other examples of what you've observed regarding who and when these things take place. Real examples based on your own observations and experience help you to ask relevant questions. They also serve to keep the conversation moving. See what the community member thinks of your examples and observations.*

3) Ask the person to identify the benefits and difficulties of the topic. What are the reasons for and results from the difficulties and benefits? Who is responsible and who bears the consequences?

> What does the community member find beneficial about each of these sources of information? Are there any difficulties that arise as a result of the information communicated? Which sources of information do they find most reliable and which are the least reliable? Which do they feel are always true? Which do they feel almost always turn out to be true? Which are the ones that are least likely to be true?

> What makes them think of that source of information as reliable or unreliable?

> Why does difficulty arise when people pass misinformation? Is there benefit when people pass good information? What are the results either way? Who is responsible and who bears the consequences?

> If the community member hears contradictory information from two sources or even the same source, how do they decide which to believe? Is there a way that they might both be true?

> *You can also talk about what you've noticed about how others in the local community are helped or hindered in this area from what you've observed. Remember not to try to teach people what they should be thinking or pass judgment on their ideas, but just try to encourage conversation. Ask the person again for their opinion of what you are saying.*

4) Ask questions that show the opposite of the person's opinion and allow them to respond.

Perhaps you've heard some people say that the government information isn't all that helpful and comes from sources who may only be looking out for themselves. What do they think of that idea? What would they say to a person that says that?

Perhaps you've heard some people say that rumors are a good source of information. What do they think about that idea?

5) Ask the person what they think would help avoid the difficulties and add to the benefits. This would include events related to the topic that haven't happened but that they'd like to see take place, advice they would give to others about the topic, or how others could make the topic more successful.

If the community member finds that certain of these sources of information are reliable, what can be done to promote those sources over others that are less reliable?

If they find that these sources of information are unreliable, what do they think could be done to make them more reliable?

What would they like to see as the real sources of information in the community? Which would they like to make less important?

What advice would the community member give to children, young people, and adults about their behavior in this area? To the more traditional community members? To the less traditional?

What kinds of people make for good information sources? What kinds of people do they tend to trust and not to trust when they hear information through or from them?

6) Ask about unfamiliar contexts related to the activity that the person might know something about. What is their opinion of that context?

Do they know of other places where people give and trust information differently? Have them tell you about those situations and what their opinion is of them.

Level 4 Daily Learning Plan 46

*What is considered shameful behavior and what
is considered behavior to be proud of*

1) Spend a few minutes just talking with the person.

2) Set the stage for the conversation by asking about the person's life experience in relationship to the life perspectives topic. Ask other general questions.

> Perhaps you've noticed that there are those in the community that do things that others really are ashamed of or don't like at all. Can the community member think of any examples for you of these kinds of behaviors? What about the opposite? What kinds of behavior are people really proud of?

> *You can give other examples of what you've observed regarding who and when these things take place. Real examples based on your own observations and experience help you to ask relevant questions. They also serve to keep the conversation moving. See what the community member thinks of your examples and observations.*

3) Ask the person to identify the benefits and difficulties of the topic. What are the reasons for and results from the difficulties and benefits? Who is responsible and who bears the consequences?

> What does the community member think are the biggest problems that arise due to shameful behavior? What are the consequences for the individual and the community? Who is responsible?

> What do they think are the benefits that people and the community receive from behavior that they are proud of? Who is responsible to see that happen and who bears the consequences if it doesn't?

> What makes this difficult? What makes that beneficial? Why is that considered shameful? Why is this considered behavior to be proud of? What is the result of either?

> *You can also talk about what you've noticed about how others in the local community are helped or hindered in this area from what you've observed. Remember not to try to teach people what they should be thinking or pass judgment on their ideas, but just try to encourage conversation. Ask the person again for their opinion of what you are saying.*

4) Ask questions that show the opposite of the person's opinion and allow them to respond.

> Perhaps you've heard some people give different opinions about this. For example, perhaps some said that yelling at another person in public is actually okay. What would they say about that?

> Perhaps you've heard some people say that fighting physically over a disagreement isn't such a big deal. What do they think about that idea?

5) Ask the person what they think would help avoid the difficulties and add to the benefits. This would include events related to the topic that haven't happened but that they'd like to see take place, advice they would give to others about the topic, or how others could make the topic more successful.

> For behavior that is shameful, what does the community member think can be done to make it occur less?

For behavior to be proud of, what do they think can be done to promote that?

What would they like to see as the way that shameful behavior is handled by the community? Which behaviors would they eliminate if they could?

What advice would the community member give to children, young people, and adults about their behavior in this area? To the more traditional community members? To the less traditional?

What kinds of people make for good examples for others in the way they behave? What kinds of people make for bad examples?

6) Ask about unfamiliar contexts related to the activity that the person might know something about. What is their opinion of that context?

Do they know of other places where these behaviors are thought of differently? Have them tell you about those situations and what their opinion is of them.

Level 4 Daily Learning Plan 47

The value of individual versus group actions and decisions, cooperation versus competition

1) Spend a few minutes just talking with the person.

2) Set the stage for the conversation by asking about the person's life experience in relationship to the life perspectives topic. Ask other general questions.

Perhaps you've noticed that there is a lot of cooperation amongst members of the community for decisions made and for the tasks done each day. Like when a person is doing leaves for their house roof, lots of people help to get that done. However, there are some people who do what they want and don't seem to cooperate with others very much. Can the community member think of any examples of these kinds of behaviors? What do people tend to do together and what do they do by themselves? Who helps whom and in what situations?

You can give other examples of what you've observed regarding who and when these things take place. Real examples based on your own observations and experience help you to ask relevant questions. They also serve to keep the conversation moving. See what the community member thinks of your examples and observations.

Perhaps you also notice that people don't seem to compete with each other very much. Even when the community plays games, people tend to just have fun and not worry about who wins. Is this true in general, do they think? Can they think of any situations where people tend to compete with each other over things, land, and so on?

3) Ask the person to identify the benefits and difficulties of the topic. What are the reasons for and results from the difficulties and benefits? Who is responsible and who bears the consequences?

What does the community member think are the benefits or difficulties that people and the community receive from cooperating?

What do they think are the benefits or difficulties that arise when people act individually?

What do they think are the benefits and difficulties to competing?

Do they think that people tend to feel pressure from others to act together instead of on their own? What happens when people make individual instead of group decisions about their lives?

Why do they say that trouble comes to the group when people act individually? Who is responsible and who bears the consequences for that?

Why do they say that more is accomplished when people work together or decide together? Have them explain that to you.

What is the reason for why they think that competition only causes difficulty? What is the result?

You can also talk about what you've noticed about how others in the local community are helped or hindered in this area from what you've observed. Remember not to try to teach people what they should be thinking or pass judgment on their ideas, but just try to encourage conversation. Ask the person again for their opinion of what you are saying.

4) Ask questions that show the opposite of the person's opinion and allow them to respond.

Perhaps you've heard some people say that it would be a lot easier to function if they could just decide and do things for themselves without worry about what the group thinks. What do they say to that idea?

Maybe some people say that competing helps people to try harder and do better. What would they say to someone who tells them that?

5) Ask the person what they think would help avoid the difficulties and add to the benefits. This would include events related to the topic that haven't happened but that they'd like to see take place, advice they would give to others about the topic, or how others could make the topic more successful.

What would the community member like to see as the way in which group and individual actions actually take place? What procedure should be followed?

What advice would the community member give to children, young people, and adults about their behavior in this area? To the more traditional community members? To the less traditional?

What kinds of people make for good examples for others in the way they include others? What kinds of people make for bad examples of this?

What kinds of competition are okay and what kinds are not? What kinds of people are good and bad examples in these areas?

6) Ask about unfamiliar contexts related to the activity that the person might know something about. What is their opinion of that context?

Does the community member know of other places where people handle these issues differently? Have them tell you about those situations and what their opinion is of them.

Level 4 Daily Learning Plan 48

Ownership, borrowing and loaning in the community

1) Spend a few minutes just talking with the person.

2) Set the stage for the conversation by asking about the person's life experience in relationship to the life perspectives topic. Ask other general questions.

> Perhaps you've noticed that each household has possessions, land, and trees that they claim the right to. How did they come by these rights? Does the community member have any of these things?

> What does the community member feel is the proper process for borrowing and loaning things?

> What kinds of items can be loaned and borrowed? What items are never loaned and borrowed?

> *You can give other examples of what you've observed regarding who and when these things take place. Real examples based on your own observations and experience help you to ask relevant questions. They also serve to keep the conversation moving. See what the community member thinks of your examples and observations.*

3) Ask the person to identify the benefits and difficulties of the topic. What are the reasons for and results from the difficulties and benefits? Who is responsible and who bears the consequences?

> What does the community member think are the benefits and difficulties of loaning items to others? What are the benefits and difficulties of owning things, land, trees, and so on?

> What makes others borrowing their tools difficult? Who is responsible and who bears the consequences for creating the difficulty?

> Why do they say that having people always ask to borrow things from them is a benefit? Have them explain the good that results from that.

> Why do they say that you are actually better off owning very little yourself but always borrowing from others?

> *You can also talk about what you've noticed about how others in the local community are helped or hindered in this area from what you've observed. Remember not to try to teach people what they should be thinking or pass judgment on their ideas, but just try to encourage conversation. Ask the person again for their opinion of what you are saying.*

4) Ask questions that show the opposite of the person's opinion and allow them to respond.

> Perhaps you've heard some people say that it would be better if all the tools and land were owned and shared by the whole community. What does the community member think of that idea?

> Perhaps some people act as if the difference between borrowing and stealing isn't very clear, and that taking something without asking and not returning it isn't stealing. What do they think of that idea?

5) Ask the person what they think would help avoid the difficulties and add to the benefits.

This would include events related to the topic that haven't happened but that they'd like to see take place, advice they would give to others about the topic, or how others could make the topic more successful.

What would the community member like to see as the way in which people in the community own and borrow property or tools?

What advice would the community member give to children, young people, and adults about their behavior in this area? To the more traditional community members? To the less traditional?

What kinds of people make for good examples for others in this area? What kinds of people make for bad examples of this?

6) Ask about unfamiliar contexts related to the activity that the person might know something about. What is their opinion of that context?

Doe they know of other places where people handle these issues differently? Have them tell you about those situations and what their opinion is of them.

Level 4 Daily Learning Plan 49

The factors that identify members of the people group in contrast to others and how the group thinks of and deals with those who don't display these characteristics, people who display disability or difference from others

1) Spend a few minutes just talking with the person.

2) Set the stage for the conversation by asking about the person's life experience in relationship to the life perspectives topic. Ask other general questions.

Perhaps you've noticed that members of the community are quick to identify those who are from other places, even when those people have lived in this community a long, long time. What are the things that make a person part of this group? What are the things that mark someone as not from this community? Are there cases where people who are group outsiders have actually become part of the group and community members don't think of them or their children as outsiders anymore?

Perhaps you've also noticed that some people tend not to accept others with disabilities of some kind and poke fun at them because they are different. Perhaps you've heard also that mothers and fathers of twins or of children born with noticeable disabilities usually get rid of them when they are born. Is this true? Have them explain that to you.

You can give other examples of what you've observed regarding how and when these things take place. Real examples based on your own observations and experience help you to ask relevant questions. They also serve to keep the conversation moving. See what the community member thinks of your examples and observations.

3) Ask the person to identify the benefits and difficulties of the topic. What are the reasons for and results from the difficulties and benefits? Who is responsible and who bears the consequences?

What are the reasons why the community member thinks it a benefit to be a part of the group? What are the difficulties of being considered part of the group? What kinds of behaviors show that people aren't really acting like part of the group, even if they look and sound like group members?

What are the benefits and difficulties of being a group outsider? How about for being a person born with a disability of some kind?

Why is it a benefit to all have the same ancestry? To all speak the same language? To all look the same? To do things in the same way and to have the same traditions?

Why is it so difficult for outsiders to become a real part of the group, do they think? What are the reasons why they never really can become insiders? What is the result of them never becoming insiders?

What do they think motivates people to make fun of others who are different? What is the result in their lives?

What do they think motivates the parents to get rid of children with disabilities when they are born? Who is responsible and who bears the consequences for the person being born in that condition? What is the result?

You can also talk about what you've noticed about how others in the local community are helped or hindered in this area from what you've observed. Remember not to try to teach people what they should be thinking or pass judgment on their ideas, but just try to encourage conversation. Ask the person again for their opinion of what you are saying.

4) Ask questions that show the opposite of the person's opinion and allow them to respond.

Perhaps some people say that it would be better if communities were actually made up of people from lots of different places so that new thoughts and ideas could be introduced. What would they say to a person that says that?

Perhaps some people think that language is the most important marker of being part of the group, while they might think that how someone looks is more important. What would they tell a person who says that?

5) Ask the person what they think would help avoid the difficulties and add to the benefits. This would include events related to the topic that haven't happened but that they'd like to see take place, advice they would give to others about the topic, or how others could make the topic more successful.

What would they like to see as the way in which people think about those who are a part of the group and those who are not?

What advice would the community member give to children, young people, and adults about their behavior in this area? To the more traditional community members? To the less traditional?

What kinds of people make for good example for others in representing the group? What kinds of people make for bad examples of the group?

6) Ask about unfamiliar contexts related to the activity that the person might know something about. What is their opinion of that context?

Do they know of other places where people handle these issues differently? Have them tell you about those situations and what their opinion is of them.

Level 4 Daily Learning Plan 50

The prestige associated with being a group insider, as well as the attitudes of those within the group toward outsiders and the attitudes of outsiders toward those within the group. The attitudes of the group toward other races and cultures

1) Spend a few minutes just talking with the person.

2) Set the stage for the conversation by asking about the person's life experience in relationship to the life perspectives topic. Ask other general questions.

Perhaps you've noticed that some members of the community don't enjoy the idea of being part of this group when they compare themselves with others from the outside. For example, it seems to be the case that some think that people with lighter skin have greater value than those with dark skin. Also, that those who speak the outside language are thought of more highly and are treated with respect. Do they think this is true? How do they think of these things?

Perhaps you've noticed that sometimes those from the outside poke fun at communities like this one. Do they think that happens? How do they think those from the other groups think about this community?

How do people in the group here think of other races and cultures? Are there some who are thought of more highly than others? Which ones are thought of the best and which the worst?

You can give other examples of what you've observed regarding who and when these things take place. Real examples based on your own observations and experience help you to ask relevant questions. They also serve to keep the conversation moving. See what the community member thinks of your examples and observations.

3) Ask the person to identify the benefits and difficulties of the topic. What are the reasons for and results from the difficulties and benefits? Who is responsible and who bears the consequences?

What are the reasons why the community member thinks the high prestige groups that they have identified are thought of in that way? What are the benefits to being a part of those higher prestige groups?

What are the reasons why they think the lower prestige groups that they have identified are thought of in that way? What are the stigmas of being a part of those lower prestige groups?

Why does the community member think it is a benefit to speak the majority language and have lighter skin? Who is responsible and who bears the consequences for this kind of thinking, the higher prestige groups or those of lower prestige, or both? What is the result of that thinking?

Why do they think that it is difficult to be a part of certain of the races that they has identified? Who is responsible and who bears the consequences for this idea? Is it widespread?

You can also talk about what you've noticed about how others in the local community are helped or hindered in this area from what you've observed. Remember not to try to teach people what they should be thinking or pass judgment on their ideas, but just try to encourage conversation. Ask the person again for their opinion of what you are saying.

4) Ask questions that show the opposite of the person's opinion and allow them to respond.

Perhaps some people say that it would be better if there were no race differences and all people were exactly the same in every way. What do they think of that idea?

Perhaps some people say that having darker skin and knowing a local language shows that you are really from the community, and that is more important than having lighter skin and a language from the outside. What would they say to a person who thinks that?

5) Ask the person what they think would help avoid the difficulties and add to the benefits. This would include events related to the topic that haven't happened but that they'd like to see take place, advice they would give to others about the topic, or how others could make the topic more successful.

How would the community member like for those from the outside to think of members of this community?

How would they like for members of the community to think of those outside, including other races and cultures?

What advice would the community member give to children, young people, and adults about their behavior in this area? To the more traditional community members? To the less traditional?

What kinds of people make for good example for others in this area? What kinds of people make for bad examples?

6) Ask about unfamiliar contexts related to the activity that the person might know something about. What is their opinion of that context?

Do they know of other places where people handle these issues differently? Have them tell you about those situations and what their opinion is of them.

Level 4 Daily Learning Plan 51

The roles and responsibilities of different members of society
and the perceived value of the different roles and individuals;
my role in the society and how that is viewed

1) Spend a few minutes just talking with the person.

2) Set the stage for the conversation by asking about the person's life experience in relationship to the life perspectives topic. Ask other general questions.

> Perhaps you've noticed that different members of the community have different roles and jobs. For example, the women carry wood and harvest garden produce, while the men cut down the big trees in new gardens and build houses. Young people, too, have certain jobs, as do children and others. Can the community member think of the specific roles that each of the different groups has and describe those for you?

> *You can give other examples of what you've observed regarding who and when these things take place. Real examples based on your own observations and experience help you to ask relevant questions. They also serve to keep the conversation moving. See what the community member thinks of your examples and observations.*

3) Ask the person to identify the benefits and difficulties of the topic. What are the reasons for and results from the difficulties and benefits? Who is responsible and who bears the consequences?

> What does the community member think is good and what is hard about being a man or woman (whatever gender they are) in this society? What about being a man, woman, or a child, or a young person? What are the things they face that are hard for them? What kinds of advantages do they have?

> Are some of these groups more important or thought of more highly than others? Why is that the case? What is the result?

> Why do they think that it is better to be a man/woman, over man/woman in this society or vice-versa? What is the result for the men and the women?

> Why do they think that it is good to be a child? Why are young people better off than adults in their opinion?

> *You can also talk about what you've noticed about how others in the local community are helped or hindered in this area from what you've observed. Remember not to try to teach people what they should be thinking or pass judgment on their ideas, but just try to encourage conversation. Ask the person again for their opinion of what you are saying.*

4) Ask questions that show the opposite of the person's opinion and allow them to respond.

> Perhaps some people say that if a man goes and carries firewood for his wife, that is a good thing, even though that is her job. What does the community member say about that?

> Perhaps some people say that children should work more and play less. What would they say to a person that says that?

5) Ask the person what they think would help avoid the difficulties and add to the benefits.

This would include events related to the topic that haven't happened but that they'd like to see take place, advice they would give to others about the topic, or how others could make the topic more successful.

What kinds of things does the community member think can be done to see that others fulfill their roles in the community? Men and women? Children? Young people?

What advice would the community member give to children, young people, and adults about their behavior in this area? To the more traditional community members? To the less traditional?

What kinds of people make for good examples for others in this area? What kinds of people make for bad examples?

6) Ask about unfamiliar contexts related to the activity that the person might know something about. What is their opinion of that context?

Do they know of other places where people handle these issues differently? Have them tell you about those situations and what their opinion is of them.

Level 4 Daily Learning Plan 52

Information and individuals who are confrontational in the community, and how bringing embarrassment to others is generally viewed and dealt with

1) Spend a few minutes just talking with the person.

2) Set the stage for the conversation by asking about the person's life experience in relationship to the life perspectives topic. Ask other general questions.

Perhaps you've noticed that most people in this community try not to directly yell at or speak to a person who has offended or irritated them with something. Does the community member see that public confrontation ever happen? When does it happen the most? Is that a good thing?

If someone does something to embarrass another person, how do people think of that? For example, if a young person is doing something that the community member doesn't like, would they tell them to stop? Or if an older man borrows their axe and doesn't bring it back, would they ask him to return it? Or if their brother says something about them that they don't like, what should they do?

Perhaps some people just really seem to be willing to confront others in public like this. How do most people in the community think of that?

You can give other examples of what you've observed regarding who and when these things take place. Real examples based on your own observations and experience help you to ask relevant questions. They also serve to keep the conversation moving. See what the community member thinks of your examples and observations.

3) Ask the person to identify the benefits and difficulties of the topic. What are the reasons for and results from the difficulties and benefits? Who is responsible and who bears the consequences?

Does the community member think that there is anything good about embarrassing another person publicly? Maybe you can recall a time when one adult brother built a fence around the property to show his other adult brother that he was unhappy with him. Is that a good way to do things? The other brother seemed really ashamed and embarrassed. What are the bad results of embarrassing others publicly? What are the good results? Who is responsible and who bears the consequences?

Does the community member think that a person should care if another person gets embarrassed? Why should they care and when is this most important?

You can also talk about what you've noticed about how others in the local community are helped or hindered in this area from what you've observed. Remember not to try to teach people what they should be thinking or pass judgment on their ideas, but just try to encourage conversation. Ask the person again for their opinion of what you are saying.

4) Ask questions that show the opposite of the person's opinion and allow them to respond.

Perhaps some people say that if a person does something wrong, they should be embarrassed and others shouldn't feel bad about that. What would the community member say to a person who says that?

Perhaps some people say that the most important thing is the age of person. Once others get married, care needs to be taken not to embarrass them. What would their response be?

5) Ask the person what they think would help avoid the difficulties and add to the benefits. This would include events related to the topic that haven't happened but that they'd like to see take place, advice they would give to others about the topic, or how others could make the topic more successful.

> What kinds of things does the community member think can be done to see that people don't get publicly embarrassed like this?

> What advice would the community member give to children, young people, and adults about their behavior in this area? To the more traditional community members? To the less traditional?

> What kinds of people make for good example for others in this area? What kinds of people make for bad examples?

6) Ask about unfamiliar contexts related to the activity that the person might know something about. What is their opinion of that context?

> Do they know of other places where people handle these issues differently? Have them tell you about those situations and what their opinion is of them.

Level 4 Daily Learning Plan 53

The kinds of close relationships between ages and genders and how these relationships are maintained and broken

1) Spend a few minutes just talking with the person.

2) Set the stage for the conversation by asking about the person's life experience in relationship to the life perspectives topic. Ask other general questions.

> Perhaps you've noticed that certain people in the community tend to spend their time with certain other people. This happens with children, with young people, and with adults as well. What does the community member think that these times of spending time with others are based on? Family relationships, clan relationships, kinship?

> *Again, you will need to give examples of what you've observed regarding who and when these things take place. Real examples based on your own observations and experience help you to ask relevant questions. They also serve to keep the conversation moving. See what the community member thinks of your examples and observations.*

3) Ask the person to identify the benefits and difficulties of the topic. What are the reasons for and results from the difficulties and benefits? Who is responsible and who bears the consequences?

> In the relationships that the community member has described to you for children, young people, and adults, what are the benefits in the different relationships? What do they think the biggest difficulties are?

> What does the community member think that different ones need to do to maintain the relationship? What are their obligations?

> What are the reasons that the community member thinks that these different relationships are broken? Are there any reasons why a relationship should be broken? What is the proper or normal way to do this? What are the results of doing this and not doing this? Who is responsible if this does not occur and who bears the consequences?

> *You can also talk about what you've noticed about how others in the local community are helped or hindered in this area from what you've observed. Remember not to try to teach people what they should be thinking or pass judgment on their ideas, but just try to encourage conversation. Ask the person again for their opinion of what you are saying.*

4) Ask questions that show the opposite of the person's opinion and allow them to respond.

> Perhaps some people say that relationships between young people are always fraught with difficulty because of the danger of immorality. But maybe the community member has said that they think some aspects of these relationships are helpful. What would the community member say to a person that thinks they should stay apart all the time?

> Perhaps some people say that children should only play with those from their own clans. But maybe the community member has said that any opportunity for them to play with others is fine. What would the community member say to a person that holds to the other opinion?

5) Ask the person what they think would help avoid the difficulties and add to the benefits. This would include events related to the topic that haven't happened but that they'd like to see take place, advice they would give to others about the topic, or how others could make the topic more successful.

> What kinds of things does the community member think should be done to see that relationships don't get broken?

> What advice would the community member give to children, young people, and adults about their behavior in this area? To the more traditional community members? To the less traditional?

> What kinds of people make for good example for others in this area? What kinds of people make for bad examples?

6) Ask about unfamiliar contexts related to the activity that the person might know something about. What is their opinion of that context?

> Do they know of other places where people handle these issues differently? Have them tell you about those situations and what their opinion is of them.

Level 4 Daily Learning Plan 54

The ways to disagree and reconcile in times of relationship conflict, as well as the value of private versus public confrontation

1) Spend a few minutes just talking with the person.

2) Set the stage for the conversation by asking about the person's life experience in relationship to the life perspectives topic. Ask other general questions.

> Perhaps you've noticed that relationships in the community undergo times of conflict. This happens with children, with young people, and with adults as well. What does the community member notice about times of relationship conflict? Family relationships, clan relationships, kinship?

> *Again, you will need to give examples of what you've observed regarding who and when these things take place. Real examples based on your own observations and experience help you to ask relevant questions. They also serve to keep the conversation moving. See what the community member thinks of your examples and observations.*

3) Ask the person to identify the benefits and difficulties of the topic. What are the reasons for and results from the difficulties and benefits? Who is responsible and who bears the consequences?

> In the relationships that the community member has described to you for children, young people, and adults, what do they think the biggest difficulties are that arise as a result of conflict?

> Do they think there are any benefits that come from times of conflict?

> What do they feel is the proper process of reconciliation in each case? What is the result of following the proper process? What is the result of not doing so? Who is responsible and who bears the consequences?

> What do they think are the reasons that people tend to have conflicts? Who are the parties that are most responsible in each case?

> *You can also talk about what you've noticed about how others in the local community are helped or hindered in this area from what you've observed. Remember not to try to teach people what they should be thinking or pass judgment on their ideas, but just try to encourage conversation. Ask the person again for their opinion of what you are saying.*

4) Ask questions that show the opposite of the person's opinion and allow them to respond.

> Perhaps some people say that relationships between young people are always fraught with difficulty because of the danger of immorality. But maybe the community member has said that they think some aspects of these relationships are helpful. What would the community member say to a person that thinks they should stay apart all the time?

> Perhaps some people say that children should only play with those from their own clans. But maybe the community member has said that any opportunity for them to play with others is fine. What would the community member say to a person that holds to the other opinion?

5) Ask the person what they think would help avoid the difficulties and add to the benefits. This would include events related to the topic that haven't happened but that they'd like to see take place, advice they would give to others about the topic, or how others could make the topic more successful.

> What does the community member think that different ones need to do to avoid these conflicts? What are their obligations to one another?

> What advice would the community member give to children, young people, and adults about their behavior in this area? To the more traditional community members? To the less traditional?

> What kinds of people make for good example for others in this area? What kinds of people make for bad examples?

6) Ask about unfamiliar contexts related to the activity that the person might know something about. What is their opinion of that context?

> Do they know of other places where people handle these issues differently? Have them tell you about those situations and what their opinion is of them.

Level 4 Daily Learning Plan 55

Those with authority who lead and make decisions for the group and the level of respect given to them. How these leaders gained their authority and to what extent people heed their leadership

1) Spend a few minutes just talking with the person.

2) Set the stage for the conversation by asking about the person's life experience in relationship to the life perspectives topic. Ask other general questions.

Perhaps you've noticed some of the decisions that get made in the community and have noted some of the leaders who typically speak out. Maybe at times leaders clearly give their opinions and so people follow these ideas. Sometimes perhaps other people speak and nothing comes of the idea. Still other times a decision is made but you are unclear about what caused the decision to be made. For the various examples that you give to the community member, can they explain the process for these decisions? Who has the authority to make them? Where do they get that authority? Who gives it to them?

Again, you will need to give examples of what you've observed regarding who and when these things take place. Real examples based on your own observations and experience help you to ask relevant questions. They also serve to keep the conversation moving. See what the community member thinks of your examples and observations.

3) Ask the person to identify the benefits and difficulties of the topic. What are the reasons for and results from the difficulties and benefits? Who is responsible and who bears the consequences?

In the various decision-making situations that the community member has described for you, have them explain to you the benefits and difficulties with each of the different decision-making processes.

For example, maybe some decisions are made because individuals come back from their gardens claiming to have seen spirits of those who have died, so the whole community has to take action to cleanse the spirit. What does the community member think are the benefits of following that person's idea about the spirit? What are the consequences if people do not? What are the difficulties that arise from following these kinds of opinions? Who are the parties that are most responsible in each case?

Maybe you notice other decisions made because older people in the community stand up and tell others what they've seen in a dream or been told by a spirit about what should be done. What does the community member think are the benefits of following that person's idea about the spirit? What are the consequences if people do not? What are the difficulties that arise from following these kinds of opinions? Who are the parties that are most responsible in each case?

You can also talk about what you've noticed about how others in the local community are helped or hindered in this area from what you've observed. Remember not to try to teach people what they should be thinking or pass judgment on their ideas, but just try to encourage conversation. Ask the person again for their opinion of what you are saying.

4) Ask questions that show the opposite of the person's opinion and allow them to respond.

Perhaps some people say that those who claim to have seen the spirits of the dead are usually just trying to make trouble and they shouldn't be believed. What does the community member think of that opinion?

Perhaps some people say that listening to elder community members is a good idea sometimes, but not when they all think that his idea is going to bring hardship on the others in the community. What does the community member think of that opinion?

5) Ask the person what they think would help avoid the difficulties and add to the benefits. This would include events related to the topic that haven't happened but that they'd like to see take place, advice they would give to others about the topic, or how others could make the topic more successful.

What does the community member think that different ones need to do to avoid the difficulties and reap the benefits with regard to leaders and decisions?

What advice would the community member give to children, young people, and adults about their behavior in this area? To the more traditional community members? To the less traditional?

What kinds of people make for good example for others in this area? What kinds of people make for bad examples?

6) Ask about unfamiliar contexts related to the activity that the person might know something about. What is their opinion of that context?

Do they know of other places where people handle these issues differently? Have them tell you about those situations and what their opinion is of them.

Level 4 Daily Learning Plan 56

Influential or successful members of society and why these individuals are viewed in such a light, as well as the level of appreciation shown to them for their success. The attitudes of these influential individuals toward others

1) Spend a few minutes just talking with the person.

2) Set the stage for the conversation by asking about the person's life experience in relationship to the life perspectives topic. Ask other general questions.

Perhaps you've noticed that certain people in society are viewed as more successful than others. Can the community member think of people in the society who are thought of in this way? Why do they think they are considered successful? Do people appreciate their success or are they envious? Do the attitudes of successful people tend to be positive or negative toward those who aren't successful? What are their obligations toward others in society? Toward their family members?

Again, you will need to give examples of what you've observed regarding who and when these things take place. Real examples based on your own observations and experience help you to ask relevant questions. They also serve to keep the conversation moving. See what the community member thinks of your examples and observations.

3) Ask the person to identify the benefits and difficulties of the topic. What are the reasons for and results from the difficulties and benefits? Who is responsible and who bears the consequences?

What does the community member see as the main benefits of being successful? For each benefit, what do they think causes that benefit? What are the results of that benefit? Who is responsible for that benefit?

What do they think are the main difficulties? For each difficulty, what do they think causes that difficulty? What are the results of the difficulty? Who is responsible and who bears the consequences for that difficulty?

You can also talk about what you've noticed about how others in the local community are helped or hindered in this area from what you've observed. Remember not to try to teach people what they should be thinking or pass judgment on their ideas, but just try to encourage conversation. Ask the person again for their opinion of what you are saying.

4) Ask questions that show the opposite of the person's opinion and allow them to respond.

Perhaps some people say that success only brings trouble and bad attitudes on both sides, so is best not to happen. What does the person think of that opinion?

Perhaps some people say that successful people should pour all of their success and profit back into the community so that all are equally benefitting. What do they think of that opinion?

5) Ask the person what they think would help avoid the difficulties and add to the benefits. This would include events related to the topic that haven't happened but that they'd like to see take place, advice they would give to others about the topic, or how others could make the topic more successful.

What does the community member think that successful people should do to behave rightly toward others? What do they think that less successful people should do to behave rightly toward the successful?

What advice would the community member give to children, young people, and adults about their behavior in this area? To the more traditional community members? To the less traditional?

What kinds of people make for good example for others in this area? What kinds of people make for bad examples?

6) Ask about unfamiliar contexts related to the activity that the person might know something about. What is their opinion of that context?

Do they know of other places where people handle these issues differently? Have them tell you about those situations and what their opinion is of them.

Level 4 Daily Learning Plan 57

The community view of time and making and breaking time commitments, as well as how people use their time based on their societal roles

1) Spend a few minutes just talking with the person.

2) Set the stage for the conversation by asking about the person's life experience in relationship to the life perspectives topic. Ask other general questions.

Perhaps you've noticed that people in the community have a very loose view of time and time commitments. Often when you plan to do something at a certain time with them, the plan changes and people don't seem to be bothered by that fact. Can the community member give some examples of this happening? Why do they think that this happens? How do they think that most people in the society view time and the use of time? Do they feel that they are committed to only working as much as they have to in order to complete tasks, or are there some people who work longer hours than are expected? Why does the community member think that happens?

Does the community member feel that how people use their time is related to their role in society? For example, are children expected to use their time in certain ways? Young people? Adults? Married people? Elderly people?

Again, you will need to give examples of what you've observed regarding who and when these things take place. Real examples based on your own observations and experience help you to ask relevant questions. They also serve to keep the conversation moving. See what the community member thinks of your examples and observations.

3) Ask the person to identify the benefits and difficulties of the topic. What are the reasons for and results from the difficulties and benefits? Who is responsible and who bears the consequences?

What does the community member see as the main benefits of meeting or not meeting time commitments?

What do they think are the main difficulties of meeting or not meeting time commitments? Who is responsible and who bears the consequences?

What do they feel causes people to decide not to meet time commitments? What are the common reasons and results?

What do they feel most motivates people to meet time commitments? What are the common results?

For each benefit, what do they think causes that benefit? What are the results of that benefit? Who is responsible for that benefit?

For each difficulty, what do they think causes that difficulty? What are the results of the difficulty? Who is responsible and who bears the consequences for that difficulty?

You can also talk about what you've noticed about how others in the local community are helped or hindered in this area from what you've observed. Remember not to try to teach people what they should be thinking or pass judgment on their ideas, but just try to encourage conversation. Ask the person again for their opinion of what you are saying.

4) Ask questions that show the opposite of the person's opinion and allow them to respond.

Perhaps some people say that those who use their time better are more successful. What does the community member think of that opinion?

Perhaps some people say that it is better to tell a person you will do something if they ask rather than offend them by saying you won't, even if you don't plan on being there. What does the community member think of that opinion?

5) Ask the person what they think would help avoid the difficulties and add to the benefits. This would include events related to the topic that haven't happened but that they'd like to see take place, advice they would give to others about the topic, or how others could make the topic more successful.

What would the community member like to see as people's attitudes toward time commitments?

What advice would the community member give to children, young people, and adults about their behavior in this area? To the more traditional community members? To the less traditional?

What kinds of people make for good example for others in this area? What kinds of people make for bad examples?

6) Ask about unfamiliar contexts related to the activity that the person might know something about. What is their opinion of that context?

Do they know of other places where people handle these issues differently? Have them tell you about those situations and what their opinion is of them.

Level 4 Daily Learning Plan 58

The seasons for life activities and how and why community members follow those seasons

1) Spend a few minutes just talking with the person.

2) Set the stage for the conversation by asking about the person's life experience in relationship to the life perspectives topic. Ask other general questions.

Perhaps you've noticed over the past year that people in the community have a well-defined schedule of seasonal activities. Can the community member describe the cycle of seasonal activities for you? Are there seasonal activities that must take place at certain times and that people tend to participate in more consistently?

Which members of society are expected to participate in which activities? Children, young people, adults?

Again, you will need to give examples of what you've observed regarding who and when these things take place. Real examples based on your own observations and experience help you to ask relevant questions. They also serve to keep the conversation moving. See what the community member thinks of your examples and observations.

3) Ask the person to identify the benefits and difficulties of the topic. What are the reasons for and results from the difficulties and benefits? Who is responsible and who bears the consequences?

What does the community member see as the main benefits of following this seasonal cycle?

What do they think are the main difficulties of not following this seasonal cycle?

What do they feel causes people to decide not to follow the seasonal cycle? What are the common reasons and results? Who is responsible and who bears the consequences for the results?

What do they feel most motivates people to follow the seasonal cycle? What are the common results? Who is responsible for the results?

For each benefit, what do they think causes that benefit? What are the results of that benefit? Who is responsible for that benefit?

For each difficulty, what do they think causes that difficulty? What are the results of the difficulty? Who is responsible and who bears the consequences for that difficulty?

You can also talk about what you've noticed about how others in the local community are helped or hindered in this area from what you've observed. Remember not to try to teach people what they should be thinking or pass judgment on their ideas, but just try to encourage conversation. Ask the person again for their opinion of what you are saying.

4) Ask questions that show the opposite of the person's opinion and allow them to respond.

Perhaps some people say that those who don't follow the seasonal activities don't only affect themselves, but also those around them in a negative way. What does the community member think of that opinion?

Perhaps some people say that even those who strictly follow the seasons encounter disaster and difficulty. What does the community member think of that opinion?

5) Ask the person what they think would help avoid the difficulties and add to the benefits. This would include events related to the topic that haven't happened but that they'd like to see take place, advice they would give to others about the topic, or how others could make the topic more successful.

What would the community member like to see as people's attitudes toward seasonal commitments?

What advice would the community member give to children, young people, and adults about their behavior in this area? To the more traditional community members? To the less traditional?

What kinds of people make for good example for others in this area? What kinds of people make for bad examples?

6) Ask about unfamiliar contexts related to the activity that the person might know something about. What is their opinion of that context?

Do they know of other places where people handle these issues differently? Have them tell you about those situations and what their opinion is of them.

Level 4 Daily Learning Plan 59

Opinions of personal and public space and how that space is determined, marked, and violated

1) Spend a few minutes just talking with the person.

2) Set the stage for the conversation by asking about the person's life experience in relationship to the life perspectives topic. Ask other general questions.

Perhaps you've noticed that when people are talking to one another, they don't sit very close and don't make eye contact often. Also, when men, women, and children are sitting together in an area, that the men and women sit separately often, as do the children. Does the community member think these things are true? What do they think about the reason why this happens?

Maybe you've also noticed that people are welcome anytime to come sit in the cooking houses and on benches under the houses of others, but they don't go into the sleeping area. Does the community member think these observations are true? What do they think is the reason for this?

What areas in the community or on the property of others are open for just anyone to visit anytime? What areas or pieces of property are closed to others? How do people mark the space of their property? Are there any visible signs like fences, bushes, clearings, and trees? Or are the signs understood but not visible in this way?

Does the community member know of ways that mark people's personal space? What are the ways this is done? Does the amount of personal space depend on age and status in the society? If so, how?

Again, you will need to give examples of what you've observed regarding who and when these things take place. Real examples based on your own observations and experience help you to ask relevant questions. They also serve to keep the conversation moving. See what the community member thinks of your examples and observations.

3) Ask the person to identify the benefits and difficulties of the topic. What are the reasons for and results from the difficulties and benefits? Who is responsible and who bears the consequences?

What does the community member see as the main benefits of these ways of marking space? What are the common reasons and results? Who is responsible for the results?

What do they think are the main difficulties of not doing these things? What are the common reasons and results? Who is responsible and who bears the consequences for the results?

You can also talk about what you've noticed about how others in the local community are helped or hindered in this area from what you've observed. Remember not to try to teach people what they should be thinking or pass judgment on their ideas, but just try to encourage conversation. Ask the person again for their opinion of what you are saying.

4) Ask questions that show the opposite of the person's opinion and allow them to respond.

Perhaps some people say that property and space boundaries don't need to be respected all that much. What does the community member think of that opinion?

Perhaps some people say that husbands and wives can never sit side-by-side in any public setting. What does the community member think of that opinion?

5) Ask the person what they think would help avoid the difficulties and add to the benefits. This would include events related to the topic that haven't happened but that they'd like to see take place, advice they would give to others about the topic, or how others could make the topic more successful.

What would the community member like to see as people's attitudes toward space and boundaries?

What advice would the community member give to children, young people, and adults about their behavior in this area? To the more traditional community members? To the less traditional?

What kinds of people make for good example for others in this area? What kinds of people make for bad examples?

6) Ask about unfamiliar contexts related to the activity that the person might know something about. What is their opinion of that context?

Do they know of other places where people handle these issues differently? Have them tell you about those situations and what their opinion is of them.

Level 4 Daily Learning Plan 60

Visitors and visiting others, the rules for visiting, and the level of priority given to showing hospitality to group insiders and outsiders

1) Spend a few minutes just talking with the person.

2) Set the stage for the conversation by asking about the person's life experience in relationship to the life perspectives topic. Ask other general questions.

Perhaps you've noticed that people in the community visit one another often throughout the day. Ask the community member any general questions you have. Can they give you an idea of who visits whom and what time of day this usually takes place? Who do they tend to visit the most often? How often and on what occasions?

When people visit, what do they usually do and talk about? Do they bring anything with them? Do they often ask for things from the community member? What kind of things do they ask for? How does the community member usually respond?

When people come in from other communities, how are they received and by whom? Is there any ceremony or ritual? Does the community member think it is important for them to be taken in and cared for? What if they are someone's family members? What if they are from an outside group?

Again, you will need to give examples of what you've observed regarding who and when these things take place. Real examples based on your own observations and experience help you to ask relevant questions. They also serve to keep the conversation moving. See what the community member thinks of your examples and observations.

3) Ask the person to identify the benefits and difficulties of the topic. What are the reasons for and results from the difficulties and benefits? Who is responsible and who bears the consequences?

What are the main benefits of visiting others? Of being visited? What are the common reasons why people visit and results when this doesn't happen? Who is responsible and who bears the consequences for the results?

What do they think are the main difficulties of visiting others? Of being visited? What are the common reasons for the difficulty and results from that? Who is responsible and who bears the consequences for the results?

Does the community member see benefit to taking in people from outside the community? What are the common reasons why people visit and results from their visits?

What are the difficulties in visitors coming in from outside the community? Why do they visit and what are the consequences to those who don't look after them properly? Who is responsible for the consequences?

You can also talk about what you've noticed about how others in the local community are helped or hindered in this area from what you've observed. Remember not to try to teach people what they should be thinking or pass judgment on their ideas, but just try to encourage conversation. Ask the person again for their opinion of what you are saying.

4) Ask questions that show the opposite of the person's opinion and allow them to respond.

Perhaps some people say that visiting isn't really very important. What does the community member think of that opinion?

Perhaps some people say that caring for outsiders isn't really very important. What does the community member think of that opinion?

5) Ask the person what they think would help avoid the difficulties and add to the benefits. This would include events related to the topic that haven't happened but that they'd like to see take place, advice they would give to others about the topic, or how others could make the topic more successful.

What would the community member like to see as people's attitudes toward visiting others and toward caring for visitors themselves?

What advice would the community member give to children, young people, and adults about their behavior in this area? To the more traditional community members? To the less traditional?

What kinds of people make for good example for others in this area? What kinds of people make for bad examples?

6) Ask about unfamiliar contexts related to the activity that the person might know something about. What is their opinion of that context?

Do they know of other places where people handle these issues differently? Have them tell you about those situations and what their opinion is of them.

Level 4 Daily Learning Plan 61

The definition of a good and bad son and man. What community members think of those who are irresponsible in these areas

1) Spend a few minutes just talking with the person.

2) Set the stage for the conversation by asking about the person's life experience in relationship to the life perspectives topic. Ask other general questions.

Perhaps you've noticed that people think and talk about people who are considered good male examples in fulfilling their roles in society.

Can the community member tell you what they think of what makes a good son versus a bad son? How should that person act and behave? What behavior and attitudes should the son demonstrate in the different phases of growing up? What marks the transitions from one phase of life to another? What does the community member think of those who don't measure up to this standard?

Can the community member tell you what they think of what makes a good adult man versus a bad man? How should that person act and behave? What does the community member think of those who don't measure up to this standard?

Again, you will need to give examples of what you've observed regarding who and when these things take place. Real examples based on your own observations and experience help you to ask relevant questions. They also serve to keep the conversation moving. See what the community member thinks of your examples and observations.

3) Ask the person to identify the benefits and difficulties of the topic. What are the reasons for and results from the difficulties and benefits? Who is responsible and who bears the consequences?

What are the main benefits of being a good son? Of having a good son? What are the reasons sons are good? Who is responsible for this taking place?

What are the main difficulties of being a bad son? Of having a bad son? What are the reasons sons are bad? Who is responsible for this taking place and who bears the consequences?

What are the main benefits of being a good man? What are the reasons men turn out good? Who is responsible for this taking place?

What are the main difficulties of being a bad man? What are the reasons men are bad? Who is responsible for this taking place and who bears the consequences?

You can also talk about what you've noticed about how others in the local community are helped or hindered in this area from what you've observed. Remember not to try to teach people what they should be thinking or pass judgment on their ideas, but just try to encourage conversation. Ask the person again for their opinion of what you are saying.

4) Ask questions that show the opposite of the person's opinion and allow them to respond.

Perhaps some people say that being a good son isn't very important. What does the community member think of that opinion?

Perhaps some people say that being a good man isn't very important. What does the community member think of that opinion?

5) Ask the person what they think would help avoid the difficulties and add to the benefits. This would include events related to the topic that haven't happened but that they'd like to see take place, advice they would give to others about the topic, or how others could make the topic more successful.

> What would the community member like to see as people's attitudes toward being good sons or men?

> What advice would the community member give to children, young people, and adults about their behavior in this area? To the more traditional community members? To the less traditional?

6) Ask about unfamiliar contexts related to the activity that the person might know something about. What is their opinion of that context?

> Do they know of other places where people handle these issues differently? Have them tell you about those situations and what their opinion is of them.

Level 4 Daily Learning Plan 62

The definition of a good and bad father and grandfather. What community members think of those who are irresponsible in these areas

1) Spend a few minutes just talking with the person.

2) Set the stage for the conversation by asking about the person's life experience in relationship to the life perspectives topic. Ask other general questions.

Perhaps you've noticed that people think and talk about people who are considered good male examples in fulfilling their roles in society.

Can the community member tell you what they think of what makes a good father versus a bad father? How should that father act and behave? What does the community member think of those fathers who don't measure up to this standard?

Can the community member tell you what they think of what makes a good grandfather versus a bad grandfather? How should that person act and behave? What does the community member think of those who don't measure up to this standard?

Again, you will need to give examples of what you've observed regarding who and when these things take place. Real examples based on your own observations and experience help you to ask relevant questions. They also serve to keep the conversation moving. See what the community member thinks of your examples and observations.

3) Ask the person to identify the benefits and difficulties of the topic. What are the reasons for and results from the difficulties and benefits? Who is responsible and who bears the consequences?

What are the main benefits of being a good father? Of having a good father? What are the reasons fathers are good? Who is responsible for this taking place?

What are the main difficulties of being a bad father? Of having a bad father? What are the reasons fathers are bad? Who is responsible for this taking place and who bears the consequences?

What are the main benefits of being a good grandfather? What are the reasons grandfathers turn out good? Who is responsible for this taking place?

What are the main difficulties of being a bad grandfather? What are the reasons grandfathers are bad? Who is responsible for this taking place and who bears the consequences?

You can also talk about what you've noticed about how others in the local community are helped or hindered in this area from what you've observed. Remember not to try to teach people what they should be thinking or pass judgment on their ideas, but just try to encourage conversation. Ask the person again for their opinion of what you are saying.

4) Ask questions that show the opposite of the person's opinion and allow them to respond.

Perhaps some people say that being a good father isn't very important. What does the community member think of that opinion?

Perhaps some people say that being a good grandfather isn't very important. What does the community member think of that opinion?

5) Ask the person what they think would help avoid the difficulties and add to the benefits.

This would include events related to the topic that haven't happened but that they'd like to see take place, advice they would give to others about the topic, or how others could make the topic more successful.

What would the community member like to see as people's attitudes toward being good fathers or grandfathers?

What advice would the community member give to children, young people, and adults about their behavior in this area? To the more traditional community members? To the less traditional?

6) Ask about unfamiliar contexts related to the activity that the person might know something about. What is their opinion of that context?

Do they know of other places where people handle these issues differently? Have them tell you about those situations and what their opinion is of them.

Level 4 Daily Learning Plan 63

The definition of a good and bad daughter and woman. What community members think of those who are irresponsible in these areas

1) Spend a few minutes just talking with the person.

2) Set the stage for the conversation by asking about the person's life experience in relationship to the life perspectives topic. Ask other general questions.

Perhaps you've noticed that people think and talk about people who are considered good female examples in fulfilling their roles in society.

Can the community member tell you what they think of what makes a good daughter versus a bad daughter? How should that person act and behave? What behavior and attitudes should a daughter demonstrate in the different phases of growing up? What marks the transitions from one phase of life to another? What does the community member think of those who don't measure up to this standard?

Can the community member tell you what they think of what makes a good woman versus a bad woman? How should that person act and behave? What does the community member think of those who don't measure up to this standard?

Again, you will need to give examples of what you've observed regarding who and when these things take place. Real examples based on your own observations and experience help you to ask relevant questions. They also serve to keep the conversation moving. See what the community member thinks of your examples and observations.

3) Ask the person to identify the benefits and difficulties of the topic. What are the reasons for and results from the difficulties and benefits? Who is responsible and who bears the consequences?

What are the main benefits of being a good daughter? Of having a good daughter? What are the reasons daughters are good? Who is responsible for this taking place?

What are the main difficulties of being a bad daughter? Of having a bad daughter? What are the reasons daughters are bad? Who is responsible for this taking place and who bears the consequences?

What are the main benefits of being a good woman? What are the reasons women turn out good? Who is responsible for this taking place?

What are the main difficulties of being a bad woman? What are the reasons women are bad? Who is responsible for this taking place and who bears the consequences?

You can also talk about what you've noticed about how others in the local community are helped or hindered in this area from what you've observed. Remember not to try to teach people what they should be thinking or pass judgment on their ideas, but just try to encourage conversation. Ask the person again for their opinion of what you are saying.

4) Ask questions that show the opposite of the person's opinion and allow them to respond.

Perhaps some people say that being a good daughter isn't very important. What does the community member think of that opinion?

Perhaps some people say that being a good woman isn't very important. What does the community member think of that opinion?

5) Ask the person what they think would help avoid the difficulties and add to the benefits. This would include events related to the topic that haven't happened but that they'd like to see take place, advice they would give to others about the topic, or how others could make the topic more successful.

> What would the community member like to see as people's attitudes toward being good daughters and women?

> What advice would the community member give to children, young people, and adults about their behavior in this area? To the more traditional community members? To the less traditional?

6) Ask about unfamiliar contexts related to the activity that the person might know something about. What is their opinion of that context?

> Do they know of other places where people handle these issues differently? Have them tell you about those situations and what their opinion is of them.

Level 4 Daily Learning Plan 64

The definition of a good and bad mother and grandmother. What community members think of those who are irresponsible in these areas

1) Spend a few minutes just talking with the person.

2) Set the stage for the conversation by asking about the person's life experience in relationship to the life perspectives topic. Ask other general questions.

Perhaps you've noticed that people think and talk about people who are considered good female examples in fulfilling their roles in society.

Can the community member tell you what they think of what makes a good mother versus a bad mother? How should that mother act and behave? What does the community member think of those mothers who don't measure up to this standard?

Can the community member tell you what they think of what makes a good grandmother versus a bad grandmother? How should that person act and behave? What does the community member think of those who don't measure up to this standard?

Again, you will need to give examples of what you've observed regarding who and when these things take place. Real examples based on your own observations and experience help you to ask relevant questions. They also serve to keep the conversation moving. See what the community member thinks of your examples and observations.

3) Ask the person to identify the benefits and difficulties of the topic. What are the reasons for and results from the difficulties and benefits? Who is responsible and who bears the consequences?

What are the main benefits of being a good mother? Of having a good mother? What are the reasons mothers are good? Who is responsible for this taking place?

What are the main difficulties of being a bad mother? Of having a bad mother? What are the reasons mothers are bad? Who is responsible for this taking place and who bears the consequences?

What are the main benefits of being a good grandmother? What are the reasons grandmothers turn out good? Who is responsible for this taking place?

What are the main difficulties of being a bad grandmother? What are the reasons grandmothers are bad? Who is responsible for this taking place and who bears the consequences?

You can also talk about what you've noticed about how others in the local community are helped or hindered in this area from what you've observed. Remember not to try to teach people what they should be thinking or pass judgment on their ideas, but just try to encourage conversation. Ask the person again for their opinion of what you are saying.

4) Ask questions that show the opposite of the person's opinion and allow them to respond.

Perhaps some people say that being a good mother isn't very important. What does the community member think of that opinion?

Perhaps some people say that being a good grandmother isn't very important. What does the community member think of that opinion?

5) Ask the person what they think would help avoid the difficulties and add to the benefits. This would include events related to the topic that haven't happened but that they'd like to see take place, advice they would give to others about the topic, or how others could make the topic more successful.

> What would the community member like to see as people's attitudes toward being good mothers or grandmothers?

> What advice would the community member give to children, young people, and adults about their behavior in this area? To the more traditional community members? To the less traditional?

6) Ask about unfamiliar contexts related to the activity that the person might know something about. What is their opinion of that context?

> Do they know of other places where people handle these issues differently? Have them tell you about those situations and what their opinion is of them.

Level 4 Daily Learning Plan 65

The sources of peace and security in community life (such as special knowledge, jobs, education, wealth, specific relationships, the government, and other secular and religious organizations)

1) Spend a few minutes just talking with the person.

2) Set the stage for the conversation by asking about the person's life experience in relationship to the life perspectives topic. Ask other general questions.

Perhaps you've noticed that people seek certain things in order to feel secure and at peace in their society. You may notice lots of ways that this takes place, such as having a big family and lots of clan connections. Or perhaps this takes the form of family members with certain jobs, with money, with an education, or with connections to higher status people. Maybe people in the society find security in being part of the government structure or part of other secular and religious organizations.

Can the community member explain to you what they think are the most important ways that an individual finds peace and security?

Again, you will need to give examples of what you've observed regarding who and when these things take place. Real examples based on your own observations and experience help you to ask relevant questions. They also serve to keep the conversation moving. See what the community member thinks of your examples and observations.

3) Ask the person to identify the benefits and difficulties of the topic. What are the reasons for and results from the difficulties and benefits? Who is responsible and who bears the consequences?

What are the main benefits of each of the factors that contributes to peace and security? Who is responsible for this taking place?

You can also talk about what you've noticed about how others in the local community are helped or hindered in this area from what you've observed. Remember not to try to teach people what they should be thinking or pass judgment on their ideas, but just try to encourage conversation. Ask the person again for their opinion of what you are saying.

4) Ask questions that show the opposite of the person's opinion and allow them to respond.

Perhaps some people say that jobs and education aren't very important for peace and security. What does the community member think of that opinion?

Perhaps some people say that big families actually bring insecurity. What does the community member think of that opinion?

5) Ask the person what they think would help avoid the difficulties and add to the benefits. This would include events related to the topic that haven't happened but that they'd like to see take place, advice they would give to others about the topic, or how others could make the topic more successful.

What would the community member like to see change in their own current level of peace and security?

What advice would the community member give to children, young people, and adults about their behavior in this area? To the more traditional community members? To the less traditional?

What does a good example of peace and security look like? A bad example?

6) Ask about unfamiliar contexts related to the activity that the person might know something about. What is their opinion of that context?

Do they know of other places where people think of these issues differently? Have them tell you about those situations and what their opinion is of them.

Level 4 Daily Learning Plan 66

The sources of fear and insecurity for community life (such as sickness, death, weakness, childlessness, divorce, being parentless, and poverty)

1) Spend a few minutes just talking with the person.

2) Set the stage for the conversation by asking about the person's life experience in relationship to the life perspectives topic. Ask other general questions.

Perhaps you've noticed that certain things in the society really bring fear and insecurity to the members. You may notice lots of ways that this takes place, such as sickness, death, and conflict. Or perhaps this takes the form of childlessness, divorce, having no parents, no connections, or being poor.

Can the community member explain to you what they think are the most important ways that an individual feels fear and insecurity?

Again, you will need to give examples of what you've observed regarding who and when these things take place. Real examples based on your own observations and experience help you to ask relevant questions. They also serve to keep the conversation moving. See what the community member thinks of your examples and observations.

3) Ask the person to identify the benefits and difficulties of the topic. What are the reasons for and results from the difficulties and benefits? Who is responsible and who bears the consequences?

What are the main difficulties of fear and insecurity? Who is responsible for this taking place and who bears the consequences?

You can also talk about what you've noticed about how others in the local community are helped or hindered in this area from what you've observed. Remember not to try to teach people what they should be thinking or pass judgment on their ideas, but just try to encourage conversation. Ask the person again for their opinion of what you are saying.

4) Ask questions that show the opposite of the person's opinion and allow them to respond.

Perhaps some people say that good health isn't very important for peace and security. What does the community member think of that opinion?

Perhaps some people say that poverty isn't important to peace and security. What does the community member think of that opinion?

5) Ask the person what they think would help avoid the difficulties and add to the benefits. This would include events related to the topic that haven't happened but that they'd like to see take place, advice they would give to others about the topic, or how others could make the topic more successful.

What advice would the community member give to children, young people, and adults about their behavior in this area? To the more traditional community members? To the less traditional?

6) Ask about unfamiliar contexts related to the activity that the person might know something about. What is their opinion of that context?

Do they know of other places where people think of these issues differently? Have them tell you about those situations and what their opinion is of them.

Level 4 Daily Learning Plan 67

The value given to holding and pursuing long-term goals, both by individuals and as well as the community collectively, and what kinds of goals people pursue (such as comfortable lives, family security, freedom from fear, happiness, social recognition, true friendship)

1) Spend a few minutes just talking with the person.

2) Set the stage for the conversation by asking about the person's life experience in relationship to the life perspectives topic. Ask other general questions.

Perhaps you've noticed that a few people seem to take on unique challenges in the community that most wouldn't. For instance, maybe an enterprising community member has tried to open a store. Maybe a few individuals have attempted to access and sell fuel and kerosene. Perhaps a few people harvest cash crops to sell. Maybe you even notice that certain people work longer and more intently in their gardening to market produce. Some may pursue education in the community. Perhaps there are people trying to save money toward a special project or purchase, like buying roofing tin for their house.

All of these kinds of things are possible examples of pursuing goals for the future in some way. Can the community member explain to you what they think about the idea of pursuing goals to 'get ahead' in life? What would they describe as some of the goals that people pursue, if any? How long-term are these goals? What do others think of those people if they themselves aren't doing these kinds of things?

Again, you will need to give examples of what you've observed regarding who and when these things take place. Real examples based on your own observations and experience help you to ask relevant questions. They also serve to keep the conversation moving. See what the community member thinks of your examples and observations.

3) Ask the person to identify the benefits and difficulties of the topic. What are the reasons for and results from the difficulties and benefits? Who is responsible and who bears the consequences?

What are the main benefits of the common ways of pursuing long-term goals? What are the reasons why the community member thinks of that as a benefit? What are the results of that benefit? Who is responsible for this taking place?

What are the main difficulties of the common ways of pursuing long-term goals? What are the reasons why the community member thinks of that as a difficulty? Who is responsible for the difficulty and who bears the consequences?

You can also talk about what you've noticed about how others in the local community are helped or hindered in this area from what you've observed. Remember not to try to teach people what they should be thinking or pass judgment on their ideas, but just try to encourage conversation. Ask the person again for their opinion of what you are saying.

4) Ask questions that show the opposite of the person's opinion and allow them to respond.

Perhaps some people say that doing things to get ahead is not a good idea. What does the community member think of that opinion?

Perhaps some people say that giving food from the store to those in need or to relatives who ask is more important than worrying about making a profit. What does the community member think of that opinion?

5) Ask the person what they think would help avoid the difficulties and add to the benefits. This would include events related to the topic that haven't happened but that they'd like to see take place, advice they would give to others about the topic, or how others could make the topic more successful.

What would the community member like to see as their own long-term goals?

What advice would the community member give to children, young people, and adults about their behavior in this area? To the more traditional community members? To the less traditional?

What does a good example of a person pursuing long-term goals look like? A bad example?

6) Ask about unfamiliar contexts related to the activity that the person might know something about. What is their opinion of that context?

Do they know of other places where people think of these issues differently? Have them tell you about those situations and what their opinion is of them.

Level 4 Daily Learning Plan 68

*Attitudes toward the created order and a sense of beauty,
how people feel they should preserve and care for the world
around them, including animal domestication*

1) Spend a few minutes just talking with the person.

2) Set the stage for the conversation by asking about the person's life experience in relationship to the life perspectives topic. Ask other general questions.

Perhaps you've noticed that people in the society don't seem to worry very much about caretaking in the world around them. Though they look after their gardens for food and raise chickens and pigs or goats, those animals are strictly viewed as means for food and so have practical value.

In general terms, though, garbage and litter are left lying about, people don't bathe very much, and they tend to consume all of whatever resource is available very quickly and without a lot of thought. Pets that aren't raised for food aren't treated well and are often abused by children and adults. Sometimes small animals are killed just for spite and stir laughter in others.

What does the community member think about your observations? Do they agree or disagree? What do they feel are the attitudes of people in the community toward taking care of the world around them? Do they think that they are motivated to do this by anything other than necessity?

Does the community member have an appreciation for things in the world around them as stirring an emotional response when they see them because they are nice or good to look at? What about the stars at night? What about a scene in the natural world? Anything that they would describe as 'beautiful'? How about a well-made cultural product? A certain animal or person? If so, what kinds of things would they place in that category?

Again, you will need to give examples of what you've observed regarding who and when these things take place. Real examples based on your own observations and experience help you to ask relevant questions. They also serve to keep the conversation moving. See what the community member thinks of your examples and observations.

3) Ask the person to identify the benefits and difficulties of the topic. What are the reasons for and results from the difficulties and benefits? Who is responsible and who bears the consequences?

What are the main benefits of conserving and taking care of the world around us? What are the reasons why the community member thinks of that as a benefit? What are the results of that benefit? Who is responsible for this taking place?

What are the main difficulties of not conserving and not taking care of the world around us? What are the reasons why the community member thinks of that as a difficulty? Who is responsible for the difficulty and who bears the consequences?

Can the community member think of any reasons why we should take time to view certain things as good to look at or beautiful? What might the benefits be for doing that?

You can also talk about what you've noticed about how others in the local community are helped or hindered in this area from what you've observed. Remember not to try to teach peo-

ple what they should be thinking or pass judgment on their ideas, but just try to encourage conversation. Ask the person again for their opinion of what you are saying.

4) Ask questions that show the opposite of the person's opinion and allow them to respond.

Perhaps some people say that taking the time to conserve actually wastes time to do other things that are important. What does the community member think of that opinion?

Perhaps some people say that beauty has not value because it doesn't give you anything practical in return. What does the community member think of that opinion?

5) Ask the person what they think would help avoid the difficulties and add to the benefits. This would include events related to the topic that haven't happened but that they'd like to see take place, advice they would give to others about the topic, or how others could make the topic more successful.

What would the community member like to see as their own long-term goals?

What advice would the community member give to children, young people, and adults about their behavior in this area? To the more traditional community members? To the less traditional?

What does a good example of a person pursuing long-term goals look like? A bad example?

6) Ask about unfamiliar contexts related to the activity that the person might know something about. What is their opinion of that context?

Do they know of other places where people think of these issues differently? Have them tell you about those situations and what their opinion is of them.

Level 4 Daily Learning Plan 69

How community members demonstrate affection and what kinds of physical contact are a part of showing affection

1) Spend a few minutes just talking with the person.

2) Set the stage for the conversation by asking about the person's life experience in relationship to the life perspectives topic. Ask other general questions.

> Perhaps you've noticed that people in the society show affection to one another in certain ways at different ages. For example, people like to hold babies and children, especially the mothers. One of their habits, which seems to show happiness or affection, is to smack the child on the head or pinch them really hard, in which case they may even cry. Others paint the face of new children to the community to show affection. What does the community member think are the common ways that people show affection to babies and young children?

> On the other hand, husbands and wives don't show a lot of physical affection to one another, at least not in public. Husbands don't kiss or hold hands with their wives, and they don't sit with them. What does the community member think are the common ways that husbands and wives show their care and affection for one another?

> Young people don't seem to receive physical affection from their parents or others, either. What does the community member think are the common ways that people show their care and affection for young people?

> How about visitors and first time acquaintances? What is the proper way to greet and show care for them?

> *Again, you will need to give examples of what you've observed regarding who and when these things take place. Real examples based on your own observations and experience help you to ask relevant questions. They also serve to keep the conversation moving. See what the community member thinks of your examples and observations.*

3) Ask the person to identify the benefits and difficulties of the topic. What are the reasons for and results from the difficulties and benefits? Who is responsible and who bears the consequences?

> What are the main benefits of signs of affection and physical contact? What are the reasons why the community member thinks of that as a benefit? What are the results of that benefit? Who is responsible for this taking place?

> What are the main difficulties with signs of affection and physical contact? What are the reasons why the community member thinks of that as a difficulty? Who is responsible for the difficulty and who bears the consequences?

> *You can also talk about what you've noticed about how others in the local community are helped or hindered in this area from what you've observed. Remember not to try to teach people what they should be thinking or pass judgment on their ideas, but just try to encourage conversation. Ask the person again for their opinion of what you are saying.*

4) Ask questions that show the opposite of the person's opinion and allow them to respond.

> Perhaps some people say that public physical contact to show affection only leads to dis-

grace and problems. What does the community member think of that opinion?

Perhaps some people say that people shouldn't worry about these things, should just go on with their responsibilities each day. What does the community member think of that opinion?

5) Ask the person what they think would help avoid the difficulties and add to the benefits. This would include events related to the topic that haven't happened but that they'd like to see take place, advice they would give to others about the topic, or how others could make the topic more successful.

What advice would the community member give to children, young people, and adults about their behavior in this area? To the more traditional community members? To the less traditional?

What does a good example of a person showing affection look like? A bad example?

6) Ask about unfamiliar contexts related to the activity that the person might know something about. What is their opinion of that context?

Do they know of other places where people think of these issues differently? Have them tell you about those situations and what their opinion is of them.

Level 4 Daily Learning Plan 70

The secular and religious subgroups in society and the purposes of these groups. The roles of these groups, how important they are, and how they gather and interact

1) Spend a few minutes just talking with the person.

2) Set the stage for the conversation by asking about the person's life experience in relationship to the life perspectives topic. Ask other general questions.

> Perhaps you've noticed that people in the society tend to get together in certain social groups in the society. For example, the older men meet to talk about issues and make decisions. A few people are also on a local school committee, and others are part of a local government council group. Some participate in a cash crop growers society. Still others have connections to religious institutions.

> What groups does the community member participate in? Can they describe the various groups in society and explain what they are for? How important are the groups? How often do the groups gather and interact? What do those groups talk about? What is the groups role?

> *Again, you will need to give examples of what you've observed regarding who and when these things take place. Real examples based on your own observations and experience help you to ask relevant questions. They also serve to keep the conversation moving. See what the community member thinks of your examples and observations.*

3) Ask the person to identify the benefits and difficulties of the topic. What are the reasons for and results from the difficulties and benefits? Who is responsible and who bears the consequences?

> What are the main benefits of these various groups? What are the reasons why the community member thinks of that as a benefit? What are the results of that benefit? Who is responsible for this taking place?

> What are the main difficulties with these groups, both internally as well as in the community? What are the reasons why the community member thinks of that as a difficulty? Who is responsible for the difficulty and who bears the consequences?

> *You can also talk about what you've noticed about how others in the local community are helped or hindered in this area from what you've observed. Remember not to try to teach people what they should be thinking or pass judgment on their ideas, but just try to encourage conversation. Ask the person again for their opinion of what you are saying.*

4) Ask questions that show the opposite of the person's opinion and allow them to respond.

> Perhaps some people say that the government council only tries to control every aspect of people's lives without reason. What does the community member think of that opinion?

> Perhaps some people say that the school board is too exclusive and demanding. What does the community member think of that opinion?

5) Ask the person what they think would help avoid the difficulties and add to the benefits. This would include events related to the topic that haven't happened but that they'd like to see take place, advice they would give to others about the topic, or how others could make the topic more successful.

If the community member had opportunity, what groups would they participate in and why?

What advice would the community member give to children, young people, and adults about their behavior in this area? To the more traditional community members? To the less traditional?

What does a good example of a citizen look like in this area of their participation in certain subgroups? A bad example?

6) Ask about unfamiliar contexts related to the activity that the person might know something about. What is their opinion of that context?

Do they know of other places where people think of these issues differently? Have them tell you about those situations and what their opinion is of them.

Level 4 Daily Learning Plan 71

Special kinship relationships and what the responsibilities and benefits are in these relationships, what a good relative does and is

1) Spend a few minutes just talking with the person.

2) Set the stage for the conversation by asking about the person's life experience in relationship to the life perspectives topic. Ask other general questions.

Perhaps you've noticed that certain relatives have closer and more important relationships than others. For example, children call their father's brothers 'father' as well, and their mother's sisters they call 'mother.' Give a few other examples of what you know about the kinship system to the community member in this way. What does the community member think of the various kinship relationships? What are the ones that they feel are the closest? Which are the most important? What are the primary responsibilities of each?

Again, you will need to give examples of what you've observed regarding who and when these things take place. Real examples based on your own observations and experience help you to ask relevant questions. They also serve to keep the conversation moving. See what the community member thinks of your examples and observations.

3) Ask the person to identify the benefits and difficulties of the topic. What are the reasons for and results from the difficulties and benefits? Who is responsible and who bears the consequences?

What are the main benefits of these various kinship relationships? What are the reasons why the community member thinks of that as a benefit? What are the results of that benefit? Who is responsible for this taking place?

What are the main difficulties with these various kinship relationships? What are the reasons why the community member thinks of that as a difficulty? Who is responsible for the difficulty and who bears the consequences?

You can also talk about what you've noticed about how others in the local community are helped or hindered in this area from what you've observed. Remember not to try to teach people what they should be thinking or pass judgment on their ideas, but just try to encourage conversation. Ask the person again for their opinion of what you are saying.

4) Ask questions that show the opposite of the person's opinion and allow them to respond.

Perhaps some people say that because of the kinship system, fathers often do a poor job of making a priority of caring for their own children first. What does the community member think of that opinion?

Perhaps some people say that the system is too focused on kinship ties to the exclusion of other friends and acquaintances. What does the community member think of that opinion?

5) Ask the person what they think would help avoid the difficulties and add to the benefits. This would include events related to the topic that haven't happened but that they'd like to see take place, advice they would give to others about the topic, or how others could make the topic more successful.

What advice would the community member give to children, young people, and adults about their behavior in this area? To the more traditional community members? To the less traditional?

What does a good example of a good relative at each level look like? A bad example?

6) Ask about unfamiliar contexts related to the activity that the person might know something about. What is their opinion of that context?

Do they know of other places where people think of these issues differently? Have them tell you about those situations and what their opinion is of them.

Level 4 Daily Learning Plan 72

Courtship and marriage, how it comes about, and how it is broken or violated

1) Spend a few minutes just talking with the person.

2) Set the stage for the conversation by asking about the person's life experience in relationship to the life perspectives topic. Ask other general questions.

> As in every society, men and women come together as husband and wife and have children. Can the community member describe to you the general way that marriage comes about? Who is responsible? How are the marriage candidates identified? Are they related to each other, and if so, how? What is the process for courtship? What behaviors are wrong for the courting couple? Can they see and talk with each other in private or in public? Is there a marriage ceremony? A bride price? Other observances or obligations on the part of the bride or the man?

> Are marriages ever violated through infidelity? What is usually the consequence of this?

> Are marriages ever broken off entirely? What usually happens? Where do the children end up, if there are any?

> *Again, you will need to give examples of what you've observed regarding who and when these things take place. Real examples based on your own observations and experience help you to ask relevant questions. They also serve to keep the conversation moving. See what the community member thinks of your examples and observations.*

3) Ask the person to identify the benefits and difficulties of the topic. What are the reasons for and results from the difficulties and benefits? Who is responsible and who bears the consequences?

> What are the main benefits of marriage? What are the reasons why the community member thinks of that as a benefit? What are the results of that benefit? Who is responsible for this taking place?

> What are the main difficulties in marriage? What are the reasons why the community member thinks of that as a difficulty? Who is responsible for the difficulty and who bears the consequences?

> What are the main difficulties in broken marriages? What are the reasons why the community member thinks of that as a difficulty? Who is responsible for the difficulty and who bears the consequences?

> *You can also talk about what you've noticed about how others in the local community are helped or hindered in this area from what you've observed. Remember not to try to teach people what they should be thinking or pass judgment on their ideas, but just try to encourage conversation. Ask the person again for their opinion of what you are saying.*

4) Ask questions that show the opposite of the person's opinion and allow them to respond.

> Perhaps some people say that infidelity isn't good, but it happens a lot and is just to be expected. What does the community member think of that opinion?

> Perhaps some people say that bride prices are hard on the family and new couple. What does the community member think of that opinion?

5) Ask the person what they think would help avoid the difficulties and add to the benefits. This would include events related to the topic that haven't happened but that they'd like to see take place, advice they would give to others about the topic, or how others could make the topic more successful.

> What advice would the community member give to children, young people, and adults about their behavior in this area? To the more traditional community members? To the less traditional?

> What does a good example of a courtship look like? A bad example?

6) Ask about unfamiliar contexts related to the activity that the person might know something about. What is their opinion of that context?

> Do they know of other places where people think of these issues differently? Have them tell you about those situations and what their opinion is of them.

Level 4 Daily Learning Plan 73

The definition of the family and family rules

1) Spend a few minutes just talking with the person.

2) Set the stage for the conversation by asking about the person's life experience in relationship to the life perspectives topic. Ask other general questions.

As in every society, families are generally defined by blood relationship in some way. Can the community member describe to you the general way that people define the closest level of family unit? Do people consider a family to first be a husband, wife, and children only, or is the first level of family bigger than that?

What are the responsibilities of each of the members of the family toward their other family members? Who is responsible to discipline and instruct the children?

Do husbands have the right to hit or physically correct their wives in any way? What kinds of ways does this usually happen? Do wives hit or physically correct their husbands?

Do families want to have boys or girls? How does the sex of the child get determined?

Should children be spaced or planned? What is the general rule about this?

Again, you will need to give examples of what you've observed regarding who and when these things take place. Real examples based on your own observations and experience help you to ask relevant questions. They also serve to keep the conversation moving. See what the community member thinks of your examples and observations.

3) Ask the person to identify the benefits and difficulties of the topic. What are the reasons for and results from the difficulties and benefits? Who is responsible and who bears the consequences?

What are the main benefits of being part of a family? What are the reasons why the community member thinks of that as a benefit? What are the results of that benefit? Who is responsible for this taking place?

What are the main difficulties in being part of a family? What are the reasons why the community member thinks of that as a difficulty? Who is responsible for the difficulty and who bears the consequences?

What are the main benefits of disciplining children? What are the reasons why the community member thinks of that as a benefit? What are the results of that benefit? Who is responsible for this taking place?

What are the main difficulties in disciplining children? What are the reasons why the community member thinks of that as a difficulty? Who is responsible for the difficulty and who bears the consequences?

What are the main benefits of correcting wives or husbands verbally or physically? What are the reasons why the community member thinks of that as a benefit? What are the results of that benefit? Who is responsible for this taking place?

What are the main difficulties in correcting husbands or wives verbally or physically? What are the reasons why the community member thinks of that as a difficulty? Who is responsible for the difficulty and who bears the consequences?

What are the main benefits of having a certain sex of child? What are the reasons why the community member thinks of that as a benefit? What are the results of that benefit? Who is responsible for this taking place?

What are the main difficulties in having a certain sex of child? What are the reasons why the community member thinks of that as a difficulty? Who is responsible for the difficulty and who bears the consequences?

What are the main benefits of planning well for children? What are the reasons why the community member thinks of that as a benefit? What are the results of that benefit? Who is responsible for this taking place?

What are the main difficulties in planning well for children? What are the reasons why the community member thinks of that as a difficulty? Who is responsible for the difficulty and who bears the consequences?

You can also talk about what you've noticed about how others in the local community are helped or hindered in this area from what you've observed. Remember not to try to teach people what they should be thinking or pass judgment on their ideas, but just try to encourage conversation. Ask the person again for their opinion of what you are saying.

4) Ask questions that show the opposite of the person's opinion and allow them to respond.

Perhaps some people say that the small family unit isn't as important as extended families. What does the community member think of that opinion?

Perhaps some people say that wives can be hit and yelled at because they don't have as much value as men. What does the community member think of that opinion?

5) Ask the person what they think would help avoid the difficulties and add to the benefits. This would include events related to the topic that haven't happened but that they'd like to see take place, advice they would give to others about the topic, or how others could make the topic more successful.

What advice would the community member give to children, young people, and adults about their behavior in this area? To the more traditional community members? To the less traditional?

What does a good example of a family look like? A bad example?

6) Ask about unfamiliar contexts related to the activity that the person might know something about. What is their opinion of that context?

Do they know of other places where people think of these issues differently? Have them tell you about those situations and what their opinion is of them.

Level 4 Daily Learning Plan 74

Rules for other social control systems, such as government. Any ambiguous areas in the rules and people's attitudes toward rule followers and rule breakers and the consequences for breaking and following the rules

1) Spend a few minutes just talking with the person.

2) Set the stage for the conversation by asking about the person's life experience in relationship to the life perspectives topic. Ask other general questions.

> As in every society, people control and give direction to other members of society as to how they should live and act. Can the community member describe to you the general ways that the government has influence in the community?

> How does the government give and enforce rules for how people live and behave? What kinds of rules do they give and how do they enforce these rules? What are the consequences for not following the rules?

> Are there areas in the government rules that are ambiguous and are open to interpretation from person to person? How so?

> How do people generally feel about the government and its rules?

> *Again, you will need to give examples of what you've observed regarding who and when these things take place. Real examples based on your own observations and experience help you to ask relevant questions. They also serve to keep the conversation moving. See what the community member thinks of your examples and observations.*

3) Ask the person to identify the benefits and difficulties of the topic. What are the reasons for and results from the difficulties and benefits? Who is responsible and who bears the consequences?

> What are the main benefits of each of government influence and rules in the society? What are the reasons why the community member thinks of that as a benefit? What are the results of that benefit? Who is responsible for this taking place?

> What are the main difficulties in government influence and rules in society? What are the reasons why the community member thinks of that as a difficulty? Who is responsible for the difficulty and who bears the consequences?

> *You can also talk about what you've noticed about how others in the local community are helped or hindered in this area from what you've observed. Remember not to try to teach people what they should be thinking or pass judgment on their ideas, but just try to encourage conversation. Ask the person again for their opinion of what you are saying.*

4) Ask questions that show the opposite of the person's opinion and allow them to respond.

> Perhaps some people say that the police system is corrupt and brutal when offenses are committed. What does the community member think of that opinion?

> Perhaps some people say that the government should be more involved in the community, especially in health and education. What does the community member think of that opinion?

5) Ask the person what they think would help avoid the difficulties and add to the benefits. This would include events related to the topic that haven't happened but that they'd like to see take place, advice they would give to others about the topic, or how others could make the topic more successful.

If the community member had an opportunity to work in the government system, would they do so? Why or why not?

What advice would the community member give to children, young people, and adults about their behavior in this area? To the more traditional community members? To the less traditional?

What does a good example of government involvement look like? A bad example?

What is a proper attitude toward the government and its rules?

6) Ask about unfamiliar contexts related to the activity that the person might know something about. What is their opinion of that context?

Do they know of other places where people think of these issues differently? Have them tell you about those situations and what their opinion is of them.

Level 4 Daily Learning Plan 75

*Sickness and death and its cause and effect on others,
including widows, widowers, and orphans*

1) Spend a few minutes just talking with the person.

2) Set the stage for the conversation by asking about the person's life experience in relationship to the life perspectives topic. Ask other general questions.

As in every society, people get sick and die. What are the main reasons why people get sick? What are the reasons why people die? Is there always a spiritual reason for the sickness or the death? How do people deal with this? Are there any special ceremonies or practices that should be observed in either case?

Do community or family members have any special responsibilities toward those who have died? Are there special ceremonies or rituals for this?

What about burial and burial practice? Who is involved and how so?

Again, you will need to give examples of what you've observed regarding who and when these things take place. Real examples based on your own observations and experience help you to ask relevant questions. They also serve to keep the conversation moving. See what the community member thinks of your examples and observations.

3) Ask the person to identify the benefits and difficulties of the topic. What are the reasons for and results from the difficulties and benefits? Who is responsible and who bears the consequences?

Are there any benefits at all to sickness and death? What are the reasons why the community member thinks of that as a benefit? What are the results of that benefit? Who is responsible for this taking place?

What are the main difficulties that result from sickness and death for those left behind, including widows, widowers, and orphans? What are the reasons why the community member thinks of that as a difficulty? Who is responsible for the difficulty and who bears the consequences?

You can also talk about what you've noticed about how others in the local community are helped or hindered in this area from what you've observed. Remember not to try to teach people what they should be thinking or pass judgment on their ideas, but just try to encourage conversation. Ask the person again for their opinion of what you are saying.

4) Ask questions that show the opposite of the person's opinion and allow them to respond.

Perhaps some people say that sickness is not spiritually caused. What does the community member think of that opinion?

Perhaps some people say that sick people need to see the traditional healer, but they need also to take their medicine. What does the community member think of that opinion?

5) Ask the person what they think would help avoid the difficulties and add to the benefits. This would include events related to the topic that haven't happened but that they'd like to see take place, advice they would give to others about the topic, or how others could make the topic more successful.

What could people do to avoid getting sick and always be healthy?

What could people do to avoid dying, or to avert sickness or death for someone they care about?

What advice would the community member give to children, young people, and adults about their behavior in this area? To the more traditional community members? To the less traditional?

6) Ask about unfamiliar contexts related to the activity that the person might know something about. What is their opinion of that context?

Do they know of other places where people think of these issues differently? Have them tell you about those situations and what their opinion is of them.

Level 4 Daily Learning Plan 76

Individuals in the community who have special roles for communicating or working with the spirits, including the levels of respect and fear that community members feel toward them

1) Spend a few minutes just talking with the person.

2) Set the stage for the conversation by asking about the person's life experience in relationship to the life perspectives topic. Ask other general questions.

Perhaps you've noticed that certain members of society are respected and even feared for their roles in working with spirits. Can the community member describe to you some of those kinds of roles? What responsibilities does that person have? How do community members feel about them? What kinds of things do they consult them for and what do these consults look like? What occurs? Is any money or item of value given in payment for their services?

Again, you will need to give examples of what you've observed regarding who and when these things take place. Real examples based on your own observations and experience help you to ask relevant questions. They also serve to keep the conversation moving. See what the community member thinks of your examples and observations.

3) Ask the person to identify the benefits and difficulties of the topic. What are the reasons for and results from the difficulties and benefits? Who is responsible and who bears the consequences?

What are the main benefits of these members of society who work with the spirits? What are the reasons why the community member thinks of that as a benefit? What are the results of that benefit? Who is responsible for this taking place?

What are the main difficulties of the spirit workers? What are the reasons why the community member thinks of that as a difficulty? Who is responsible for the difficulty and who bears the consequences?

You can also talk about what you've noticed about how others in the local community are helped or hindered in this area from what you've observed. Remember not to try to teach people what they should be thinking or pass judgment on their ideas, but just try to encourage conversation. Ask the person again for their opinion of what you are saying.

4) Ask questions that show the opposite of the person's opinion and allow them to respond.

Perhaps some people say that the spirit workers are just out for a profit and sometimes deceive people or can't do what they promise. What does the community member think of that opinion?

Perhaps some people say that the spirit workers hold the society together. What does the community member think of that opinion?

5) Ask the person what they think would help avoid the difficulties and add to the benefits. This would include events related to the topic that haven't happened but that they'd like to see take place, advice they would give to others about the topic, or how others could make the topic more successful.

If the community member could be a person who works with the spirits, would they want to do so? Why or why not?

What advice would the community member give to children, young people, and adults about their behavior in this area? To the more traditional community members? To the less traditional?

What does a good example of a person who works with the spirits look like? A bad example?

6) Ask about unfamiliar contexts related to the activity that the person might know something about. What is their opinion of that context?

Do they know of other places where people think of these issues differently? Have them tell you about those situations and what their opinion is of them.

Level 4 Daily Learning Plan 77

Beliefs about how people generally interact with spirit beings, what kinds of spirit beings, when this occurs, and what the consequences are

1) Spend a few minutes just talking with the person.

2) Set the stage for the conversation by asking about the person's life experience in relationship to the life perspectives topic. Ask other general questions.

Perhaps you've noticed that certain members of society talk about having encounters with spirits. Can the community member describe to you some of those kinds of encounters? When, how, and why do they usually happen? What different kinds of spirit beings are out there? Where do they come from? Do they always exist or are they headed someplace and will eventually disappear or go away? How do people handle them? Are they good or bad? Do they help or hurt? Do they cause fear? What are their characteristics? Do they have bodies? Can they attack or injure people? Kill them?

Again, you will need to give examples of what you've observed regarding who and when these things take place. Real examples based on your own observations and experience help you to ask relevant questions. They also serve to keep the conversation moving. See what the community member thinks of your examples and observations.

3) Ask the person to identify the benefits and difficulties of the topic. What are the reasons for and results from the difficulties and benefits? Who is responsible and who bears the consequences?

What are the main benefits from the various spirit beings? What are the reasons why the community member thinks of that as a benefit? What are the results of that benefit? Who is responsible for this taking place?

What are the main difficulties from the various spirit beings? What are the reasons why the community member thinks of that as a difficulty? Who is responsible for the difficulty and who bears the consequences?

You can also talk about what you've noticed about how others in the local community are helped or hindered in this area from what you've observed. Remember not to try to teach people what they should be thinking or pass judgment on their ideas, but just try to encourage conversation. Ask the person again for their opinion of what you are saying.

4) Ask questions that show the opposite of the person's opinion and allow them to respond.

Perhaps some people say that the spirit beings are easy to deceive. What does the community member think of that opinion?

Perhaps some people say that the spirit beings are really important for keeping people in line. What does the community member think of that opinion?

5) Ask the person what they think would help avoid the difficulties and add to the benefits. This would include events related to the topic that haven't happened but that they'd like to see take place, advice they would give to others about the topic, or how others could make the topic more successful.

What can a person do to avoid the difficulty with the spirits and reap the benefits?

What advice would the community member give to children, young people, and adults about their behavior in this area? To the more traditional community members? To the less traditional?

6) Ask about unfamiliar contexts related to the activity that the person might know something about. What is their opinion of that context?

Do they know of other places where people think of these issues differently? Have them tell you about those situations and what their opinion is of them.

Level 4 Daily Learning Plan 78

Where people think that history and life are heading

1) Spend a few minutes just talking with the person.

2) Set the stage for the conversation by asking about the person's life experience in relationship to the life perspectives topic. Ask other general questions.

> How does the community member view the purpose of the time that has passed from the beginning of recorded time until now? Do they think that time just goes in circles year after year based on seasonal activities, or do they feel that the community and society are heading somewhere? Is life getting better generally? Getting worse? Staying the same?

> Are people just existing in that space of time or are they moving toward something? Do people have a destiny or destination? If so what does that destination look like? Is it a physical or a spiritual destination? Is there more than one place?

> Why do people go to the different destinations? How do they get there? What do they have to do to improve their chances of getting to a better place, if that is possible?

> Do people ever come back physically after they die? If so, how does that happen and why?

> *Again, you will need to give examples of what you've observed regarding who and when these things take place. Real examples based on your own observations and experience help you to ask relevant questions. They also serve to keep the conversation moving. See what the community member thinks of your examples and observations.*

3) Ask the person to identify the benefits and difficulties of the topic. What are the reasons for and results from the difficulties and benefits? Who is responsible and who bears the consequences?

> How are time and history a benefit to the community? What are the reasons why the community member thinks of that as a benefit? What are the results of that benefit? Who is responsible for this taking place?

> What are the main obstacles and difficulties we encounter as we try to control our lives and destinations? Who is responsible for the difficulty and who bears the consequences?

> *You can also talk about what you've noticed about how others in the local community are helped or hindered in this area from what you've observed. Remember not to try to teach people what they should be thinking or pass judgment on their ideas, but just try to encourage conversation. Ask the person again for their opinion of what you are saying.*

4) Ask questions that show the opposite of the person's opinion and allow them to respond.

> Perhaps some people say that no matter what you do on earth, you have no guarantee for your destination after death. What does the community member think of that opinion?

> Perhaps some people say that people should just live life as they want and not worry about history or life after death. What does the community member think of that opinion?

5) Ask the person what they think would help avoid the difficulties and add to the benefits. This would include events related to the topic that haven't happened but that they'd like to see take place, advice they would give to others about the topic, or how others could make the topic more successful.

What advice would the community member give to children, young people, and adults about their behavior in this area? To the more traditional community members? To the less traditional?

6) Ask about unfamiliar contexts related to the activity that the person might know something about. What is their opinion of that context?

Do they know of other places where people think of these issues differently? Have them tell you about those situations and what their opinion is of them.

Level 4 Daily Learning Plan 79

The view of history and any defining stories of the origins of people and the world

1) Spend a few minutes just talking with the person.

2) Set the stage for the conversation by asking about the person's life experience in relationship to the life perspectives topic. Ask other general questions.

> Perhaps you've noticed that people in the society refer to stories of their own origins and the origins of the world around them. If so, it is a good idea for you to hear some of those stories to have a clear idea of what this represents in their minds. You might even need additional time to collect and understand these stories, because there may be lots of them and they are often important to how people think.

> How does the community member view the way that the world up to now came into existence? Were there any beings or people who were really important to that process? If so, who are they and what are they like? Do they still exist? Do they have any current influence and control in the world? If so, in what ways?

> Do people need to pay these beings respect in some way today? Did the beings suggest or demand that people follow any rules? Which ones? Are the beings trustworthy? Unchanging? All-powerful? What are their faults and limitations?

> *Again, you will need to give examples of what you've observed regarding who and when these things take place. Real examples based on your own observations and experience help you to ask relevant questions. They also serve to keep the conversation moving. See what the community member thinks of your examples and observations.*

3) Ask the person to identify the benefits and difficulties of the topic. What are the reasons for and results from the difficulties and benefits? Who is responsible and who bears the consequences?

> How are these stories of origins and spirit beings a benefit to the community? What are the reasons why the community member thinks of that as a benefit? What are the results of that benefit? Who is responsible for this taking place?

> What are the main obstacles and difficulties with the stories and spirit beings? Are the stories and beings consistent and trustworthy? Who is responsible for the difficulty and who bears the consequences?

> *You can also talk about what you've noticed about how others in the local community are helped or hindered in this area from what you've observed. Remember not to try to teach people what they should be thinking or pass judgment on their ideas, but just try to encourage conversation. Ask the person again for their opinion of what you are saying.*

4) Ask questions that show the opposite of the person's opinion and allow them to respond.

> Perhaps some people say that no matter what you do on earth, you have no guarantee for your destination after death. What does the community member think of that opinion?

> Perhaps some people say that people should just live life as they want and not worry about history or life after death. What does the community member think of that opinion?

5) Ask the person what they think would help avoid the difficulties and add to the benefits.

This would include events related to the topic that haven't happened but that they'd like to see take place, advice they would give to others about the topic, or how others could make the topic more successful.

What advice would the community member give to children, young people, and adults about their behavior in this area? To the more traditional community members? To the less traditional?

6) Ask about unfamiliar contexts related to the activity that the person might know something about. What is their opinion of that context?

Are all the stories that the community member knows about how the community and world came into existence the same, or do they vary from place to place? Do they vary within the community or society where they live? If so, how? What is their opinion of this?

Level 4 Daily Learning Plan 80

Any taboos and special rituals related to daily activities and spirit beings. Any ambiguous areas in the rules and people's attitudes toward rule followers and rule breakers and the consequences for breaking and following the rules

1) Spend a few minutes just talking with the person.

2) Set the stage for the conversation by asking about the person's life experience in relationship to the life perspectives topic. Ask other general questions.

> Perhaps you've noticed that people in the society follow other special regular rituals and observe other taboos. Can the community member talk about the taboos and rituals in different categories of life activities for you? Where does the community member think these things came from?

> *Again, you will need to give examples of what you've observed regarding who and when these things take place. Real examples based on your own observations and experience help you to ask relevant questions. They also serve to keep the conversation moving. See what the community member thinks of your examples and observations.*

3) Ask the person to identify the benefits and difficulties of the topic. What are the reasons for and results from the difficulties and benefits? Who is responsible and who bears the consequences?

> What are the benefits from each of the taboos and rituals? What are the reasons why the community member thinks of that as a benefit? What are the results of that benefit? Who is responsible for this taking place?

> What are the main obstacles and difficulties with not following the rituals and taboos? What are the results? Who is responsible for the difficulty and who bears the consequences?

> *You can also talk about what you've noticed about how others in the local community are helped or hindered in this area from what you've observed. Remember not to try to teach people what they should be thinking or pass judgment on their ideas, but just try to encourage conversation. Ask the person again for their opinion of what you are saying.*

4) Ask questions that show the opposite of the person's opinion and allow them to respond.

> Perhaps some people say that the rituals or taboos don't always work to guarantee success. What does the community member think of that opinion?

> Perhaps some people say that even a single person not following the taboos can be disastrous for the whole community. What does the community member think of that opinion?

5) Ask the person what they think would help avoid the difficulties and add to the benefits. This would include events related to the topic that haven't happened but that they'd like to see take place, advice they would give to others about the topic, or how others could make the topic more successful.

> What advice would the community member give to children, young people, and adults about their behavior in this area? To the more traditional community members? To the less traditional?

6) Ask about unfamiliar contexts related to the activity that the person might know something about. What is their opinion of that context?

Do they know of other places where people think of these issues differently? Have them tell you about those situations and what their opinion is of them.

Level 4 Daily Learning Plans 81-100

In the last section of learning plans, you will think of additional or expanded life perspectives topics to create your own learning plans by applying the question framework. Focus on discussing topics that you've observed as important life issues for those in the community and talk with two people for each daily plan. Think also about special ceremonies or religious practices that you have questions about the reasons for and results from that you have yet to investigate.

For each daily learning plan, first write down the plan number and plan topic in your *Daily Learning Plan Notebook*. Then write out in your notebook the framework questions and examples that you will use to talk through this topic with two different individuals.

Don't forget to also include three hours each day for listening and reflecting on the recordings of your conversations. Make notes in your *Life Perspectives Notebook* as you do this. Also you will need to spend time each day preparing for the next day.

1. Spend a few minutes just talking with the person.

2. Set the stage for the conversation by asking about the person's life experience in relationship to the life perspectives topic.

3. Ask the person to identify the benefits and difficulties of the topic. What are the reasons for and results from the difficulties and benefits? Who is responsible and who bears the consequences?

4. Ask questions that show the opposite of the person's opinion and allow them to respond.

5. Ask the person what they think would help avoid the difficulties and add to the benefits. This would include events related to the topic that haven't happened but that they'd like to see take place, advice they would give to others about the topic, or how others could make the topic more successful.

6. Ask about unfamiliar contexts related to the topic that the person might know something about.

Self-evaluation for Level 4

In the following Level 4 self-evaluation, read each statement and mark the number that represents your current ability.

1. I have completed all 100 Level 4 daily learning plans.

1 ☐	2 ☐	3 ☐	4 ☐	5 ☐
not at all well	barely well	somewhat well	adequately well	extremely well

2. I can understand and summarize the benefits and difficulties of many common activities in the community.

1 ☐	2 ☐	3 ☐	4 ☐	5 ☐
not at all well	barely well	somewhat well	adequately well	extremely well

3. I can understand and summarize the opinions of others as to the causes and solutions for the difficulties of many common activities in the community. I can also understand and summarize the causes for the benefits of the activities and ways to reap those benefits.

1 ☐	2 ☐	3 ☐	4 ☐	5 ☐
not at all well	barely well	somewhat well	adequately well	extremely well

4. I can understand and summarize the opinions of others about common community activities as they defend them against opposing views.

1 ☐	2 ☐	3 ☐	4 ☐	5 ☐
not at all well	barely well	somewhat well	adequately well	extremely well

5. I can understand and summarize the speculations of others about common community activities, such as what that person would like to see take place, advice they would give to others about the activity, and how the activity could be made more successful.

1 ☐	2 ☐	3 ☐	4 ☐	5 ☐
not at all well	barely well	somewhat well	adequately well	extremely well

6. I can understand and summarize the accounts of others as they talk about unfamiliar contexts related to common activities in the community that they are aware of.

1 ☐	2 ☐	3 ☐	4 ☐	5 ☐
not at all well	barely well	somewhat well	adequately well	extremely well

7. I can give my opinions of the benefits and difficulties of many common activities in the community.

1 ☐	2 ☐	3 ☐	4 ☐	5 ☐
not at all well	barely well	somewhat well	adequately well	extremely well

8. I can give my opinions of the causes and solutions for the difficulties of many common activities in the community. I can also explain the causes for the benefits of the activities and ways to reap those benefits.

1 ☐	2 ☐	3 ☐	4 ☐	5 ☐
not at all well	barely well	somewhat well	adequately well	extremely well

9. I can defend my opinions about common activities against opposing views.

1 ☐ not at all well 2 ☐ barely well 3 ☐ somewhat well 4 ☐ adequately well 5 ☐ extremely well

10. I can speculate about common community activities, such as what I would like to see take place, advice I would give to others about the activity, and how the activity could be made more successful.

1 ☐ not at all well 2 ☐ barely well 3 ☐ somewhat well 4 ☐ adequately well 5 ☐ extremely well

11. I can talk about unfamiliar contexts related to common activities in the community that I am aware of.

1 ☐ not at all well 2 ☐ barely well 3 ☐ somewhat well 4 ☐ adequately well 5 ☐ extremely well

12. I can effectively use the life perspectives question framework to talk with others about the ways that languages are used in the community and the attitudes of community members toward those languages. I can also give and defend my own opinions on these matters.

1 ☐ not at all well 2 ☐ barely well 3 ☐ somewhat well 4 ☐ adequately well 5 ☐ extremely well

13. I can effectively use the life perspectives question framework to talk with others about the attitudes of community members toward information coming in from outside the community as well as their attitudes toward outside influence and societal change. I can also give and defend my own opinions on these matters.

1 ☐ not at all well 2 ☐ barely well 3 ☐ somewhat well 4 ☐ adequately well 5 ☐ extremely well

14. I can effectively use the life perspectives question framework to talk with others about the value of formal learning and education to community members, including literacy. I can also give and defend my own opinions on these matters.

1 ☐ not at all well 2 ☐ barely well 3 ☐ somewhat well 4 ☐ adequately well 5 ☐ extremely well

15. I can effectively use the life perspectives question framework to talk with others about any avoidance relationships in the society, as well as the overall degree and freedom of interaction between different members of society. I can also give and defend my own opinions on these matters.

1 ☐ not at all well 2 ☐ barely well 3 ☐ somewhat well 4 ☐ adequately well 5 ☐ extremely well

16. I can effectively use the life perspectives question framework to talk with others about formal and informal sources of information. This includes what kind of information and people that others listen to and how to present information so that others believe it to be true and important, as well as how people handle instances of contradictory information. I can also give and defend my own opinions on these matters.

1 ☐ not at all well   2 ☐ barely well   3 ☐ somewhat well   4 ☐ adequately well   5 ☐ extremely well

17. I can effectively use the life perspectives question framework to talk with others about what is considered shameful behavior and what is considered behavior to be proud of. I can also give and defend my own opinions on these matters.

1 ☐ not at all well   2 ☐ barely well   3 ☐ somewhat well   4 ☐ adequately well   5 ☐ extremely well

18. I can effectively use the life perspectives question framework to talk with others about the value of individual versus group actions and attitudes toward cooperation and competition. I can also give and defend my own opinions on these matters.

1 ☐ not at all well   2 ☐ barely well   3 ☐ somewhat well   4 ☐ adequately well   5 ☐ extremely well

19. I can effectively use the life perspectives question framework to talk with others about ownership, borrowing and loaning in the community. I can also give and defend my own opinions on these matters.

1 ☐ not at all well   2 ☐ barely well   3 ☐ somewhat well   4 ☐ adequately well   5 ☐ extremely well

20. I can effectively use the life perspectives question framework to talk with others about the factors that identify members of the people group in contrast to others and how the group thinks of and deals with those who don't display these characteristics. I can also talk about attitudes toward people who display disability or difference from others. I can also give and defend my own opinions on these matters.

1 ☐ not at all well   2 ☐ barely well   3 ☐ somewhat well   4 ☐ adequately well   5 ☐ extremely well

21. I can effectively use the life perspectives question framework to talk with others about the prestige associated with being a group outsider or insider, as well as the attitudes of those within the group toward outsiders and the attitudes of outsiders toward those within the group. I can also talk about the attitudes of the group toward other races and cultures. I can give and defend my own opinions on these matters.

1 ☐ not at all well   2 ☐ barely well   3 ☐ somewhat well   4 ☐ adequately well   5 ☐ extremely well

22. I can effectively use the life perspectives question framework to talk with others about the roles and responsibilities of different members of society and the perceived value of the different roles and individuals. I can also talk about my role in the society and how that is viewed. I can give and defend my own opinions on these matters.

1 ☐ not at all well   2 ☐ barely well   3 ☐ somewhat well   4 ☐ adequately well   5 ☐ extremely well

23. I can effectively use the life perspectives question framework to talk with others about information and individuals who are confrontational in the community, and how bringing embarrassment to others is generally viewed and dealt with. I can give and defend my own opinions on these matters.

1 ☐ not at all well   2 ☐ barely well   3 ☐ somewhat well   4 ☐ adequately well   5 ☐ extremely well

24. I can effectively use the life perspectives question framework to talk with others about kinds of close relationships between ages and genders and how these relationships are maintained and broken. I can give and defend my own opinions on these matters.

1 ☐ not at all well   2 ☐ barely well   3 ☐ somewhat well   4 ☐ adequately well   5 ☐ extremely well

25. I can effectively use the life perspectives question framework to talk with others about the ways to disagree and reconcile in times of relationship conflict, as well as the value of private versus public confrontation. I can give and defend my own opinions on these matters.

1 ☐ not at all well   2 ☐ barely well   3 ☐ somewhat well   4 ☐ adequately well   5 ☐ extremely well

26. I can effectively use the life perspectives question framework to talk with others about those with authority who lead and make decisions for the group and the level of respect given to them. I can also talk about how these leaders gained their authority and to what extent people heed their leadership. I can give and defend my own opinions on these matters.

1 ☐ not at all well   2 ☐ barely well   3 ☐ somewhat well   4 ☐ adequately well   5 ☐ extremely well

27. I can effectively use the life perspectives question framework to talk with others about influential or successful members of society and why these individuals are viewed in such a light, as well as the level of appreciation shown to them for their success. I can talk about the attitudes of these influential individuals toward others. I can also give and defend my own opinions on these matters.

1 ☐ not at all well   2 ☐ barely well   3 ☐ somewhat well   4 ☐ adequately well   5 ☐ extremely well

28. I can effectively use the life perspectives question framework to talk with others about their view of time and making and breaking time commitments, as well as how people use their time based on their societal roles. I can also give and defend my own opinions on these matters.

1 ☐ not at all well   2 ☐ barely well   3 ☐ somewhat well   4 ☐ adequately well   5 ☐ extremely well

29. I can effectively use the life perspectives question framework to talk with others about the seasons for life activities and how and why they follow those seasons. I can also give and defend my own opinions on these matters.

1 ☐ not at all well   2 ☐ barely well   3 ☐ somewhat well   4 ☐ adequately well   5 ☐ extremely well

30. I can effectively use the life perspectives question framework to talk with others about their opinions of personal and public space and how that space is determined, marked, and violated. I can also give and defend my own opinions on these matters.

1 ☐	2 ☐	3 ☐	4 ☐	5 ☐
not at all well	barely well	somewhat well	adequately well	extremely well

31. I can effectively use the life perspectives question framework to talk with others about visitors and visiting others, the rules for visiting, and the level of priority given to showing hospitality to group insiders and outsiders. I can also give and defend my own opinions on these matters.

1 ☐	2 ☐	3 ☐	4 ☐	5 ☐
not at all well	barely well	somewhat well	adequately well	extremely well

32. I can effectively use the life perspectives question framework to talk with others about how they define a good and bad son and man and what their attitudes are toward those who are irresponsible in these areas. I can also give and defend my own opinions on these matters.

1 ☐	2 ☐	3 ☐	4 ☐	5 ☐
not at all well	barely well	somewhat well	adequately well	extremely well

33. I can effectively use the life perspectives question framework to talk with others about how they define a good and bad father and grandfather and what their attitudes are toward those who are irresponsible in these areas. I can also give and defend my own opinions on these matters.

1 ☐	2 ☐	3 ☐	4 ☐	5 ☐
not at all well	barely well	somewhat well	adequately well	extremely well

34. I can effectively use the life perspectives question framework to talk with others about how they define a good and bad daughter and woman and what their attitudes are toward those who are irresponsible in these areas. I can also give and defend my own opinions on these matters.

1 ☐	2 ☐	3 ☐	4 ☐	5 ☐
not at all well	barely well	somewhat well	adequately well	extremely well

35. I can effectively use the life perspectives question framework to talk with others about how they define a good and bad mother and grandmother and what their attitudes are toward those who are irresponsible in these areas. I can also give and defend my own opinions on these matters.

1 ☐	2 ☐	3 ☐	4 ☐	5 ☐
not at all well	barely well	somewhat well	adequately well	extremely well

36. I can effectively use the life perspectives question framework to talk with others about the sources of peace and security in community life (such as special knowledge, jobs, education, wealth, specific relationships, the government, and other secular and religious organizations). I can also give and defend my own opinions on these matters.

1 ☐	2 ☐	3 ☐	4 ☐	5 ☐
not at all well	barely well	somewhat well	adequately well	extremely well

37. I can effectively use the life perspectives question framework to talk with others about the sources of fear and insecurity for community life (such as sickness, death, weakness, childlessness, divorce, being parentless, and poverty). I can also give and defend my own opinions on these matters.

1 ☐   2 ☐   3 ☐   4 ☐   5 ☐
not at all   barely   somewhat   adequately   extremely
well   well   well   well   well

38. I can effectively use the life perspectives question framework to talk with others about the value of holding and pursuing long-term goals, both by individuals as well as the community collectively, and what kinds of goals people pursue (such as comfortable lives, family security, freedom from fear, happiness, social recognition, true friendship). I can give and defend my own opinions on these matters.

1 ☐   2 ☐   3 ☐   4 ☐   5 ☐
not at all   barely   somewhat   adequately   extremely
well   well   well   well   well

39. I can effectively use the life perspectives question framework to talk with others about their attitudes toward the created order and a sense of beauty, how people feel they should preserve and care for the world around them, including animal domestication. I can give and defend my own opinions on these matters.

1 ☐   2 ☐   3 ☐   4 ☐   5 ☐
not at all   barely   somewhat   adequately   extremely
well   well   well   well   well

40. I can effectively use the life perspectives question framework to talk with others about how they demonstrate affection and what kinds of physical contact are a part of showing affection. I can also give and defend my own opinions on these matters.

1 ☐   2 ☐   3 ☐   4 ☐   5 ☐
not at all   barely   somewhat   adequately   extremely
well   well   well   well   well

41. I can effectively use the life perspectives question framework to talk with others about the secular and religious subgroups in society and the purposes of these groups as well as the roles of these groups, how important they are, and how they gather and interact. I can also give and defend my own opinions on these matters.

1 ☐   2 ☐   3 ☐   4 ☐   5 ☐
not at all   barely   somewhat   adequately   extremely
well   well   well   well   well

42. I can effectively use the life perspectives question framework to talk with others about special kinship relationships and what the responsibilities and benefits are in these relationships, as well as what a good relative does and is. I can also give and defend my own opinions on these matters.

1 ☐   2 ☐   3 ☐   4 ☐   5 ☐
not at all   barely   somewhat   adequately   extremely
well   well   well   well   well

43. I can effectively use the life perspectives question framework to talk with others about courtship and marriage, how it comes about, and how it is broken and violated. I can also give and defend my own opinions on these matters.

1 ☐ not at all well 2 ☐ barely well 3 ☐ somewhat well 4 ☐ adequately well 5 ☐ extremely well

44. I can effectively use the life perspectives question framework to talk with others about the definition of the family and about family rules. I can also give and defend my own opinions on these matters.

1 ☐ not at all well 2 ☐ barely well 3 ☐ somewhat well 4 ☐ adequately well 5 ☐ extremely well

45. I can effectively use the life perspectives question framework to talk with others about the rules for other social control systems, such as government, as well as any ambiguous areas in the rules and people's attitudes toward rule followers and rule breakers and the consequences for breaking and following the rules. I can also give and defend my own opinions on these matters.

1 ☐ not at all well 2 ☐ barely well 3 ☐ somewhat well 4 ☐ adequately well 5 ☐ extremely well

46. I can effectively use the life perspectives question framework to talk with others about sickness and death and its cause and effect on others, including, widows, widowers, and orphans. I can also give and defend my own opinions on these matters.

1 ☐ not at all well 2 ☐ barely well 3 ☐ somewhat well 4 ☐ adequately well 5 ☐ extremely well

47. I can effectively use the life perspectives question framework to talk with others about the individuals in the community who have special roles for communicating or working with the spirits, including the levels of respect and fear that community members feel toward them. I can also give and defend my own opinions on these matters.

1 ☐ not at all well 2 ☐ barely well 3 ☐ somewhat well 4 ☐ adequately well 5 ☐ extremely well

48. I can effectively use the life perspectives question framework to talk with others about their beliefs about how people generally interact with spirit beings, what kinds of spirit beings, when this occurs, and what the consequences are. I can also give and defend my own opinions on these matters.

1 ☐ not at all well 2 ☐ barely well 3 ☐ somewhat well 4 ☐ adequately well 5 ☐ extremely well

49. I can effectively use the life perspectives question framework to talk with others about where they think that history and life are heading. I can also give and defend my own opinions on these matters.

1 ☐ not at all well 2 ☐ barely well 3 ☐ somewhat well 4 ☐ adequately well 5 ☐ extremely well

50. I can effectively use the life perspectives question framework to talk with others about their view of history and any defining stories of the origins of people and the world. I can also give and defend my own opinions on these matters.

1 ☐   2 ☐   3 ☐   4 ☐   5 ☐
not at all   barely   somewhat   adequately   extremely
well   well   well   well   well

51. I can effectively use the life perspectives question framework to talk with others about any taboos and special rituals related to daily activities and spirit beings, as well as any ambiguous areas in the rules and people's attitudes toward rule followers and rule breakers and the consequences for breaking and following the rules. I can also give and defend my own opinions on these matters.

1 ☐   2 ☐   3 ☐   4 ☐   5 ☐
not at all   barely   somewhat   adequately   extremely
well   well   well   well   well

52. I can effectively use the life perspectives question framework to talk with others about twenty other life perspectives topics, including:

1) ....
1 ☐   2 ☐   3 ☐   4 ☐   5 ☐
not at all   barely   somewhat   adequately   extremely
well   well   well   well   well

2) ....
1 ☐   2 ☐   3 ☐   4 ☐   5 ☐
not at all   barely   somewhat   adequately   extremely
well   well   well   well   well

3) ....
1 ☐   2 ☐   3 ☐   4 ☐   5 ☐
not at all   barely   somewhat   adequately   extremely
well   well   well   well   well

4) ....
1 ☐   2 ☐   3 ☐   4 ☐   5 ☐
not at all   barely   somewhat   adequately   extremely
well   well   well   well   well

5) ....
1 ☐   2 ☐   3 ☐   4 ☐   5 ☐
not at all   barely   somewhat   adequately   extremely
well   well   well   well   well

6) ....
1 ☐   2 ☐   3 ☐   4 ☐   5 ☐
not at all   barely   somewhat   adequately   extremely
well   well   well   well   well

7) ....
1 ☐   2 ☐   3 ☐   4 ☐   5 ☐
not at all   barely   somewhat   adequately   extremely
well   well   well   well   well

8) ....
1 ☐   2 ☐   3 ☐   4 ☐   5 ☐
not at all   barely   somewhat   adequately   extremely
well   well   well   well   well

9) ....
1 ☐   2 ☐   3 ☐   4 ☐   5 ☐
not at all   barely   somewhat   adequately   extremely
well   well   well   well   well

10) ....
1 ☐   2 ☐   3 ☐   4 ☐   5 ☐
not at all   barely   somewhat   adequately   extremely
well   well   well   well   well

11) ....
1 ☐   2 ☐   3 ☐   4 ☐   5 ☐
not at all   barely   somewhat   adequately   extremely
well   well   well   well   well

12) ....
1 ☐   2 ☐   3 ☐   4 ☐   5 ☐
not at all   barely   somewhat   adequately   extremely
well   well   well   well   well

13) ....
1 ☐   2 ☐   3 ☐   4 ☐   5 ☐
not at all   barely   somewhat   adequately   extremely
well   well   well   well   well

14) ....
1 ☐   2 ☐   3 ☐   4 ☐   5 ☐
not at all   barely   somewhat   adequately   extremely
well   well   well   well   well

15) ....
1 ☐   2 ☐   3 ☐   4 ☐   5 ☐
not at all   barely   somewhat   adequately   extremely
well   well   well   well   well

16) ....
1 ☐   2 ☐   3 ☐   4 ☐   5 ☐
not at all   barely   somewhat   adequately   extremely
well   well   well   well   well

17) ....
1 ☐   2 ☐   3 ☐   4 ☐   5 ☐
not at all   barely   somewhat   adequately   extremely
well   well   well   well   well

18) ....
1 ☐   2 ☐   3 ☐   4 ☐   5 ☐
not at all   barely   somewhat   adequately   extremely
well   well   well   well   well

19) ....
1 ☐   2 ☐   3 ☐   4 ☐   5 ☐
not at all   barely   somewhat   adequately   extremely
well   well   well   well   well

20) ....
1 ☐   2 ☐   3 ☐   4 ☐   5 ☐
not at all   barely   somewhat   adequately   extremely
well   well   well   well   well